ACHIEVING THE RADICAL REFORM OF SPECIAL EDUCATION

ESSAYS IN HONOR OF JAMES M. KAUFFMAN

ACHIEVING THE RADICAL REFORM OF SPECIAL EDUCATION

Essays in Honor of
James M. Kauffman

Edited by

Jean B. Crockett
University of Florida

Michael M. Gerber
University of California at Santa Barbara

Timothy J. Landrum
University of Virginia

 Lawrence Erlbaum Associates
Taylor & Francis Group

New York   London

Cover design by Tomai Maridou.

Lawrence Erlbaum Associates
Taylor & Francis Group
270 Madison Avenue
New York, NY 10016

Lawrence Erlbaum Associates
Taylor & Francis Group
2 Park Square
Milton Park, Abingdon
Oxon OX14 4RN

Printed in the United States of America on acid-free paper
10 9 8 7 6 5 4 3 2 1

International Standard Book Number-13: 978-0-8058-5859-4 (Hardcover)

Library of Congress Cataloging-in-Publication Data

Achieving the radical reform of special education : essays in honor of James M.
Kauffman / edited by Jean B. Crockett, Michael M. Gerber, Timothy J. Landrum.
        p. cm.
    Includes bibliographical references and index.
    ISBN 978-0-8058-5859-4 — 0-8058-5859-8 (cloth : alk. paper)
    ISBN 978-1-4106-1678-4 — 1-4106-1678-9 (e book)
    1. Special education. I. Kaufmann, James M. II. Crockett, Jean B. III. Gerber,
Michael M. IV. Landrum, Timothy J.

    LC3965.A24 2007
    371.9'04—dc22   2006001822

Visit the Taylor & Francis Web site at
http://www.taylorandfrancis.com

For James M. Kauffman—scholar, special educator, and advocate for children and youth

Contents

Preface

Special education should and will be reshaped. The central question is this: How will it change? … The profession could confront its problems in ways likely to bring truly substantive, lasting change—reform that is radical in that its failure is not highly predictable. (Kauffman, 1993, p. 6)

This book is about the reshaping of special education in ways that aim to achieve what James M. Kauffman called radical educational reform in a classic article published in *Exceptional Children* in the last decade of the 20th century. Most of us would use the term *radical reform* to describe changes that are remarkably new or that extend far beyond the norm, and most of the time our usage would be correct. Kauffman (1993), however, used the adjective *radical* as derived from the Latin word *radix*, meaning "root," and employed the term radical reform to mean "arising from or going to the root" of something. (*American Heritage Dictionary of the English Language*, 2006). As a result, this book is not about making novel or extensive alterations to special education, but about investing in basic renovations that attend to fundamental "learner–teacher interactions that are at the core of effective instruction" (Kauffman, p. 7).

This book is also a Festschrift (fĕst'shrĭft'), a volume of learned articles and essays by colleagues and admirers offered as a tribute to a scholar in honor of a special occasion. As three of his colleagues, admirers, and former students, it is our privilege to serve as the editors of this Festschrift in honor of the scholar James M. Kauffman, on the occasion of his retirement as the Charles S. Robb Professor of Education at the University of Virginia.

Not only is this volume a tribute to the mentor we call Jim, and to his prodigious influence on the education of children and youth with disabilities, it is intended to highlight and to examine issues central to the continued growth and maturation of the field of special education—issues Jim has raised pointedly and repeatedly in his writing over the past three decades. We are very grateful to the impressive collection of top scholars who have contributed chapters to this volume. Their learned articles and essays provide a valuable synopsis of the status of special education and the progress toward the achievement of its radical reform at the outset of the 21st century.

Most of us became acquainted with the name James M. Kauffman in print, and some of us continue to seek out his writing as much for its candor and elegance as its insights into the education and treatment of children and youth with behavior disorders. As was said of the American author Mark Twain, his "unerring sense of the right word and not its second cousin taught people to pay attention when he spoke, whether in person or in print. He said things that were smart and things that were wise and he said them incomparably well" (Fishkin, 1996, pp. 8–9). These words rephrased in the present apply easily to Jim Kauffman who like Mark Twain also hailed from Hannibal, Missouri. Kauffman's provocative prose provides the moral compass for thousands of readers, and continues to influence the practice of special education worldwide as it has for more than 30 years. Just as Twain "became the voice of the new land, the leading translator of 'who' and 'what' the 'American' was, and to a large extent, still is" (p. 8), Kauffman lit out ahead of the rest for new territory in the 1960s, becoming the voice for the field of behavior disorders and a leading translator of who and what the "special educator" was and ought to be.

Jim Kauffman was among the first cadre of young scholars to earn a doctoral degree in special education in 1969 supported by federal funding from what was then called the U.S. Office of Education,

Bureau for the Education of the Handicapped (BEH). We spoke with Richard Whelan, of the University of Kansas and Kauffman's doctoral advisor, to capture his recollections of Jim's early career as a teacher and a scholar (personal communication, June 14, 2006).

Whelan remembers meeting Jim during the summer of 1962 at the Southard School for children with severe emotional and behavioral disorders at the Menninger Clinic in Topeka, Kansas. Dick Whelan was the school's principal; Jim Kauffman was a newly hired teacher, spending the months before school started as a child care worker teaching/modeling self-control and social skills, and arranging recreational activities. Whelan recalled that "Jim and his colleagues were like surrogate parents. The school was a secure facility but you'd never know it. In the approach we used students were surrounded with people rather than barriers." Whelan left Southard School to study for his doctorate with Norris Haring but continued his affiliation as a consultant working closely with Kauffman and other members of the school's faculty. "Jim was a splendid professional, a leader, and a natural," recalled Whelan; "he cared deeply about others—the students and his co-workers—and they cared about him. He was a listener and learner." Two years later, Jim left Southard School for public school teaching in Tecumseh, Kansas, but Whelan and Kauffman kept close ties.

Dick Whelan confirmed that Jim Kauffman considered leaving the Midwest to pursue a doctorate in the philosophy of education, but that Jim also showed interest in the advanced study of behavior disorders. Whelan, by then a faculty member at the University of Kansas, picked up on Kauffman's interest, making him aware of new federal funding for doctoral students in special education: "Universities were scrambling to bring good people in for doctoral level preparation. Teacher education programs throughout the nation needed competent teacher educators and researchers to prepare empathic and capable teachers to instruct students with many needs." The first fellowships were awarded by the BEH in 1964–1965 and Whelan recalled that the stipends were about $2,400 per year, with a bonus of $600 for each dependent (including spouse and children). "The doctoral fellows did not pay tuition or fees, and there was no requirement to work for this award, other than the academic rigors of being a doctoral student." Whelan downplayed his guiding role, but Jim has told us otherwise and credits Whelan and the opportunities that came with fiscal support from federal leadership training grants at the University of Kansas with pointing him toward the study of special education.

We are grateful to Dick Whelan for contributing his unique perspective of Jim Kauffman as a teacher, doctoral student, and eminent scholar. Referring to his friend and former student Whelan remarked that "Jim's aim and vision as a young man was to excel and to keep acquiring knowledge and practical wisdom. He has remained *constant* in pursuit of knowledge; this has never tapered off." As his friends and former students we appreciated Whelan's references to Jim's sense of humor and his characterizations of Jim as being collaborative and very serious about the quality of his work. We recognized the references to Jim's sense of history and his commitment to being grounded in good science. When Whelan said that Jim Kauffman has always been willing to take on "the flavor of the month," we recognized our colleague who resists with passion the seduction of nonsense and empty rhetoric that poses threats to special education students and their teachers.

Jim Kauffman is, as Whelan says, our field's true Renaissance man, a constant scholar who relies on the wisdom of science and empirical evidence, and who draws on the knowledge of history, literature, and philosophy in advancing the fields of special education and behavior disorders. His extensive scholarship is fueled by his passion for rational investigation coupled with his calling to ask or to answer challenging questions, and to comment on what he sees as troublesome policies and practices. Kauffman's concern for good thinking and rational statements, reflected in the following excerpt from an editorial he wrote in 1981, remains as compelling today in stopping nonsense and improving education:

> Special education does not exist in splendid isolation from politics, economics, regular education, legislation, litigation, research findings, and the social ecologies that shape all social welfare programs. Special education professionals have been remarkably unsuccessful, however, in conceptualizing special education in its social context and understanding how it is shaped by forces outside itself. Our "philosophy" has amounted to little more than advocacy based on humanistic sentiment ...

Special education has had its politicians and bureaucrats, its test-makers, its curriculum-builders, its organizers and administrators, its advocates, and its attorneys. Perhaps what it needs more than anything today is its philosophers—special educators who are capable of understanding special education in its historical and contemporary social and cultural contexts, articulating a coherent set of relevant premises about the education of exceptional children in our society, and elaborating the implications of various courses of action. Only our most capable scholars will be adequate for the task. (Kauffman, 1981, p. 4)

It is in this spirit that this Festschrift was created. We hope that it meets its dual purpose of serving as both an honor to James M. Kauffman, and as a guide for those capable scholars who will accept Kauffman's challenge in achieving what he called the radical reform of special education.

OVERVIEW AND ORGANIZATION OF THE VOLUME

This text is intended for the use of scholars, policymakers, and graduate students in special education and associated disciplines who seek to improve schools and to improve the education of students whose behavior and exceptional learning needs prevent their academic and social development. In framing this volume, we selected a topic central to much of Jim Kauffman's scholarship and advocacy in recent years, and on which his writing has wielded a good measure of influence. As a guide for this effort, we adopted the three long-term strategies for substantive reform articulated in Kauffman's 1993 article, *How We Might Achieve the Radical Reform of Special Education*: (a) disaggregating special education populations; (b) repairing and elaborating special education's conceptual foundations; and (c) strengthening the field's empirical base. We divided the volume into three parts corresponding to these themes, with a fourth part addressing principles of advocacy and reform in special education. Each part begins with a brief introduction that provides an overview of the theme and its relationship to Kauffman's work. The chapters that follow make reference to the status of the field of special education and its progress, pitfalls, and promising next steps in the years following the article's original publication.

PART I: DISAGGREGATING SPECIAL EDUCATION POPULATIONS

Special education in public schools is little more than a century old. Modern special education began 30 years ago in the United States with the passage of P. L. 94–142. At the time of this writing, it has been 13 years since Kauffman proffered his view of the radical steps needed to reform special education. And yet, surprisingly, the most fundamental premises of special education are still under debate. Among these premises, one that was the cornerstone of Kauffman's call to action, is the notion that students with disabilities need to be disaggregated from the general school population if they are to have a hope of receiving an appropriate education, one with reasonable chances of having a positive influence on their learning and life outcomes. Schools, in the principled foundations of special education, ought to treat individuals with disabilities *differently* because of objectively identifiable characteristics and learning needs that differ in important, practical ways from those of students without disabilities.

In this section, the authors who write on this theme give reason to be concerned, but also reason to hope. Oswald and Coutinho offer no apology that special education is founded on a "practical," rather than "natural" taxonomy of educationally relevant disabilities. Taxonomies of human differences, like all taxonomies of living things, in fact, are never present in the world awaiting discovery. Believing otherwise misrepresents science and its progress. Rather taxonomies are theoretical inventions of the human mind meant to promote order, clarity, and understanding of endless variation (see Gerber, 2000).

Oswald and Coutinho also argue for the importance of disaggregation within the population of students with disabilities. Boardman and Vaughn illustrate both the need and its practicality in their discussion of proposals to identify students with learning disabilities not by intrinsic characteristics, but rather by their relative ability to respond to good instruction. This argument is extended by Walker and Sprague whose chapter demonstrates a similar attention to the practicality of disaggregating students with significant behavior disorders for differentiated treatment by schools. Finally, Lewis and Wehby, citing a significant knowledge base for teaching students with emotional/behavior disorders in schools, argue that only more and better science will build the knowledge we need. There are no shortcuts to circumvent the barriers and challenges schools present to special education. Special education exists in that system, is part of it, is defined by it. Reform efforts that propose merging regular and special education disregard the historical foundation of special education on the observation of nontrivial and practical differences in the kind and amount of support required if some students are to achieve important learning and life goals. How the diverse learning needs of students with disabilities will be addressed in a reformed system will remain unclear if we cannot achieve consensus on the fundamental principle of disaggregation.

PART II: REPAIRING AND ELABORATING SPECIAL EDUCATION'S CONCEPTUAL FOUNDATIONS

In addressing the second step toward achieving radical reform Kauffman (1993) noted that despite criticisms that special education does not work, most critics concede that it works "in some ways, but not well enough" (p. 11). What was needed, he argued, were elaborations on conceptual foundations that would lead to coherent and logical statements about what special education is, what its goals are, and how its success can be defined. In the current context, the alignment of the Individuals with Disabilities Education Act of 2004 with provisions of the No Child Left Behind Act of 2001 has blurred distinctions between special and general education increasing the need for clarity in assessing the contribution of each to the greater achievement of students with disabilities in higher performing schools.

The authors addressing historical, legal, and philosophical foundations in this section extend Kauffman's advocacy and scholarship by elaborating on the purpose of special education and its goals as an integral component of public schooling. Mark Mostert offers a tribute to those he calls special education's "historical distinctives"—people with disabilities, their parents, advocates, and educators from the past who grappled with the meaning of human differences and who helped to build special education's conceptual foundations. Mostert draws on sources from the Disability Museum Web site to bring the history of special education to life in the words of notables including Horace Mann, Anne Sullivan, Helen Keller, Dorothea Dix, Joseph Carey Merrick, Gunnar Dybwad, and Eunice Kennedy Shriver.

Barbara Bateman and Naomi Zigmond address the intersection of educational policies and practices in their chapters. Bateman examines special education's conceptual foundations as they have evolved in law since 1975 discussing 10 basic premises that both reflect and shape the foundations of special education practice. Bateman explains that law can "provide insights into the foundations of practice and into the connection between practice and research, but it does not provide a foundation for research." From her perspective the foundation for research is the province of science, which guides special education, rather than law, which governs its practice. Naomi Zigmond examines the conceptual foundations that inform the role and responsibilities of the special educator—"the teacher with a special certification who is specially trained to do special things with special students." In challenging the co-teaching model frequently used in restructuring schools, Zigmond calls for unconventional thinking in endorsing nine propositions that guide policies more likely to improve the practice of educators who teach students with learning and behavior disorders.

Concluding this section, Gary Sasso addresses the philosophical foundations of special education as grounded in the scientific method. Sasso like Kauffman is a vocal proponent for supporting rational inquiry as the best guide for ethical and practical decision-making in special education. In his critique of the postmodern philosophies of Derrida and Foucault, he challenges cultural and cognitive relativism as a bankrupt and unsupportable position corrosive to the tenets that guide research and practice in special education. How historical understanding, legal reasoning, instructional prowess, and rational inquiry reform special education in the 21st century remains to be seen but in Bateman's words, "we can all hope that special education practice moves ever closer to the legal precepts that govern it, and that it follows ever more closely the research that guides it."

PART III: STRENGTHENING SPECIAL EDUCATION'S EMPIRICAL BASE

Part III includes chapters that address the straightforward, yet remarkably complex, concern about the extent to which a useful empirical foundation exists on which special education practice, and potentially reform, can be built. Kauffman has noted that the accumulation of a body of research data is a tedious process, and that the important questions special education researchers pose have neither quick nor easy answers. The chapters here attest to this fact. In the lead essay, Forness and Beard point out that our sister disciplines of child psychiatry and mental health are more advanced than special education in conducting randomized controlled trials (RCTs), which many argue are necessary to establish a true evidence base. Although research with special education interventions in schools can be exceedingly difficult, and randomized controlled trials present even greater challenges for researchers in the field, Forness and Beard force us to consider the implications of the types of research we do for the evidence base we ultimately claim.

An important step in furthering the goal of establishing an evidence base in special education was the publication of a set of quality indicators papers in *Exceptional Children* in 2005. These papers elaborated sets of quality indicators against which research evidence might be evaluated across four types of research designs: group experimental designs, single-subject designs, correlational designs, and qualitative research. Cook and Tankersley provide a field test of the quality indicators for group experimental research designs, using as examples intervention studies with students at risk of developing emotional or behavioral disorders. Their chapter represents perhaps the most comprehensive look to date at one set of these quality indicators as applied to published research studies. Because the quality indicators will prove ultimately useful only to the extent that they can be interpreted and applied, Cook and Tankersley have taken a critical next step in advancing toward a true evidence base. Similarly, Lane, Barton-Arwood, Rogers, and Robertson use the quality indicators for both group experimental designs and single subject designs in their overview of academic intervention research with students with EBD. Lane et al. not only apply rigorous standards to the evidence they review, but validate Kauffman's comment in 2003 that he has "younger colleagues who understand both the primary role of instruction in special education for students with emotional and behavioral disorders and the importance of empirically validated instructional methods" (p. 327). Taken together, the chapters in this section present a striking and honest look at the progress of our field with regard to establishing an evidence base on which to stand, and offer precisely what Kauffman described as the types of advances that "are key to the substantive reform of special education" (p. 13).

PART IV: KAUFFMAN'S CONTRIBUTIONS TO SPECIAL EDUCATION

The Festschrift concludes with a summary chapter contributed by Jim Kauffman's longtime colleagues John Wills Lloyd and Daniel P. Hallahan that examines advocacy in special education and its relationship to reform. Echoing themes Kauffman has represented for three decades, Lloyd and Hallahan argue that advocacy and reform should be guided by several principles: "legality, empiricism, rationality, and continuing concern for providing beneficial services at a given time while seeking to improve the quality of services available in the future." They note that our field has seen its share of advocates whose positions or proposals are not based on strong evidence, whose passionate advocacy may exceed reasonable limits imposed by rationality and empiricism. But to us their elegantly simple statement that "advocating reform requires someone to act as advocate and something to advocate, a person and a position or issue" speaks directly to both the unwavering advocacy that Jim Kauffman's professional career has embodied, as well as Kauffman's frequent appeal that we base reform efforts—indeed, all research and practice—on principles as simple as logic and rational thinking.

The chapters were solicited from scholars whose research and commentary addresses special education reform, and who are well-suited to provide empirically sound analyses of the key issues. Each contributor had considerable leeway within the framework of the text, and we purposefully left it to them to contribute original research, reviews of the literature, critical analyses, or reflective chapters.

We are grateful to this host of most capable scholars for their contributions to this volume. We are grateful to Mary Theresa Kiely at the University of Florida for help with compiling the indexes. We are also grateful to John Lloyd, Special Education and Disability Series Editor for Lawrence Erlbaum Associates, for his encouragement. We are especially grateful to editor Lane Akers and to publisher Lawrence Erlbaum for their support of this project and for sharing our enthusiasm in the development of a Festschrift in honor of James M. Kauffman. Of course we are most grateful to Jim for becoming the philosopher he told us in 1981 that we needed, especially as he has applied his dialectic with the practice of special education to the study of behavior disorders. As he predicted, we will need our most capable scholars to achieve the radical reform of special education, and, happily, for the field of special education, Kauffman is among them.

—Jean B. Crockett
—Michael M. Gerber
—Timothy J. Landrum

Note. All royalty earnings from the sale of this book are assigned to the Eli M. Bower Endowed Fellowship Fund at the University of Virginia. This fund provides an annual stipend to a graduate student in the Curry School of Education who is preparing to work with children with emotional or behavioral disorders.

REFERENCES

Fishkin, S. F. (1996). *Lighting out for the territory: Reflections on Mark Twain and American culture*. New York: Oxford University Press.

Gerber, M. M. (2000). An appreciation of learning disabilities: The value of blue-green algae. *Exceptionality, 8*, 29–42.

Kauffman, J. M. (1981). From the editor. *Exceptional Education Quarterly, 2*(2), 3–4.

Kauffman, J. M. (1993). How we might achieve the radical reform of special education. *Exceptional Children, 60*, 6–16.

DISAGGREGATING SPECIAL EDUCATION POPULATIONS

Science, not only everyday life, at the beginning of the 21st century inches closer to new understandings both about what makes us similar and what makes each of us unique. Human beings are not only diverse in the ethnic, linguistic, and sociological senses of that term, we are also bio-diverse. We are, at the level of our genetic endowment and our biological development, radically different from one another, radically individual (Edelman, 1987). The wonder of it is the invisible but pervasive "means by which [life] created so much diversity from so little physical matter" (Wilson, 1992, p. 35). Even before the Genome Project and the parallel advances in neuroscience, careful behavioral science had already marked the passing of any simple nature versus nurture explanations for human diversity or the flaws, imperfections, and failures of adaptive development (see Sameroff & Chandler, 1975). The environment that surrounds and nurtures—or fails to nurture—us transacts with the genetic engine that creates us (Ridley, 2003). We and our environments— our caregivers, our teachers, interested and indifferent others—are mutually modifying.

It is a cause for some frustration that our political capabilities do not keep pace with our scientific knowledge. We are still challenged to build social—specifically educational—systems and institutions that are fully responsive to individual differences when and where they matter. Special education is constructed on a science as well as a political conviction that, although many differences entail serious, tangible risks for poor learning and life outcomes for many children, we can do something about it.

On the other hand, the near simultaneous worldwide recognition 30 years ago of the needs and responsibilities in modern societies for educating students with disabilities, and the variety of progressive legislative responses it produced, should be cause for pride and some hope. Special education is still a work in progress. And as the authors of the following chapters argue, although we have done much, there is still much to do.

Specifically, we need to embrace the inescapable reality that children whose characteristics we identify with disability, developmental delay, or risk are deeply and inextricably embedded but also defined by their immediate environments—families, schools, neighborhoods. The science of this generation must be as attentive to the mutually modifying influences of these contexts as the science of the previous generation was attentive to individual differences. When parents receive additional education and support, they are better at preventing maladaptive development in their children despite any intellectual, behavioral, or sensory limitations. If we imagine a school in which students with disabilities thrive, it is likely we have imagined a different kind of school.

However, to build that kind of science requires a foundational assumption that individual differences, however complex their etiology, are real and meaningful. Each of the following authors has produced a thoughtful response to Kauffman's assertion of a "first premise," namely that "disaggregation of students is necessary to assure appropriateness of education for all" (p. 11). Moreover, they provide concrete examples of how an applied science of special education has worked and will work to the benefit of students with disabilities when it is founded on this premise.

PART I

REFERENCES

Edelman, G. M. (1987). *Neural Darwinism: The theory of neuronal group selection.* New York: Basic Books.

Kauffman, J. M. (1993). How we might achieve the radical reform of special education. *Exceptional Children, 60,* 6–16.

Ridley, M. (2003). *Nature via nurture: Genes, experience, and what makes us human.* New York: Harper Collins.

Sameroff, A., & Chandler, M. (1975). Reproductive risk and the continuum of caretaking casualty. In F. D. Horowitz, (Ed.), *Review of child development research* (4th ed., pp. 187–244). Chicago: The University of Chicago Press.

Wilson, E. O. (1992). *The diversity of life.* New York: Norton.

Chapter 1

On Disaggregating Disability, Whatever That Means

Donald P. Oswald
Virginia Commonwealth University

Martha J. Coutinho
East Tennessee State University

It has been said that those who are uncomfortable with portions of the orthodox language of the church (any church), can ease their discomfort in the public recitation of prayers or the creed by periodically mentally inserting the phrase "whatever that means" (e.g., "Our Father who art in heaven, whatever that means, hallowed be Thy name. Thy kingdom come, whatever that means ...," etc.). This remedy for the anxiety associated with using a word or phrase that carries a heavy freight of popular misunderstanding and whose meaning is somewhat ambiguous, has now passed into popular culture; a Google search for the phrase "whatever that means" on the pages of the World Wide Web yields more than 2 million hits.

This ambiguity-of-meaning problem applies to the term *disability*. Although we may believe of disability that, like pornography, we know it when we see it, we may be challenged to offer a water-tight definition that unerringly divides the human race into "those who is, and those who ain't." Further, we are increasingly confronted by self-advocates, labeled by society as people with disabilities, who reject the application of the term to their personal experience. Advocacy for "deaf culture" is one example of this phenomenon (Ladd, 2003) and recent first-person accounts of Asperger's Disorder represent another (see Baron-Cohen, 2002). Although few would reject the term *disability* as a meaningless construct, these alternative voices profitably call us to re-examine what it means when we use it, how others are likely to understand it, and how congruent are the meaning and the understanding.

In the face of this ambiguity, Kauffman (1993) has been an unapologetic voice crying in the wilderness in support of the principle of disaggregation of disability. Kauffman has persistently promoted as "special education's first premise: Disaggregation of students is necessary to ensure the appropriateness of education for all" and further that "Disaggregating general from special education is not sufficient; students with disabilities must be disaggregated" (p. 11). Thus, disaggregation means distinguishing disability within the general population and distinguishing among the different categories of disability.

Thus, to disaggregate requires that we be able to meaningfully define disability and the subtypes of disability. This process of disaggregation is commonly referred to as *diagnosis* and Kauffman's position is based on an assumption that valid and reliable diagnosis is possible (Kauffman & Hallahan, 2005).

What is not clear is whether the position put forward by Kauffman and others also demands that the categories into which one sorts disability must be in some sense "natural" categories. Popular understanding of diagnoses, and to some extent of special education categories, is that they "carve nature at the joints"; that is, that these are real conditions that students "have" (whatever that means) and that the lines that divide students with disabilities from the general population of students, as well as those that divide one category from the next, are present in nature.

Such popular understanding assumes that science has identified the essence of a category or "kind" so that individuals can be reliably sorted into kinds that are mutually exclusive. Natural kinds of this sort are best exemplified by the periodic table of elements; here we have discrete categories of substances that can be described in their essence with no overlap or "gray areas." These kinds have "fixed internal properties that make them be what they are, [and] they can potentially be identified with perfect reliability" (Zachar, 2000, p. 168).

Few educators would argue that special education categories are kinds of this sort (see Gerber, 2000). Even if we are not certain whether our categories have "fixed internal properties," we can be fairly confident about a lack of "perfect reliability." But if they are not natural kinds, then what sort of categories are they? And should we be worried about basing diagnosis and instruction on a system that cannot be located in nature?

Our thinking here is strongly influenced by Zachar's (2000) discussion of natural kinds and practical kinds. Zachar points out that essentialists' wont is to label the only alternative to the natural kind an "arbitrary kind;" but he also notes that this designation is unnecessarily pejorative and proposes as an alternative the less affectively laden "practical kinds." "Practical kinds are fuzzier than natural kinds, but they are not arbitrary. … classification of practical kinds requires balancing criteria that change their values in different contexts" (p. 168).

One might inquire whether there are any "natural kinds" subsets among *homo sapiens*. Race has clearly been discredited as a candidate; sex comes close but even here biological anomalies and gender identities muddy the water considerably. As Zachar (2000) points out, if this seems too much like academic waffling, we need look no further than evolutionary biology for evidence that seeming classical categories are, in fact, not so hard-and-fast after all. In biology, species are perhaps the closest thing we have to natural kinds; but Darwin based his work on the assumption that the immutability of species was a fiction. And evolutionary theory has generally accepted that the notion of "species" is not as straightforward as popular thinking suggests (Gould, 2002).

The practical kinds concept is based on a prototype model of classification. Prototype categories do not have necessary or sufficient conditions that serve to define membership; rather categories are based on a family resemblance and there may be several different criteria one could meet in order to be considered a member of the class. One can identify instances that are more, or less, prototypical of a category (e.g., the robin is more prototypical of the class "bird" than is the ostrich; Zachar, 2000).

Contrary to the inclination of some biologically minded mental health professionals, Zachar (2000) argues that psychiatric disorders should not be viewed as natural kinds, indeed that "this kind of essentialistic thinking is scientifically malignant" (p. 169). In fact, recent versions of the *Diagnostic and Statistical Manual of Mental Disorders* have institutionalized an anti-essentialist view. Diagnoses are described by prototype, and although individuals with a given diagnosis are presumed to match a subset of the designated diagnostic criteria, a single necessary or sufficient criterion, or set of criteria, is generally not specified.

The features that render psychiatric diagnoses practical, rather than natural, kinds are even more clearly evident with respect to special education categories. The categories codified in IDEA regulations are as fuzzy as the fuzziest of mental health diagnoses. Leaving aside the point that the number of categories has changed over the years, the categories cannot be said to be based on essential differences (i.e., differences of essence) among students.

An important feature of practical kinds is that they often exist in overlapping systems based on level of analysis. This feature is manifestly important with regard to children with disabilities. Understanding the "levels of analysis" aspect of categorization can take us a long ways toward a more productive understanding of special education disability categories; it may also help us understand some of the challenges of disaggregation and the struggles that the educational system has faced in placing students into categories.

Some of the special education categories, for example, are based on physical features that are objectively measurable and thus, relatively reliably identifiable. "Deafness," "visual impairment including blindness," and "orthopedic impairment" for example, refer to observable physical differences in sensory or motor functioning. These categories are not mutually exclusive (witness the "deaf-blindness" category) but, taken one at a time, it is a reasonably objective decision as to whether the student falls into the category, or not, based on those observable physical differences. Thus, if we label one level of analysis "sensory and motor functioning" there is, among the categories, a subset that is reasonable easily determinable.

As an aside, we would still not label these categories natural kinds. Children with visual impairment are not different in essence from their peers. However, one can imagine a prototypical child for the category and a set of characteristics that could be used to describe the category and define the boundaries, even if those boundaries are fuzzy.

However, the largest group of special education categories is based on the assessment of constructs that are more abstract. This group includes autism, mental retardation, developmental delay, emotional disturbance, and learning disability. In these categories, we encounter a huge issue related to the validity of the assessment of individual differences, and the meaning of such individual variation. The level of analysis for these categories may be described as the observation of behavior in the presence of a structured, standardized set of stimuli. Observations at this level of analysis lead to judgments with respect to such constructs as intelligence, achievement, and behavior disturbance that are then translated into categorical determinations.

It is instructive to consider that for some of the categories, for example, mental retardation, the diagnostic process requires taking inherently variable measures, such as full-scale IQ and adaptive behavior scores, themselves the composite of several subconstructs (e.g., verbal ability, nonverbal problem-solving ability, and the various adaptive domains), and establishing an arbitrary cut-point (e.g., 2 SD below the mean) as the definitional dividing line between disability and "normal" or "typical" functioning. Further, arguments that justify any given cut-point are sparse, and cut-points have changed frequently over the years (e.g., for mental retardation), altering with a stroke of the pen the status of thousands of individuals with respect to the diagnostic category. Some amount of controversy about the identity of those individuals near the cut-off is inevitable.

Truth be told, if we are most interested in accurately reflecting nature in our descriptive systems, we would perhaps not create categories at all. Categories, with few exceptions, are artificially created and imposed on a system of near-continuous variability in nearly every conceivable aspect of morphology and behavior. However, although the logical and philosophical basis for a decision to create categories from more or less continuous variation can be debated, there are clear administrative, clinical, educational, and intervention-related reasons for doing so. In the absence of specified cut-points, disability decisions become excessively arbitrary and even more subject to systemic factors that foster discrimination, denial of service, or inappropriate labeling.

In truth, however, even when our assessments emphasize measurement of diagnosis-relevant constructs, classification decisions generally emerge by a prototype-matching process. Scores above or below the cut-points may be treated as indicators of the match but are treated as neither necessary nor sufficient.

Another level of analysis in categorizing special education disability conditions refers to etiology. Most of the special education categories are neutral with respect to etiology; one category, however, "traumatic brain injury," explicitly refers to a specific etiology, that is, "an acquired injury to the brain caused by an external physical force" (Assistance to States for the Education of Children With Disabilities: Proposed Rule, 2005), rather than to the differences in behavior or functioning that may result.

A comparable situation has arisen in the scientific literature on autism in that a sizeable subset of children with autism has a specific chromosomal abnormality (Fragile X) that is objectively identifiable. The field has struggled with the complications that arise in moving between the behavioral-characteristics level of analysis (autism as a syndrome) and the etiology level of analysis (Fragile X). Issues surrounding the TBI category are, if anything, more complicated because of the wide variety of cognitive, behavioral, and functional impairment characteristics that children with brain injury may manifest.

These examples illustrate the levels-of-analysis problem. The present system of the special education categories depends on negotiating several different levels of analysis in determining a disability category. Thoughtful consideration of the disability categorization system may leave us astonished that it works as well as it does.

However, the recognition that special education categories are not natural kinds relieves us of the burden of expecting educational diagnostic processes to identify the "real" disorder. In dealing with practical kinds, we are not searching for differences of essence by which to unerringly classify types of individuals. Rather, we are seeking distinctions "that help us navigate through the world. Their validity is in their usefulness" (Zachar, 2000, p. 170).

This assistance in navigation through the world of education for all children is the primary, and essential, contribution that disaggregation offers. Children's problems in learning differ in meaningful ways and the evolution of the descriptions of those differences has moved the field forward immeasurably.

Many of the disadvantages of the special education classifications in use 30 years ago are as relevant today (Hobbs, 1975a, 1975b). Some children, particularly those near cut-scores, may be mistakenly identified as disabled by educators. The use of a diagnostic label can lead to stigma, stereotyping, a misrepresentation of someone's potential, and denial of opportunities (Kauffman, 1997; MacMillan & Hendrick, 1993; Reynolds, 1991). Nonetheless, definitions of disabilities based on a clear conceptual framework, technically sound measures, and professional judgment have proven crucial for determining who will be served, what educational interventions to consider, prevalence estimates, who will be trained to meet the needs, and how much money will be spent (Kauffman, 1997). More importantly, appropriate disaggregation culminates in outcomes for students with disabilities that are better than if special services were not provided (Hanushek, Kain, & Rivkin, 2002). Without special education, most students with disabilities fail to achieve satisfactory learning and adult life outcomes (Kauffman & Hallahan, 2005).

In many ways, and for many reasons, the system of categorizing student disabilities is imperfect and approximate. It fails to separate children neatly into mutually exclusive groups that reflect inherent differences of essence. It does not always provide useable prototypes that can characterize groups of children that share important characteristics that are likely to require similar responses from the educational system. The present system of categories displays some of the features of unplanned cities that have grown faster than the structure of the community can accommodate. Such areas are frequently characterized by governmental, and other, divisions in ways that seem to defy logic but persist because such characterizations made sense at one time.

Professional opinions continually evolve with respect to students who fail to make satisfactory progress, leaving the disaggregation of students susceptible to categorical drift (Ysseldyke, Algozzine, & Thurlow, 1992). The categorization of disability for the purposes of special education is not a system of natural kinds; but there exists a philosophically defensible alternative approach that has proven effective in better understanding and responding to the needs of children.

CONCLUSIONS

The system is not perfect, but there is significant risk involved in leaping to the conclusion that it must be abandoned as hopeless. In the spirit of continued evolution of that system, the field might consider the issues and alternatives we have discussed above.

The levels-of-analysis question is one that grows ever more complex with evolving research into the causes and manifestations of disability. If we wait to solve this issue, a system of categories will never see the light of day. Given the present state of knowledge, we cannot avoid overlapping levels of analysis and the system must be flexible enough to accommodate such overlap.

Nonetheless, a careful philosophical analysis may be a first step toward a more coherent system. It may be fruitful to clarify what are the levels of analysis that are most functional in defining educational disability. This is a pragmatic question that can be answered only by educators thoughtfully examining the philosophical issues and responding in terms of what works best for schools. A benefit of such examination may be that public goals for education, and the consequences these have for children with disabilities, become explicit (Edgar & Hayden, 1984/1985). Decisions about who is disabled, and definitions of free and appropriate education, may vary depending on whether the goal is accountability for results related to academic content standards or preparation for major adult life roles through academic, career-technical, and community-based learning (Kochhar-Bryant & Bassett, 2002; Sitlington & Clark, 2006).

The alternative to thoughtful examination and systematic evolution of the system for disaggregation is to have no system at all. There is little reason to revert to Ground Zero with all of the attendant issues of civil rights and human suffering that preceded the present era. The answer to "Can't we all just be people?" is "No." The human race has tried that solution in countless variations and has always failed; categorizing is a natural human impulse and, in the absence of categories that are deliberately created with prosocial intent, history tells us that other categories will be created and promulgated, most often for the purposes of control, of preserving the power of the powerful and the wealth of the wealthy. In a democracy, distribution of resources occurs through application of criteria that are explicit and subject to change. The present system cries for revision, even fundamental reconceptualization, but not destruction.

Science proceeds via a process of disaggregation and re-aggregation, splitting things into subgroups and lumping them into supersets. This process is essential to the advancement of knowledge (Adelman, 1996). It calls for a certain tolerance for ambiguity in that systems are never perfect and rarely map squarely onto pragmatic concerns with education and rehabilitation. Disaggregation of special populations is a necessary, if controversial, act. It is unrealistic to hope for a classification system that identifies natural kinds among children with disabilities; but we can hope for a solution focused on "practical kinds" that is functional.

REFERENCES

Adelman, H. S. (1996). Appreciating the classification dilemma. In W. Stainback & S. Stainback. (Eds.), *Controversial issues confronting special education: Divergent perspectives* (2nd ed., pp. 96–112). Boston: Allyn & Bacon.

Assistance to States for the Education of Children With Disabilities: Proposed Rule, 70 Fed. Reg., 35,837 (June 21, 2005; to be codified at 34 C.F.R. pt. 300).

Baron-Cohen, S. (2002). Is Asperger syndrome necessarily viewed as a disability? *Focus on Autism and Other Developmental Disabilities, 17*, 186–191.

Edgar, E., & Hayden, A. H. (1984/1985). Who are the children in special education and how many children are there? *Journal of Special Education, 18*, 523–539.

Gerber, M. M. (2000). An appreciation of learning disabilities: The value of blue-green algae. *Exceptionality, 8*, 29–42.

Gould, S. J. (2002). *The structure of evolutionary theory*. Cambridge, MA: Harvard University Press.

Hobbs, N. (1975a). *The futures of children*. San Francisco: Jossey-Bass.

Hobbs, N. (1975b). *Issues in the classification of children* (Vols. 1–2). San Francisco: Jossey-Bass.

Kauffman, J. M. (1993). How we might achieve the radical reform of special education. *Exceptional Children, 60*, 6–16.

Kauffman, J. M. (1997). *Characteristics of emotional and behavioral disorders of children and youth* (6th ed.). Upper Saddle River, NJ: Merrill.

Kauffman, J. M., & Hallahan, D. P. (2005). *Special education: What it is and why we need it*. Boston: Pearson.

Kochhar-Bryant, C. A., & Bassett, D. S. (2002). Challenge and promise in aligning transition and standards-based education. In C. A. Kochhar-Bryant & D. S. Bassett (Eds.), *Aligning transition and standards- based education: Issues and strategies* (pp. 1–23). Arlington, VA: Council for Exceptional Children.

Hanushek, E. A., Kain, J. F., & Rivkin, S. G. (2002). Inferring program effects for special populations: Does special education raise achievement for students with disabilities? *Review of Economics and Statistics, 84,* 584–599.

Ladd, P. (2003). *Understanding deaf culture: In search of deafhood*. Clevedon, UK: Multilingual Matters.

MacMillan, D. L., & Hendrick, I. G. (1993). Evolution and legacies. In J. I. Goodlad & T. C. Lovitt (Eds.), *Integrating general and special education* (pp. 23–48). Columbus, OH: Merrill/Macmillan.

Reynolds, M. C. (1991). Classification and labeling. In J. W. Lloyd, N. N. Singh, & A. C. Repp (Eds.), *The regular education initiative: Alternative perspectives on concepts, issues and models* (pp. 29–41). Sycamore, IL: Sycamore.

Sitlington, P. L., & Clark, G. M. (2006). *Transition education and services for students with disabilities* (4th ed.). Boston: Pearson.

Ysseldyke, J. E., Algozzine, B., & Thurlow, M. L. (1992). *Critical issues in special education* (2nd ed., pp. 92–136). Boston: Houghton Mifflin.

Zachar, P. (2000). Psychiatric disorders are not natural kinds. *Philosophy, Psychiatry, & Psychology* (7), 167–182.

Chapter 2

Response to Intervention as a Framework for the Prevention and Identification of Learning Disabilities: Which Comes First, Identification or Intervention?

Alison Gould Boardman
University of Colorado

Sharon Vaughn
University of Texas

School reform and special education have been closely linked, often with a tension that has not been readily resolved (Crockett & Kauffman, 1998). The notion of providing a free and appropriate education to all children and youth was a historical step in education requiring changes in both general and special education. Related to these changes are concepts such as mainstreaming and inclusion that Kauffman (Crockett & Kauffman, 1999) identifies as practices that could be inappropriately used for undermining education for students with disabilities.

A full educational opportunity—an appropriate public education that is firmly fixed on productive learning for each student, that acknowledges the dynamic reciprocity between student and setting, and that marshals its resources under the guiding principle of social justice—has much to offer America's youth. If, and when, these benefits can be assured for all, the dynamic mechanism inherent in the concept of LRE [least restrictive environment] and implemented through its continuum can be set aside for a dynamic reciprocity that rests with confidence on the primary value of social institutions—social justice. (Crockett & Kauffman, 1999, p. 202)

Over the years, Kauffman has reminded us that educational decision-making can be influenced by both research and values (Kauffman, 1993, 2003). The scientific base of special education is an essential foundation for influencing decision-making. The values we have about equity and social justice, particularly as they relate to individuals with disabilities, are also essential elements (Kauffman, 2003).

Recently, through reauthorization of IDEA (2004), the issue of using Response To Intervention (RTI) for identifying students with learning disabilities has been presented. This chapter attempts to represent issues related to RTI within the context of Kauffman's advice about the role of science and social justice when making decisions regarding individuals with disabilities.

ISSUES IN IDENTIFYING STUDENTS WITH LEARNING DISABILITIES

Recently, researchers involved with school reform efforts in both general and special education have argued that the number of students identified with learning disabilities (LD) is greatly influenced by the quality of reading instruction that students receive (Fletcher, Coulter, Reschly, & Vaughn, 2004). Furthermore, there has been extensive discussion and research on *how* students are identified with LD. It is now commonly agreed that the traditional IQ-discrepancy model is not essential to determining the existence of an LD in reading (e.g., Donovan & Cross, 2002; Fletcher et al., 1994; Stuebing, Fletcher, Ledoux, & Shaywitz, 2002).

RTI has been proposed as a viable alternative to prevent learning difficulties and to provide data to support decision-making that is an IQ-discrepancy formula for the identification of LD. Furthermore, it provides a framework for the delivery of high-quality, core reading instruction and more intensive interventions to students who are learning how to read. It has been estimated that about 80% of students with learning disabilities have disabilities in reading (National Research Council, 1998). Although the RTI approach can be used to frame intensive interventions for math and behavior problems (cf. Fuchs, 2005; Walker et al., 1996), this chapter limits its focus to its application in reading.

The RTI framework as applied to reading is based on two key assumptions about reading and reading disabilities. First, those applying an RTI framework presume that there are a set of essential components that are systematically taught to students so they can develop a strong base in academic areas such as reading and math (Fuchs, 2005; Gresham, 2002; Jenkins & O'Connor, 2002). Furthermore, in this framework, reading disability is thought to fall along a continuum from poor reading to superior reading with biological, instructional, and environmental influences having some bearing on proficiency at all levels (Fletcher et al., 2002; Shaywitz, Fletcher, Holahan, & Shaywitz, 1992).

Rather than imposing a discrete set of characteristics in which someone is judged either to have or not to have a reading disability, a cut-point is used to differentiate those who need help from those who do not. If reading proficiency is normally distributed across all students, then poor readers would fall at the tail of the distribution. This tail would represent those students who read at substantially lower levels than would be expected given their reading instruction, age, and grade level. This view of reading disabilities uses a dimensional representation rather than a categorical one to operationalize struggling readers.

The dimensional view of reading disabilities works well in an RTI framework because the assessment of, and assistance for students is based directly on reading performance (Vaughn, Linan-Thompson, & Hickman-Davis, 2003; Vellutino et al., 1996). Furthermore, because assistance is for relatively brief periods, students are not part of a remediation program of indeterminate duration where exit is infrequent. In general, most RTI frameworks use criterion referenced assessments to determine who needs additional support in reading, regardless of the cause. Specifically, students who do not demonstrate expected skills in reading for their age and grade level at specific times during the year are at risk for reading failure and are provided with additional support in reading. Furthermore, those students who fail to make adequate gains when they are provided with high-quality reading instruction are likely to need ongoing intensive support and would be candidates for referral for special services (e.g., special education). In summary, RTI frameworks seek first to prevent reading failure and then, for those students who do not respond to intervention, assessment data linked to instruction are used to accurately identify those students who may require special education services. In this way, many students who might otherwise meet criteria for "rule-out" from special education, but still fail to achieve in reading and fail to receive needed support, will learn to read when provided with effective instruction in reading within an RTI framework.

RTI AND THE PREVENTION OF READING FAILURE

RTI is a framework that focuses on two critical features of schooling for students with learning difficulties. First, RTI is a means for preventing reading difficulties. Students who respond to high-quality instruction or intervention in reading may no longer require special education services. Accordingly, RTI has been referred to as a "safety net" of sorts to catch struggling readers before they fail in school and in some cases, making the referral and identification of LD unnecessary (Fletcher et al., 2004; University of Texas Systems/Texas Education Agency, 2005). And second, for students who fail to make adequate progress even after receiving high quality interventions, RTI data can be used as one of several criteria for the identification of a learning disability and may be one of the data sources used in place of the traditional IQ-discrepancy formula. Essential to the prevention and accurate identification of learning disabilities is the ongoing assessment of students and the delivery of effective instruction and interventions based in current reading research.

Providing High Quality Instruction

What exactly is RTI and what does it look like? The implementation of an RTI framework can take many forms and specific models of implementation are designed based on the needs, resources, and preferences of particular schools or school districts (Batsche et al., 2005). Though not designed to capture every possible implementation of RTI, the National Association of State Directors of Special Education (Batsche et al., 2005) summarizes two primary models that serve as the basis for many of the iterations on RTI: standard protocol through data-based program modification (Deno, 1985; Deno & Mirkin, 1977) and behavioral consultation or problem-solving (Bergan, 1977; Bergan & Kratochwill, 1990). The problem-solving model and the standard protocol implementation share many common elements including defining the problem, measuring the problem, determining how students' learning problems compare with peers, identifying expectations, implementing interventions, monitoring progress and making decisions about continuing instruction or other interventions/placements (see Table 2.1). By identifying the key ideas from both the problem-solving and standard protocol interventions, it is possible to design a framework that integrates the approaches, determining when and how each would be used.

We describe one of these frameworks that we hereafter refer to as the *three-tier reading framework* (University of Texas System/Texas Education Agency, 2005). The three-tier reading framework has been implemented with students in grades K–3, both in research settings (in which research staff delivers interventions and collects assessment data) as well as in practice (in which sites have implemented the model with their own personnel and resources).

Tier I, Primary Intervention: Core Reading Instruction, Screening and Assessment, Ongoing Professional Development.

Tier I is the prevention element of a multitiered approach. It is perhaps the most important element because effective primary intervention provides the means for reducing risk by assuring all students are "on track" from the beginning. Through progress monitoring and differentiated instruction, effective teachers identify early students who need additional instruction, practice, or support and provide it. This careful consideration of the needs of all learners allows for a minimum number of students who are not making grade-level or higher gains. The goal is to improve the quality of reading instruction and thus, to avoid the overrepresentation of students with LD that can occur as a result of inadequate instruction in reading.

TABLE 2.1

The Bergan and Deno Models

Bergan Model: Modern Problem-Solving Steps	Deno Model: Modern Standard Protocol Reading Interventions
Define the problem behaviorally.	Define problems in terms of performance level and skills deficits.
Measure performance in the natural setting.	Assess reading skills through progress-monitoring, CBM and criterion-referenced skills inventories.
Determine current status and performance gap compared to peers.	Determine current status and performance gap compared to peers.
State a goal based on peer performance expectations.	State goals in terms of benchmarks for reading performance and peer expectations.
Design intervention plan, applying scientific instructional and behavior change principles.	Apply scientifically based instruction emphasizing five components of reading.
Implement intervention over a reasonable period of time with good treatment integrity.	Implement intervention over a reasonable period of time with good treatment integrity.
Monitor progress frequently using a time series analysis graph and make changes in the intervention as needed to improve effectiveness or raise goals, as indicated by data.	Monitor progress frequently using a time series analysis graph and make changes in the intervention as needed to improve effectiveness or raise goals, as indicated by data.
Evaluate results compared to goals and peer performance.	Evaluate results based on attainment of reading benchmarks.
Make decisions based on data to continue, fade, discontinue or seek more intense interventions.	Make decisions about discontinuing or phasing out small group instruction if benchmarks are attained *or* after consideration of further, more intense interventions, including possible special education eligibility.

Note: From *Response to Intervention: Policy Considerations and Implementation* (p. 8) by G. Batsche, J. Elliott, J. L. Graden, J. Grimes, J. F. Kovaleski, D. Prasse, D. J. Reschly, J. Schrag, & W. D. Tilly, III., (2005), Alexandria, VA: National Association of State Directors of Special Education. Copyright © 2005 by NASDSE. Reprinted with permission.

There are several critical elements of a core reading program. First, the core reading program is based on research and contains the critical components of beginning reading. These critical elements vary by grade level but include phonemic awareness, phonics, fluency, vocabulary, comprehension, spelling, and writing. Second, benchmark assessments that provide for screening and progress monitoring are given to all students at least three times a year to identify those students who are in need of supplemental reading intervention. And finally, ongoing professional development and follow-up support is provided to teachers to equip them with the support necessary to provide the high-quality reading instruction those students need. Essential to the success of the core reading program is using multiple grouping formats (e.g., one-on-one instruction, student pairing, small groups, whole group) as well as frequent progress monitoring to track student progress and to adjust instruction accordingly. Many schools implement a minimum of 90 minutes of core reading instruction everyday.

Tier II, Secondary Intervention.   Tier II instruction targets students who are not making adequate progress in the core reading program (Tier I). Decisions about who will receive supplemental instruction are made based on the results of benchmark assessments and progress monitoring. The goal of Tier II is to identify students and target their intervention so that their progress is accelerated and additional intervention is minimized. Typically, students who are provided secondary intervention continue in the core reading program so that the secondary intervention is "in addition" to their typical instruction. In many schools, students who are in need of supplemental instruction are provided this instruction for a designated amount of time. There are many examples of how secondary intervention may be provided. A few of these examples include: (a) students may receive one-on-one instruction for 5 days per week for 20 days and then based on their progress, further decisions may be made; and (b) students may receive small group instruction for a designated amount of time (20 to 60 sessions) and then student progress determines whether further intervention is provided or student data may be used for other purposes (e.g., placement, different program).

Over the past 5 years, we (e.g., Vaughn, Coleman, & Linan-Thompson, 2002) have been implementing and evaluating a three-tier framework in which students whose progress in their primary instruction (Tier I) is less than adequate are provided one 10 to 12 week round (approximately 50 sessions) of Tier II intervention. Then, based on assessment data, those students who meet benchmark goals no longer require supplemental intervention and continue on with core reading instruction only. Those students who are making slower progress receive a second round of Tier II intervention. Tier II instruction is generally 30 minutes daily (in addition to the core reading program) and can be provided by the classroom teacher, a reading specialist or another trained professional. Tier II instruction is tailored to the needs of small groups of students and contains frequent progress monitoring and refinement of instruction to meet individual student needs.

Tier III, Tertiary Intervention.   For many students, one or two rounds of secondary intervention are all they need to obtain a strong foundation in reading. These students, who without intervention might eventually have met eligibility criteria for special education services, are considered remediated. For other students, progress continues to be slow and assessment data suggests that they are not responding adequately to the core reading instruction, even with additional specialized support. Often termed *nonresponders*, these students show minimal gains during Tier I and II, or make progress but continue to read well below expectations. These low responders are the students who are most likely to be referred for special education services. It is expected that the progress monitoring and other assessment data obtained on these students while participating in the secondary intervention would be a useful data source for identifying these students as learning/reading disabled.

Students may enter Tier III intervention after one or two rounds of Tier II intervention in which little or no progress is made. In addition, students may go in and out of Tier III intervention depending on the type of support they need. Students who require Tier III intervention are likely to need ongoing support to be successful in the general education curriculum even when they have gained a strong foundation in early reading skills. Tier III reading intervention may or may not be part of special education services—depending on the framework and decision-making practices of the school and district.

Schools or districts must determine the relationship between Tier III intervention and placement in special education. When students become eligible for Tier III intervention, many schools also convene a pre-referral intervention team or an individualized education planning team to review progress and make recommendations for a student's continued educational needs.

RTI and Eligibility Determination

Assessment information including data from progress monitoring of benchmarks, and other evaluations administered in an RTI framework, can be used as part of LD determination. One potential issue related to using data from RTI as a source of information in determining the eligibility of students for special services is that it will promote variability in the prevalence rates of learning disabilities. The thinking is that because criteria for what constitutes adequate progress could vary from school to school, district to district, and/or state to state—the prevalence of students with learning disabilities will also vary considerably. Interestingly, there is already large variation across and within states on the prevalence of students with learning disabilities—as great as 2.9% to 9.4% (Reschly & Hosp, 2004). Districts that are currently using RTI report minimal changes in the percentage of students identified as learning disabled (Batsche et al., 2005).

All things being more or less equal, it is generally understood that students with LD do not achieve at the rate or level that would be expected given their age, ability level, or educational opportunity. Special education legislation mandates the identification of students who meet the criteria for LD so that these students can receive a special education. Until recently, the IQ-discrepancy formula was a defining feature of LD determination. That is, students were only eligible for special education services if it was found that they had a severe discrepancy between their ability (as measured by an IQ or an IQ equivalent score) and their performance (most commonly measured by standardized basic skill assessments). However, many researchers have questioned both the validity and utility of the IQ-discrepancy formula, particularly as a tool to differentiate poor readers with LD from poor readers without LD (Fletcher et al., 2004; Steubing, Fletcher, LeDoux, & Shaywitz, 2002). Although research syntheses and consensus reports outline a host of problems in the IQ-discrepancy formula (e.g., Bradley, Danielson, & Hallahan, 2002; Donovan & Cross, 2002; Lyon et al., 2001; Steubing et al., 2002), objections to the IQ-discrepancy formula have been challenged by others (see American Academy of School Psychology, 2004; Kavale, Holdnack, & Mostert, 2005). The prevailing views on the shortcomings of using an IQ-discrepancy formula to determine LD are summarized by Vaughn and Fuchs (2003):

1. The degree of discrepancy does not correlate to the severity of a learning disability.
2. Academic performance may not differ between those with and those without a discrepancy.
3. Discrepancy does not always yield reliable information (e.g., over-representing certain student populations and under-representing others).
4. The nature and degree of discrepancy do not inform instruction.
5. IQ-discrepancy is not necessary to determine a learning disability.

We address a few of the key issues associated with IQ-discrepancy but refer the reader to a complete discussion of the IQ-discrepancy debate elsewhere (Steubing et al., 2002). The failure of the IQ-discrepancy model to adequately identify students with LD is reflected in the most recent amendments to the Individuals with Disabilities Education Improvement Act (IDEA; 2004) that states that, " ... a local educational agency shall not be required to take into consideration whether a child has a severe discrepancy between achievement and intellectual ability ..." And further, that "... in determining whether a child has a specific learning disability, a local educational agency may use a process that determines if the child responds to scientific, research-based intervention" (sec 614).

Although IDEA (2004) does not preclude districts from using an IQ-discrepancy formula for determining LD, it allows for the use of an RTI framework as an alternative. Because RTI provides a way to assess the unexpected underachievement of students with LD and it is linked to instruction, RTI allows students to receive more immediate attention (Mellard, Byrd, Johnson, Tollefson, & Boesche, 2004).

Whereas in the more traditional models of LD determination, students often have to wait for the referral process to run its course (i.e., referral, assessment, eligibility determination, program planning) before receiving intervention, RTI works to differentiate students with learning disabilities from other learners at the same time as they are receiving instruction and interventions. Rather than providing instruction, waiting to see if a student fails and then beginning the special education referral process, in RTI frameworks, professionals seek first to provide high-quality instruction in the general education classroom in conjunction with the use of precise assessment tools to identify early those students at risk for reading failure and to monitor the progress of those students as they receive more intensive reading interventions matched to their particular learning needs. All students who are at risk are provided immediate intervention as early as kindergarten to address their needs in reading, much earlier than most students would be identified, referred, and placed in special education programs.

Another critical component of the discussion of eligibility determination is the utility, if any, of being identified with a learning disability. In essence, what good is the identification of an LD if it does not afford the student better learning opportunities? Gresham (2002) and others have used the term *treatment validity* to describe this phenomena and call for the use of assessment procedures that lead directly to positive outcomes for students. Just as assessments used in the classroom should inform instructional decisions, so too should the process for identifying a learning disability lead to recommendations for remediation. In an RTI framework, professionals come to the discussion of LD eligibility equipped with often extensive assessment data as well as instructional techniques that have been implemented and then a student's response or outcomes from the intervention. These data assist the IEP team in making well-informed decisions about areas of weakness or disability as well as recommendations for an appropriate special education program, if necessary.

The data-driven component of RTI addresses another important issue in LD identification—the misrepresentation of students from culturally or ethnically diverse backgrounds. If identification procedures were accurate enough, then students who read below expected levels due to other factors such as cultural or ethnic differences and environmental deprivation would not be labeled with LD. However, IQ-discrepancy eligibility determination often fails to distinguish real LD from poor readers (that might result from poor instruction in reading for example) and "rule-out" factors are written into the IDEA definition (IDEA, 2004) to avoid identifying students with LD who are not reading at expected levels but do not have a learning disability.

However, as a position statement from the International Reading Association (2003) states

> If quality instruction combined with timely and appropriately intense reading interventions does not solve the reading problem that is the source of the referral, then it is time to consider alternative programs such as special education. If educators deliver excellent reading instruction to children before considering a special education placement, they will identify more of the children for whom special education is truly appropriate. (p. 2)

RTI addresses the issue of educational opportunity and environmental disadvantage by calling attention to the training of teachers and specialists to provide high-quality research-based reading instruction and intensive intervention for those who need it, regardless of the cause and prior to a determination of eligibility for special education. In essence, when the RTI framework works, then the "rule-out" won't be utilized as students will be "ruled-out" once they are on track for learning to read.

In addition to bias in traditional eligibility assessments, potential biases exist at the classroom level as well. Teachers have commonly been the ones to identify students who are referred for special education eligibility determination. However, this has resulted in an overrepresentation of boys and African-American students who are referred for special education, most likely due to classroom behavior management issues (Donovan & Cross, 2002). When RTI is used appropriately, identification for intervention and/or referral to special education is data driven and thus does not rely on teacher opinion and potential bias about student functioning (Fletcher et al., 2004). Teachers' views are an important part of eligibility determination, but in RTI they are based in data on ability and growth in reading that are collected as part of progress monitoring and other assessments in reading.

In sum, RTI has provided a framework for promising solutions to many of the problems associated with reading failure in schools. However, implementing the features of RTI effectively may require shifts in how resources are allocated, teacher training, implementation of instruction, as well as the pedagogy of reading and the meaning of special education. In the next section, we report on several key issues related to research and implementation of RTI frameworks.

RTI Research and Practice

There is little question that additional research on the effective implementation of RTI frameworks is required. Perhaps the strongest research base is on practices related to early reading interventions for students with reading difficulties (e.g., Blachman et al., 2004; Felton, 1993; Jenkins & O'Connor, 2002; Lovett, Steinbach, & Frijters, 2000; Torgesen et al., 1999; Vellutino et al., 1996). The two areas where the most significant research is required are: (a) establishing evidence of the appropriate use of assessment methods and establishing cut-offs for the identification of students with learning disabilities, and (b) identifying and implementing effective interventions with older students (Grades 4–12).

Need for More Empirical Evidence of Assessment Methods. Several studies have looked at the role of the RTI framework in identifying students as nonresponders, those students who do not respond to effective instruction and intervention. Of importance in this area is identifying what types of assessments yield information about what it means to respond or not respond to intervention. Several studies have demonstrated the effectiveness of a dual discrepancy approach (Fuchs & Fuchs, 1998). A dual discrepancy occurs when students are discrepant from their peers in both reading skills (performance level) and the rate at which they make gains in reading (growth rate). For example, Speece and Case (2001) focused on the utility of using criterion-based reading measures to identify students with LD using a dual-discrepancy format. In this study, students who were given a battery of curriculum-based measures (CBM; criterion referenced assessments linked to instruction) in reading were compared with students who received assessments to identify IQ-achievement discrepancy. Students who fell in the lowest quartile in the CBM group demonstrated more reading deficits and more closely matched the ethnic distribution of the school than did students who demonstrated an IQ-achievement discrepancy. In another study, McMaster and colleagues (McMaster, Fuchs, Fuchs, & Compton, 2005) also used a dual-discrepancy approach to identify and intervene with nonresponders in reading and found that this approach was a reliable and valid way to distinguish between nonresponders and peers who were either "at-risk" readers who were responsive to intervention or normally achieving readers. Although these studies provide evidence to support the use of a dual-discrepancy approach to identify nonresponders, less research actually has taken this information to determine eligibility for LD and then followed the progress of these students relative to students who have been identified with LD using an IQ-discrepancy approach.

Another relevant issue is whether students who fail to respond to effective instruction and intervention are learning disabled. Because reading failure often is comorbid with other disabilities, such as attention deficit hyperactivity disorder or behavior disorder, referrals and testing for special education should take into account possible alternative explanations for reading failure (Vaughn & Fuchs, 2003). Students who have mental retardation, for example, also may be nonresponders, requiring identification and services that match their specific needs. Implementation of RTI models should include collaboration between professionals in various programs, including but not limited to special education, to ensure that LD does not become a catchall category for nonresponders. Although several large-scale interventions have identified students with LD within an RTI framework (e.g., Donovan & Cross, 2002; Gresham, 2002), there is still a need to further validate specific methods and procedures for identifying which nonresponders meet criteria for LD determination (Mellard et al., 2004; Vaughn & Fuchs, 2003).

Advantages to using RTI as a prevention practice and a resource for eligibility for students with learning disabilities can be summarized as reducing reliance on the teacher as the sole source for referral, focusing on academic skills rather than processing difficulties, reducing the number of students who require special education support but are not identified and referred by teachers, and increasing the focus on current learning under positive instructional conditions (Speece, Case, & Molloy, 2003).

Identifying and Implementing an RTI Framework with Older Students. Considering the rather extensive database on effective interventions for struggling readers in the early grades, considerably less is known about the factors associated with effective interventions for older students. In part, this is because the variation in reading-related difficulties is greater in older students. Although students may require instruction in many of the elements related to reading difficulties in younger students (e.g., alphabetic principle, word-reading strategies, fluency), additional factors also may need to be addressed. Older students' difficulties may result from the accumulated negative outcomes associated with low levels of reading, such as limited vocabulary and concept knowledge, few comprehension strategies for reading diverse text types, especially expository/information texts, and low motivation for reading (e.g., see Snow & Biancarosa, 2004, for a review). In particular, research is needed regarding students with persistent and significant reading disabilities to better understand practices related to classification and definition of reading disabilities (the most prevalent type of learning disability) in older students.

There is also evidence to suggest that reading difficulties in older students, just as in young children, are often the result of inadequate instruction in reading (Torgesen et al., 2001). Furthermore, the results of research in this area suggest that intensive instruction in beginning reading skills can be an effective way to remediate reading failure in older students. Thus, there is promise for the use of an RTI framework for older students (Reschly & Hosp, 2004). The challenge of using RTI with students in middle and high schools also involves working with the demands of curricula and scheduling that make it difficult to allocate the amount of time and resources that are needed to provide effective interventions. Administrators should encourage effective reading interventions for older students, even when they also may be considered for special education services.

How Are Resources Allocated for the Reform of Current Practices?

RTI is not a reading program or even a reading model, it is in fact a reform effort that like other large-scale reforms often requires a system-wide evaluation of current practices and a reallocation of resources in a variety of areas. For example, one guide suggests that administrators conduct an evaluation of current reading practices that includes the following components prior to implementing RTI.

> Curriculum and supplemental materials; instructional practices; amount of time devoted to instruction; integration of reading and writing into other curricular domains; supplemental materials for students who are struggling; referral processes for supplemental instruction; environmental arrangement and grouping practices; professional development; and assessment processes and student outcome data. (University of Texas System/Texas Education Agency, 2004, p. 84)

The implication of evaluating this extensive list of components is that some or all may need to be altered or changed considerably in order to implement an effective RTI framework. Reworking a current program at the school, district, or state level requires buy-in by practitioners at every level as well as the resources to provide long-term professional development, appropriate materials, and the flexibility in the curriculum and scheduling to provide the amount of time needed to implement intensive interventions. In addition, RTI implementation also may require coordination of multiple programs, including general education, special education, Title I, ESL and other funding and instructional resources. This is a large, but not insurmountable, task if there is adequate leadership and commitment to ongoing professional development.

More Research Is Needed to Understand Large-Scale Implementation of RTI.   RTI has been implemented in a variety of settings, but still at a limited scale. One of the greatest needs now, is the implementation of large-scale RTI research to study its general effectiveness (Danielson, Doolittle, & Bradley, 2005). Although the National Research Council on Learning Disabilities is beginning to scale-up research efforts (Mellard et al., 2004), it will be some time before results can be disseminated. What will RTI look like once it is in the hands of schools and teachers? Will teachers and specialists be able to access the training and resources needed to effectively implement research-based reading instruction, progress monitoring, and the tiered interventions that are integral to an RTI framework? For example, Lyon and colleagues (2001) determined that many teachers do not yet have the conceptual or pedagogical skills to provide research-based instruction in reading. The implication here is that there is a basic need to provide system-wide professional development opportunities with follow-up support and resources to improve teacher quality. Ysseldyke (2005) has suggested that their may even be what he terms a "condition called 'RTI resistance'" (p. 127) as teachers are required to implement these effective but time consuming practices that may even result in higher rates of identification of LD. Although it takes a great effort to expand research and practice and wait for results, current evidence from research demonstrates that more and larger studies of RTI implementation are worth pursuing (Fletcher et al., 2004).

CONCLUSION

RTI frameworks are currently being implemented in districts throughout the United States and implementation is likely to increase in response to IDEA (2004). These frameworks hold much potential both for preventative interventions for students with and without disabilities, leading as well to more appropriate identifications. Implementation of RTI requires highly trained personnel who can provide leadership and instructional support as interventions and problem solving practices are implemented. Decisions regarding when in the RTI process students may be considered sufficiently nonresponsive to warrant referral and placement in special education requires highly knowledgeable and skilled professionals.

Kauffman (1993, 1994) has indicated that if we are to have the highly prepared and knowledgeable professionals in special education needed to implement appropriate assessments and interventions for individuals with disabilities, teacher preparation programs will have to be even more rigorous and the induction process into teaching will require adjustments (Kauffman, 1994; Gelman, Pullen, & Kauffman, 2004). Kauffman's analysis of special education reform leads to recognition that change for change sake is not the goal. Rather, when reform is instituted, the overall result should be improved services and outcomes for students with disabilities (Kauffman, 1993, 1999). We hope that the many benefits associated with RTI can be realized and the pitfalls avoided.

REFERENCES

American Academy of School Psychology. (2004). Recommendation on comprehensive evaluation for learning disabilities. *Communiquè, 32*(7), 12.

Batsche, G., Elliott, J., Graden, J. L., Grimes, J., Kovaleski, J. F., Prasse, D., et al. (2005). *Response to intervention: Policy considerations and implementation.* Alexandria, VA: National Association of State Directors of Special Education.

Bergan, J. R. (1977). *Behavioral consultation.* Columbus, OH: Merrill.

Bergan, J. R., & Kratochwill, T. R. (1990). *Behavioral consultation and therapy.* New York: Plenum.

Blachman, B. A., Schatschneider, C., Fletcher, J. M., Francis, D. J., Clonan, S. M., Shaywitz, B. A., et al. (2004). Effects of intensive reading remediation for second and third graders and a 1-year follow-up. *Journal of Educational Psychology, 96*, 441–461.

Bradley, R., Danielson, L., & Hallahan, D. P. (Eds.). (2002). *Identification of learning disabilities: Research to practice.* Mahwah, NJ: Lawrence Erlbaum Associates.

Crockett, J. B., & Kauffman, J. M. (1998). Taking inclusion back to its roots. *Educational Leadership, 56,* 74–77.

Crocket, J. B., & Kauffman, J. M. (1999). *The least restrictive environment: Its origins and interpretations in special education.* Mahwah, NJ: Lawrence Erlbaum Associates.

Danielson, L., Doolittle, J., & Bradley, R. (2005). Past accomplishments and future challenges. *Learning Disability Quarterly, 28,* 137–139.

Deno, S. (1985). Curriculum-based measurement: The emerging alternative. *Educational Children, 52,* 219–232.

Deno, S., & Mirkin, P. J. (1977). *Data-based program modification: A manual.* Washington, DC: Office of Education.

Donovan, M. S., & Cross, C. T. (Eds.). (2002). *Minority students in special and gifted education.* Washington, DC: National Academy Press.

Felton, R. (1993). Effects of instruction on the decoding skills of children with phonological processing problems. *Journal of Learning Disabilities, 26*(9), 583–589.

Fletcher, J. M., Coulter, W. A., Reschly, D. J., & Vaughn, S. (2004). Alternative approaches to the definition and identification of learning disabilities: Some questions and answers. *Annals of Dyslexia, 54*(2), 304–331.

Fletcher, J. M., Lyon, G. R., Barnes, M., Stuebing, K. K., Francis, D. J., Olson, R. K., et al. (2002). Classification of learning disabilities: An evidence-based evaluation. In R. Bradley, L. Danielson, & D. P. Hallahan (Eds.), *Identification of learning disabilities: Research to practice*, 185–250. Mahwah, NJ: Lawrence Erlbaum Associates.

Fletcher, J. M., Shaywitz, S. E., Shankweller, D. P., Katz, L., Liberman, I. Y., & Fowler, A. (1994). Cognitive profiles of reading disability: Comparisons of discrepancy and low achievement definitions. *Journal of Educational Psychology, 85,* 1–18.

Francis, D. J., Shaywitz, S. E., Stuebing, K. K., Shaywitz, B. A., & Fletcher, J. M. (1996). Developmental lag versus deficit models of reading disability: A longitudinal, individual growth curves analysis. *Journal of Educational Psychology, 88,* 3–17.

Fuchs, L. S. (2005). *Prevention research in mathematics: Improving outcomes, building identification models, and understanding disability.* Retrieved November 13, 2005, from http://oh1.csa.com/ids70/view_record.php?id=1&recnum=0&SID=ff84871fed1226119fbb0175b6c088c6. *Journal of Learning Disabilities, 38*(4), 350–352.

Fuchs, L. S., & Fuchs, D. (1998). Treatment validity: A unifying concept for reconceptualizing the identification of learning disabilities. *Learning Disabilities Research and Practice, 13*(4), 204–219.

Gelman, J. A., Pullen, P. L., & Kauffman, J. M. (2004). The meaning of highly qualified and a clear road map to accomplishment. *Exceptionality, 12*(4), 195–207.

Gresham, F. M. (2002). Responsiveness to intervention: An alternative approach to the identification of learning disabilities. In R. Bradley, L. Danielson, & D. P. Hallahan (Eds.), *Identification of learning disabilities: Research to practice* (pp. 467–564). Mahwah, NJ: Lawrence Erlbaum Associates.

Individuals with Disabilities Education Improvement Act Regulations. (2004). SEC. 614. *Evaluations, eligibility determinations, individualized education programs, and educational placements.* Retrieved from http://thomas.loc.gov/cgi-bin/query/z?c108:h.1350.enr>:

International Reading Association. (2003). *The role of reading instruction in addressing the overrepresentation of minority children in special education in the United Sates: A position statement of the International Reading Association* [Brochure]. Newark, DE: Author.

Jenkins, J. R., & O'Connor, R. E. (2002). Early identification and intervention for young children with reading/learning disabilities. In R. Bradley, L. Danielson, & D. Hallahan (Eds.), *Identification of learning disabilities* (pp. 99–149). Hillsdale, NJ: Lawrence Erlbaum Associates.

Kauffman, J. M. (1993). How we might achieve the radical reform of special education. *Exceptional Children, 60*(1), 6–16.

Kauffman, J. M. (1994). Places of change: Special education's power and identity in an era of educational reform. *Journal of Learning Disabilities, 27*(10), 610–618.

Kauffman, J. M. (1999). Places of change: Special education's power and identity in an era of educational reform. *Journal of Learning Disabilities, 27,* 610–618.

Kauffman, J. M. (2003). Reflections on the field. *Education and Treatment of Children, 26*(4), 325–329.

Kavale, K. A., Holdnack, J. A., & Mostert, M. P. (2005). Responsiveness to intervention and identification of specific learning disability: A critique and alternative proposal. *Learning Disability Quarterly, 28,* 2–16.

Lovett, M. W., Steinbach, K. A., & Frijters, J. C. (2000). Remediating the core deficits of developmental reading disability: A double-deficit perspective. *Journal of Learning Disabilities, 33*(4), 334–359.

Lyon, G. R., Fletcher, J. M., Shaywitz, S. E., Shaywitz, B. A., Torgensen, J. K., Wood, F. B., et al. (2001). Rethinking learning disabilities. In C. E. Finn, Jr., R. A. J. Rotherham, & C. R. Hokanson, Jr. (Eds.), *Rethinking special education for a new century* (pp. 259–287). Washington, DC: Thomas B. Fordham Foundation and Progressive Policy Institute.

McMaster, K. L., Fuchs, D., Fuchs, L. S., Compton, D. L. (2005). Responding to nonresponders: An experimental field trial of identification and intervention methods. *Exceptional Children, 71*, 445–463.

Mellard, D. F., Byrd, S. E., Johnson, E., Tollefson, J. M., & Boesche, L. (2004). Foundations and research on identifying model responsiveness-to-intervention sites. *Learning Disability Quarterly, 27*, 243–256.

National Research Council. (1998). *Preventing reading difficulties in young children.* Washington, DC: U.S. Department of Education.

Reschly, D. J., & Hosp, J. L. (2004). State SLD policies and practices. *Learning Disability Quarterly, 27*, 197–213.

Shaywitz, B. A., Fletcher, J. M., Holahan, J. M., & Shaywitz, S. E. (1992). Discrepancy compared to low achievement definitions of reading disability: Results from the Connecticut Longitudinal Study. *Journal of Learning Disabilities, 25*, 639–648.

Snow, C., & Biancarosa, G. (2004). *Reading next: A vision for action and research in middle and high school literacy: A report to Carnegie Corporation of New York.* Washington, DC: Alliance for Excellent Education.

Speece, D. L., & Case, L. P. (2001). Classification in context: An alternative approach to identifying early learning disability. *Journal of Educational Psychology, 93*, 735–749.

Speece, D. L., Case, L. P., & Molloy, D. E. (2003). Responsiveness to general education instruction as the first gate to learning disabilities identification. *Learning Disabilities Research and Practice, 18*(3), 147–156.

Stuebing, K. K., Fletcher, J. M., LeDoux, J. M., & Shaywitz, B. A. (2002). Validity of IQ-discrepancy classifications of reading disabilities: A meta-analysis. *American Educational Research Journal, 39*, 469–518.

Torgesen, J. K., Alexander, A. W., Wagner, R. K., Rashotte, C. A., Voeller, K. S., & Conway, T. (2001). Intensive remedial instruction for children with severe reading disabilities: Immediate and long-term outcomes from two instructional approaches. *Journal of Learning Disabilities, 34*, 33–58.

Torgesen, J. K., Wagner, R. K., Rashotte, C. A., Rose, E., Lindamood, P., Conway, T., et al. (1999). Preventing reading failure in young children with phonological processing disabilities: Group and individual response to instruction. *Journal of Educational Psychology, 91*, 579–593.

University of Texas System/Texas Education Agency. (2004). *3-Tier reading model: Reducing reading difficulties for kindergarten through third-grade students* (Rev. ed.). Austin, TX: Texas Education Agency.

University of Texas System/Texas Education Agency. (2005). *Introduction to the 3-tier reading model: Reducing reading difficulties for kindergarten through third grade students* (4th ed.). Austin, TX: Texas Education Agency.

Vaughn, S., Coleman, M., & Linan-Thompson, S. (January 2002–December 2006). *Preventing reading difficulties: A three-tiered intervention model.* The University of Texas at Austin. Retrieved November 4, 2005, from http://www.nichcy.org/directories/84.324x.asp.

Vaughn, S., & Fuchs, L. S. (2003). Redefining learning disabilities as inadequate response to instruction: The promise and potential problems. *Learning Disabilities Research and Practice, 18*(3), 137–146.

Vaughn, S., Linan-Thompson, S., & Hickman-Davis, P. (2003). Response to treatment as a means of identifying students with reading/learning disabilities. *Exceptional Children, 69*(4), 391–409.

Vellutino, F., Scanlon, D., Sipay, E., Small, S., Pratt, A., & Chen, R. (1996). Cognitive profiles of difficult-to-remediate and readily remediated poor readers: Early intervention as a vehicle for distinguishing between cognitive and experiential deficits as basic causes of specific reading disabilities. *Journal of Educational Psychology, 88*, 601–638.

Walker, H. M., Horner, R. H., Sugai, G., Bullis, M., Sprague, J. R., Bricker, D., et al. (1996). Integrated approaches to preventing antisocial behavior patterns among school-age children and youth. *Journal of Emotional and Behavioral Disorders, 4*, 193–256.

Ysseldyke, J. (2005). Assessment and decision making for students with learning disabilities: What if this is as good as it gets? *Learning Disabilities Quarterly, 28*, 125–128.

Chapter 3

Early, Evidence-Based Intervention with School-Related Behavior Disorders: Key Issues, Continuing Challenges, and Promising Practices

Hill M. Walker
Jeffrey R. Sprague
University of Oregon

In the past decade, school-related behavioral disorders, as manifested by the growing population of at-risk children and youth, has been an increasing focus of policymakers, legislators, and educators. In light of an increasingly demanding but unsupportive public, declining fiscal and political support, and the mandates and impact of the No Child Left Behind Act, the public schools' tolerance for investments in long-term prevention efforts to buffer and offset the impact of environmental risk factors affecting at-risk students has shown a corresponding decline. Given the demographic, linguistic and cultural diversity of the current school-age population, schools are required to accommodate an ever-widening spectrum of children's behavioral characteristics, school readiness levels, attitudes, and beliefs. At the same time, the tools and resources required to achieve this goal are increasingly beyond the reach of many educators due to a range of policy, bureaucratic, legal, fiscal and professional obstacles.

The conditions just discussed, when combined with the numerous risks (individual, familial, community, societal) to which our children and youth are currently exposed, substantially reduce the odds that behaviorally at-risk students can successfully navigate the many challenges and barriers facing them during their public school careers. Members of the at-risk student population frequently bring highly dysfunctional and aversive behavior patterns with them as they begin their schooling careers as well as poorly developed school readiness skills (e.g., good school work habits, the ability to cooperate with others, a willingness to accept adult directives and instructions). Because of the aversive and intractable nature of their behavior they are quickly identified as "problem students" by teachers and peers as individuals to avoid within several years of beginning schooling (Kauffman, 1999, 2005; Reid, Patterson, & Snyder, 2002; Walker, Ramsey, & Gresham, 2004). If these students remain on this path by the intermediate grades they are rejected by most of their teachers and become eligible for membership in a deviant peer group consisting of students with similar behavioral characteristics and histories. The long-term, negative consequences and destructive outcomes for such students have been well documented in longitudinal studies conducted in the United States, New Zealand, Canada, Britain, and Western Europe (Kellam, Brown, Rubin, & Ensminger, 1983; Reid et al., 2002).

Aggressive, antisocial behavior that is characterized by an early onset, severe intensity, occurrence across multiple settings, and that persists across school years, appears to be a harbinger of these destructive outcomes among large numbers of at-risk children and youth (Kellam, Rebok, Ialongo, & Mayer, 1994; Patterson, Reid, & Dishion, 1997). Early detection of these behavior patterns that are so disruptive of school adjustment and success, and implementation of proven, evidence-based interventions to teach an adaptive behavior pattern that will alter this destructive trajectory, is one of the most important policy objectives in our field.

Kauffman (1993, 2002, 2003, 2004, 2005) has been an articulate and effective advocate for the adoption of such evidence-based strategies and approaches. At the same time, he has been a realist about the cultural values and beliefs of the educational enterprise that resists adoption of potentially effective policies despite overwhelming evidence that we have the means to achieve such a goal in a cost-effective manner (Lynch, 2004). In a series of articles written over the past decade, he has provided a thoughtful and provocative analysis of the current situation and especially how the early detection and intervention of behaviorally at-risk students to achieve prevention goals can be stigmatizing, demeaning and damaging (e.g., see Kauffman, 2002, 2003, 2004, 2005). Broad numbers of educators misinterpret this argument as a rationale for resisting adoption and implementation of effective prevention policies and approaches.

Casting this dilemma in the form of an assimilation-accommodation continuum, this latter perspective registers as a highly conservative position in which all students are expected to adjust satisfactorily to the demands and expectations of the school setting without benefit of or access to special accommodations. As a result, larger and larger numbers of the at-risk student population face a rejecting and often hostile school environment that all too often merely waits for them to fail and exit the premises.

The field of medicine provides a useful and clarifying analogy in this regard. For example, from a public health perspective, one would argue that all children should be inoculated against the preventable diseases that they may contract at some point in their development. However, using the conservative approach to school-related behavior disorders just referenced, we would not inoculate these youth because (a) it would cause them to be stigmatized as possibly disease prone and (b) resources for treating those who do eventually contract the disease would be preserved for when they are actually needed. But, at such point, the risks to the patient, the cumulative damage incurred from failure to address the problem(s), as well as the cost(s) may well be extraordinary.

This chapter addresses key issues and challenges facing those who advocate for the early detection and treatment of behaviorally at-risk students in using evidence-based approaches and strategies. The remainder of the chapter addresses three major topics as follows: (a) the evidence base for detecting and intervening effectively with school-age children and youth having aggressive, disruptive, and oppositional behavior disorders; (b) the extent to which effective approaches are *not* being adopted and implemented in public school contexts and some possible reasons as to why this may be the case; and (c) presentation of some promising results from implementation of the *First Step to Success* early intervention program that was coordinated by a county mental health department-level Commission on Children and Families over a 4-year period across three Oregon school districts. The chapter concludes with a discussion of the need to further integrate school and mental health policies and practices in the context of prevention and early intervention.

THE EVIDENCE BASE FOR INTERVENING EFFECTIVELY WITH SCHOOL-RELATED BEHAVIOR DISORDERS

As Kauffman (2005) has noted, early intervention designed to offset a destructive trajectory can mean intervening either (a) early in the development of the trajectory and/or (b) early in a child's life course. The important point is to intervene as early and as effectively as possible in order to divert the at-risk child or youth away from a destructive trajectory that predicts current and future negative outcomes. Often, a child's entry into kindergarten is an opportunity for addressing his or her behavior problems; this is particularly true for children who have acquired an antisocial behavior pattern prior to school entry. Reid (1993) has observed that in order to intervene effectively at the point of school entry, it is important to involve the three most important social agents in the child's life as part of the intervention—parents, teachers, and peers. The authors' combined experience over several decades with implementing school-based interventions to solve behavior problems confirms this observation. In order to mount and sustain effective school interventions for behavior problems over the long term, it is essential to create meaningful and continuing roles for these social agents in the behavior change process.

Key Characteristics of Evidence-Based Interventions (EBIs) in Behavior Disorders

In the past decade, evidence-based intervention approaches have been defined and promoted pervasively in the professional literatures of psychology and education (see Adelman & Taylor, 2003; Hoagwood & Johnson, 2003; Kratochwill & Shernoff, 2004).

Kimberly Hoagwood has been one of the most articulate and effective advocates of such approaches within the context of schooling for addressing the mental health needs of K–12 students (Burns & Hoagwood, 2002; Hoagwood, 2003/2004; Schoenwald & Hoagwood, 2001). A generic definition of evidence-based practices, according to Hoagwood, refers to a body of scientific knowledge about treatments, prevention, and intervention approaches or service practice (Hoagwood, 2003/2004). Kratochwill and Shernoff (2004), on the other hand, argue that an intervention or practice should carry the EBI designation only when (a) information about its contextual application in actual practice is specified and (b) when it has demonstrated effectiveness under the conditions of implementation and evaluation in actual practice.

EBIs reported in the empirical literature have in common that they are research-based, structured, manualized and tested using randomized clinical trials. Many experts in prevention science insist that in order to rise to the level of a scientifically acceptable EBI, it has to be tested successfully against an untreated control group within a randomized trial (Kellam & Langevin, 2003). However, researchers within the field of applied behavior disorders often make the case that the use of single-subject methodology with multiple replications is of sufficient rigor for establishing the necessary scientific evidence for school interventions (Bingham, 2001; Strain, 2001). Such disagreement over standards for establishing scientific rigor will likely persist regarding EBIs in school settings.

An important distinction relating to EBIs involves *efficacy* versus *effectiveness*. Efficacy refers to the demonstration that an intervention works under idealized conditions (e.g., grant-funded, properly supervised, adequate fidelity, and so forth) while under the control of the developer. In contrast, effectiveness refers to the demonstration of positive outcomes for the intervention under normal or routine conditions within the target setting. Very often, these conditions are not ideal. Demonstrating effectiveness is a far more difficult task. Many promising practices or programs fail to bridge the gap between efficacy and effectiveness. Ideally, an EBI will produce acceptable outcomes even when it is implemented by practitioners with less than optimal fidelity (Walker, Golly, McLane, & Kimmich, 2005).

A final, important characteristic of EBIs refers to the magnitude or power of the treatment effect (i.e., effect size) produced by the intervention. Typically, a robust effect size favoring the intervention group is considered to be .80 and above; a moderate effect size ranges between .50 and .80; and a low or weak effect size is considered to be in the .20 to .50 range of magnitude.

The Availability of EBI Practices and Approaches for Use by School Personnel

The fields of school-related behavior disorders, prevention science, and positive behavior supports have all developed cohesive, accessible and school-relevant knowledge bases of information that are judged to be of substantial value in addressing the myriad problems that behaviorally at-risk students present to educators (Bingham, 2001; Horner, Sugai, Lewis-Palmer, & Todd, 2001; Katsiyannis & Yell, 2004; Kauffman, 2005; Kellam, Mayer, Rebok, & Hawkins, 1998; Kellam, & Rebok, 1992; Reid et. al, 2002; Stichter & Conroy, 2004; Sugai & Horner, 2002; Walker et al., 2004). The evidence-based tools, strategies and approaches described in these related literatures provide the means for educators and related services professionals to intervene effectively early on the trajectory or pathway(s) that are associated with so many destructive outcomes later on in the lives of at-risk children and youth (e.g., school failure and dropout, delinquency, violent acts, drug and alcohol abuse, early arrests for serious offenses). The empirical supports and results for these approaches are generally robust and reflect the highest scientific standards in conducting intervention studies for the purpose of achieving prevention outcomes. The work of Kellam and his colleagues has been particularly noteworthy in this regard.

The Cost-Effectiveness of Early Intervention

The case for the cost-effectiveness of early intervention is, in the authors' view, quite persuasive, particularly if young children have been enrolled in quality preschool programs. Lynch (2004) recently conducted a seminal review of the evidence for the cost–benefits of high-quality, early childhood development (ECD) programs. Long-term studies of ECD programs document the following positive outcomes or benefits for them:

1. Higher levels of academic achievement.
2. Greater school success, including less grade retention and higher graduation rates.
3. Higher employment and earnings.
4. Better health outcomes.
5. Less welfare dependency.
6. Lower crime rates.
7. Lower government expenditures.

As a rule, investments in high-quality, early childhood development programs produce very high rates of return for participants. For example, Lynch (2004) reports that benefit cost ratios for four well-known ECD programs were as follows: (1) the Perry Preschool Program ($8.74); (2) the Prenatal/Early Infancy Program ($5.06); (3) the Abecedarian Program ($3.78); and (4) the Chicago Child–Parent Program ($7.14). Typically, these ratios are calculated by subtracting the cost of program participation, adjusting dollars for inflation over the long term, and estimating the benefits in dollars of such long-term outcomes as *not* having to consume expensive services such as drug and alcohol treatment; avoiding delinquency and school dropout; avoiding welfare combined with the value-added, fiscal contributions of full employment and payment of taxes.

The Perry Preschool Program has been the subject of numerous economic analysis studies using these methods (see Barnett, 1985a, 1985b). This program was established in Ypsilanti, Michigan by David Weikart and his colleagues during the 1960s (see Weikart, Bond, & McNeil, 1978) and is regarded as model, high-quality preschool program. The Perry Preschool Program was designed to serve economically disadvantaged 3- and 4-year-old children. The participants were randomly assigned to either the Perry Preschool Program or to an equivalent control group. Children in an experimental group attended an enriched preschool program in the morning with a specially designed curriculum. In the afternoon, their teachers made home visits to the parents of participating children. Group meetings of the participating children's parents with program staff were also arranged on a regular basis. The total cost of the program for 1 year averaged $4,963 for each participant.

Through age 19, the program returned an average of $7,580 per participant (in 1986 dollars); beyond age 19, the return averaged $12,126 on average. Table 3.1 provides a comparison of these two groups on a series of socially important outcome measures. The Perry Preschoolers had substantially more positive profiles than did control participants across these long-term outcomes. The Perry Preschoolers and members of the control group have been followed well into adulthood and continue to show widely divergent life-course paths.

Similarly dramatic outcomes have been reported over a 25-year follow-up period for highly disruptive-aggressive children who were treated between the ages of 3 and 6 by a Regional Intervention Program (i.e., see Strain & Tim, 2001). Hawkins, Catalano, Kosterman, Abbott, and Hill (1999) reported results of a long-term follow-up study focused on prevention of adolescent health risk outcomes (e.g., substance abuse, violent delinquent acts, heavy drinking, sexually transmitted diseases, etc.) attributable to early intervention with

TABLE 3.1

Longitudinal Follow-Up Assessment Results
for the Perry Preschool Program

Category	Experimental	Control	ρ
Early childhood			
IQ at age 5	95	83	<.01
Late childhood			
School years in special education	16%	28%	.04
Ever classified mentally retarded	15%	35%	.01
Adolescent/early adulthood			
Age 15 mean achievement test score	122.2	94.5	<.01
High school graduation	67%	49%	.03
Postsecondary education	38%	21%	.03
Arrested or detained	31%	51%	.02
Employed at age 19	50%	32%	.03
Receiving welfare at age 19	18%	32%	.04

teachers, parents, and target children within grades 1–3. The study involved a large sample ($N = 642$) of at-risk youth at the beginning of their school careers who were randomly assigned to one of three groups (i.e., early intervention, later intervention, and control). At age 18, the authors followed up with 598 of the original sample and found no differences on any of their measures between later intervention and control youth; however, the early intervention group was favored on a broad range of outcomes when compared to the control group. The authors concluded that bonding, full engagement, and attachment to schooling served as a powerful protective factor against a host of health-risk outcomes in their study. Finally, Zigler, Taussig, and Black (1992) reviewed the evidence regarding the prevention of delinquency and concluded that *the* most effective prevention strategy was early, preschool education in which parents were involved and that focused on developing social, emotional, and academic competence skills. The just-cited studies and evidence are only a small piece of the seminal studies that have and continue to be conducted that document the powerful returns from investing in quality preschool programs and EBIs that are implemented well and early on in an at-risk student's developmental trajectory.

In the past decade, both the development and accessibility of evidence-based interventions and practices for addressing behavioral challenges in the context of schools have become much more available to educational consumers. However, substantial obstacles remain that constrain schools' willingness and ability to implement these proven and promising practices. Hoagwood (2001) has provided insightful analyses and commentary regarding their impact in preventing the delivery of needed intervention services and supports to at-risk children and youth. This issue is examined in the next section and some possible reasons are offered for their existence and continuing negative impact.

BARRIERS TO THE ADOPTION AND IMPLEMENTATION OF EVIDENCE-BASED PRACTICES IN SCHOOLS

In spite of the considerable progress that has been achieved over the past decade in the development and dissemination of evidence-based practices, the inability of educators to access, adopt and deliver them within the context of schooling persists (Hoagwood,

2001). Burns and Hoagwood (2002) argue the following in this regard: (a) that approximately 20% of today's students in K–12 would qualify for a recognized mental disorder, (b) that about one sixth of these students actually receive treatment services and supports for their problems, and (c) only 10% of these students are exposed to evidence-based practices that are matched to their disorder(s). It has been the rule rather than the exception for promising evidence-based practices and innovations to languish on the shelves of their developers due to such factors as (a) a failure to adapt them to the minimal requirements of the target settings for which they were designed or in which they could be used effectively; (b) philosophical disagreement with the basic premises or procedures of the practice by end users; (c) the perception that the practice requires more time, effort and expertise than its potential gain(s) may produce in improved child outcomes; and (d) the disruptive intrusiveness of the practice re normal operational routines (Hoagwood, 2001; 2003/ 2004).

In his now-classic text on the diffusion and adoption of innovations, Rogers (1995) shows that the continuum ranging from discovery to adoption and implementation of an innovation shows considerable time lags across all fields of inquiry and disciplines. Even simple innovations can experience long time lags from discovery to adoption. For example, Rogers reports that the simple dietary cure for scurvy, a debilitating and often fatal disorder, was discovered during the mid-1700s by a surgeon in the British Royal Navy; however, another century was required before this preventive measure was fully implemented across all British naval and merchant fleets. It is estimated that this time lag is approximately 20 years in mental health; it is likely at least this long in K–12 education.

Kauffman (1993, 1996) has been an effective and informed critic of schools' reluctance to adopt evidence-based practices that can have a positive impact on at-risk students, particularly students with behavior problems and disorders. Kauffman notes that there has been relatively little sustained improvement in educational practices over the past several decades due to the weak relationship between the availability of evidence-based practices and their dissemination and adoption within school contexts (see Walker, 2004). Schoenwald and Hoagwood (2001) and Schoenwald and Rowland (2002) have written at length on the issues involved and the need for a research agenda on the transportability of interventions and innovative practices from efficacy to effectiveness. Crossing this chasm within school settings can be an especially complex and difficult task. They recommend that when feasible and practicable, that new approaches be developed, from start to finish, within the target setting(s) for which they are ultimately designed.

A special issue of *School Psychology Review*, edited by Power in 2003, focused on the development of model demonstrations for addressing child mental health needs through interdisciplinary and community partnerships. Some researchers in our field are beginning to develop practice settings as centers of inquiry in which interventions are developed, from initial conceptualization to demonstrations of their effectiveness, within target practice settings (e.g., see Fantuzzo, McWayne, & Bulotsky, 2003; Walker, 2004). This is a highly recommended but challenging approach as it can sometimes be very difficult to achieve and maintain the necessary levels of study design control (i.e., randomization) and implementation fidelity within the relative chaos of many public school settings.

The authors have had considerable experience in the development and delivery of universal as well as selected intervention approaches within school settings (Sprague & Golly, 2005; Walker et al., 1997, 1998; Walker et al., 2004). It is our sense that educators are seeking methods and approaches that will allow them to be more effective without requiring the investment of extensive time, training or effort in order to do so. With respect to evaluating the acceptability of new interventions or practices, educators often ask themselves the following sorts of questions:

1. Does it fit seamlessly into ongoing classroom and/or school practices?
2. Is it consistent with school and personal values?
3. Is it something that can be applied equally to an entire classroom, or does it require special accommodations of individual students or small groups of students?
4. Does it solve a high-priority problem or issue (e.g., reading failure, aggression, bullying and harassing peers)?
5. Does the consumer or implementer have the skills and access to resources necessary to apply the practice effectively?

New approaches that come up lacking on these criteria risk failure in terms of being adopted and implemented effectively. Some other dimensions that should be considered in the intervention evaluation-adoption process are the cost of the intervention relative to the effect(s) it produces, whether it has a broad generalized effect or a highly localized and specific one, whether it can be feasibly and easily integrated into daily routines and operational procedures, and whether its actual effectiveness has been adequately demonstrated for its intended purpose?

Our field is urgently in need of a research agenda in this general area that addresses the critical issues of (a) the acceptability of new interventions to consumers and its influence on their adoption and usage, (b) the "nuisance" variables and setting specific factors that produce unwanted noise and that are targets for control by developers and researchers but that often powerfully mediate the application and effectiveness of an innovation once it has been released for general use, and (c) systematic studies of the research to practice process, or the transportability of new innovations, that address the needs of at-risk students within K–12 settings.

It has been suggested that we have a substantial knowledge base on whether our interventions will work. However, our understanding of how and why they do is, by comparison, far less developed. The careful study of implementation within the applied, normalized contexts and settings that our interventions are designed for, as recommended by Domitrovich and Greenberg (2000), provides an important pathway for achieving this goal.

OUTCOMES FROM A 4-YEAR IMPLEMENTATION OF THE *FIRST STEP TO SUCCESS*: EARLY INTERVENTION PROGRAM ACROSS THREE OREGON SUBURBAN SCHOOL DISTRICTS

In 2001, the authors collaborated with the Washington County, Oregon Mental Health Department and the Washington County Commission on Children and Families in an application for a 4-year prevention grant from the Substance Abuse and Mental Health Services Administration (SAMHSA) of the National Institutes of Health. The focus of this grant competition was on the prevention of school environmental conditions and child behavioral characteristics and patterns that could lead to later destructive outcomes such as drug use and abuse in adolescence. High levels of aggressive behavior in young children, for example, have been linked through longitudinal research by Kellam and his associates to later drug use (see Kellam & Anthony, 1998; Kellam et al., 1983).

The application focused on the *First Step to Success* early intervention program, developed by Walker and his associates, for reducing aggressive, antisocial behavior among at-risk children in grades K–3 (Walker et al., 1997, 1998). The specific purpose or goal of the grant was to evaluate an enhanced version of *First Step* in which the home intervention component of the program was expanded and in which mental health and support services were provided to families whose children were participating in the program.

The *First Step to Success* program[1] is a selected early intervention for achieving secondary prevention goals and outcomes. It has three components as follows: (a) universal, early screening of all students; (b) a school intervention designed to reduce aggressive, disruptive behavior; teach an adaptive behavior pattern that will contribute to school success; and develop the skills and social competencies that will allow recruitment of social support networks and friendships; and (c) a home intervention component that teaches parents and caregivers how to directly teach, practice, and reinforce school success skills at home. *First Step* is established and operated initially by a behavioral coach (e.g., school counselor, behavioral specialist, psychologist, early interventionist, social worker, etc.) who works collaboratively with the child's teacher and parents. The program requires approximately 3 months from start to finish for full implementation and consumes about 50 to 60 hours of the coach's time over this period.

The first week of the program is operated by the coach who turns it over to the regular teacher on Day 6 of the program for the remainder of the intervention period. The coach then provides support, technical assistance, and supervision on an as needed basis for the duration of the program. On Day 10 of the program, the target child's parents are invited to participate in the home component of *First Step*; approximately 65% to 70% of parents agree to do so. The

---

[1]Numerous evaluative studies, reviews, and best-practice compilations have been produced to date on the program. These compilations and a program history are available from the authors.

coach then works closely with parents and caregivers for 6 weeks in teaching them how to teach their child school success skills at home.

The Washington County Enhanced *First Step-Mental Health Project* was a collaborative effort involving three suburban school districts (Beaverton, Hillsboro, and Tigard/Tualatin) located near Portland, Oregon; the Washington County Commission on Children and Families; and the University of Oregon Institute on Violence and Destructive Behavior (IVDB). Key IVDB staff, under the direction and supervision of the second author, provided evaluation, training and technical assistance services throughout the duration of the project (i.e., from September, 2001, to June, 2005). The primary goal of this project was to expand the districts' capacity to prevent the development of behavioral and mental health problems in young, school-age children, and to promote working linkages among schools and child-family serving agencies. A supporting goal was to develop and test an evidence-based approach that could be sustained in Washington County and to provide a template or road-map for replication of this approach within Oregon and nationally. The focus of the evaluation was on (a) documenting the intervention's impact on the participating target child, teacher, and parents, where appropriate; (b) gathering information on participating students during the intervention; and (c) assessing the social acceptability of the intervention's procedures and outcomes by teachers and parents. In the following, we present descriptions of the project's participants, methods and procedures, outcomes, and a brief discussion of their implications.

Participants

Over the 4-year period of the project, a sample of 274 preschool through grade 2 children and their families, who were at risk for behavioral and mental disorders, were served by this program. Children were screened and selected as at risk using the procedures and behavioral criteria of the Early Screening Project (ESP) developed by Walker and his colleagues (Walker, Severson, & Feil, 1995). The ESP uses a combination of teacher nomination and rankings, behavioral ratings, and in vivo behavioral observations to screen and identify at-risk children. Nearly 800 students were screened across the three school districts during the project. The number of screened students served across three school districts by year was as follows: Year 1= 14; Year 2 = 77; Year 3 = 84; and Year 4 = 99. By participating school district, the numbers served were Beaverton (110), Hillsboro (94) and Tigard/Tualatin (70). In terms of demographics, approximately 77% of the students served were boys and 23% were girls. Caucasian students accounted for 57% of the total sample and Latino students comprised 25% of the sample. There were only two Native American students and three African-American students among the participating students.

Methods and Procedures

A pool of *First Step* behavioral coaches was identified and trained within each school district. Training in the *First Step* program's procedures was provided by IVDB staff in a series of staff development sessions in Year 1 of the project. Technical assistance, booster and debriefing sessions, and additional training sessions along, with e-mail and telephone communication were maintained throughout the life of the project.

Family participants received an enhanced version of the HomeBase component of the *First Step* program in which the behavioral coach instructs and coaches parents/caregivers in how to teach their child school success skills at home using a variety of games and activities (e.g., sharing, cooperating, accepting teacher directives, doing your work, and so forth). The project enhancements to the *First Step* program included revisions to the HomeBase component designed to strengthen and expand this program component so as develop better skill levels among parents and adding coordinated mental health services and supports.

A *First Step* coordinator was identified and hired within each participating district to facilitate a high-quality implementation effort. *First Step* coaches, coordinators, IVDB trainers, and project staff met regularly to debrief, to discuss and problem solve issues, and to coordinate their efforts across the three districts.

Project Outcomes

The ESP screening procedure and its measures were administered in the fall and spring of each project year during this study. Figure

3.1 illustrates pre- and post-assessments (Fall, Spring) on each of the four key ESP measures: teacher adaptive behavior ratings, teacher maladaptive behavior ratings, teacher aggression ratings, and behavioral observations of target students' academic engagement (AET) recorded during academic periods within each participating teacher's classroom. Figure 3.1 also shows the average normative score on each of these measures as derived from the national normative data base on the ESP. Inspection of Figure 3.1 shows that the Enhanced *First Step* intervention appeared to have moved the participating students to well within the normal range on two of these measures (i.e., ESP aggression and levels of observed academic engagement). The adaptive and maladaptive teacher ratings showed substantial movement in the predicted directions but did not reach normative levels.

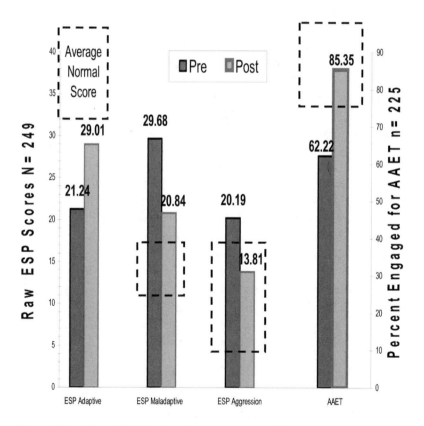

Figure 3.1.   Overall behavior change scores on key outcome measures.

The at-risk status of the participating students showed substantial reductions from pre to post assessments on ESP measures that were replicated across the three school districts. Students were assigned a risk status ranging from "no risk" to "extreme risk" based on pre-post teacher ratings on the ESP Critical Events Checklist. ESP cutoff points on this measure are as follows: no risk = 0 items checked by the teacher; low risk = 1 item checked; high risk = 2 items checked; and extreme risk = 3 or more items checked. Very similar results were observed in each school district. Although students initially classified with no or low risk showed some increase in risk at posttest, in each district dramatic decreases in risk status were observed for students in the high- and extreme risk status groups.

To assess consumer satisfaction and program acceptability for the *First Step* program and its results, a series of surveys and interviews was conducted by IVDB staff with parents, teachers, principals, coaches and the lead coach coordinators. Results of these assessments were generally quite positive. Teachers felt that 72% of the *First Step* students had improved in their compliance to rules and expectations. Fifty-three percent of parents believed their child's behavior at home had improved during the *First Step* program. Teachers, parents, and coaches were asked whether the target child's peer relationships had improved. Respectively, 56% of teachers, 43% of parents, and 78% of coaches answered "yes" to this question. Finally, 90% of participating teachers believed that the *First Step* program produced a positive impact on their classroom as a whole.

Parents were asked to specifically rate their satisfaction with the *First Step* program overall and to also rate their experience with the home and school components of *First Step* along with the behavioral coach with whom they worked. Across all three districts, overall parent satisfaction with the *First Step* program averaged 4.7 on a scale of 1–5 where a rating of 1 = disappointing and a rating of 5 = excellent. Ratings for the home and school components of *First Step* averaged 4.5 and ratings for the behavioral coach averaged 4.8. These results were closely replicated across each of the three participating school districts. Satisfaction levels for Beaverton ranged from 4.5 to 4.9; for Hillsboro, they were 4.4 to 4.7; and for Tigard-Tualatin, they were 4.5 to 4.8. Principals and the lead coaches were also generally supportive of the *First Step* program, the project and its outcomes in their interview comments.

Discussion

Although the results and outcomes of this study cannot be attributed unequivocally to *First Step* program implementation, it is unlikely that they were due to extraneous or uncontrolled, random variations. These results closely replicated those obtained by Walker and his colleagues in a randomized control trial of the *First Step* program's effects (Walker et al., 1998). Participating parents showed satisfaction with changes in their child's behavior, with the *First Step* program, and with the behavioral coaches with whom they worked. Importantly, parents said their school relationships had improved as a result of their participation; teachers and administrators rated effects of the intervention highly and indicated they would be willing to use the *First Step* program again.

Teacher ratings also indicated that the *First Step* program appears to have positively impacted classroom climate as well. This is a key finding that was first noted by Perkins-Rowe (2001) in a study of the *First Step* program. The case for prevention through early intervention can be a difficult sell to many school systems (Kauffman, 2003). Selected, targeted interventions are needed that not only focus on the severe problem behaviors of target children but concomitantly also have a positive impact on the behavior of classmates, improve peer relations, and change classroom climate for the better. Targeted interventions that produce these outcomes may be more acceptable to teachers and schools.

Studies are needed of the characteristics of coaches that predict better program outcomes. Anecdotally, we have found that coaches having a master's degree and/or who have advanced training and experience with classroom behavior management techniques tend to be more effective implementation agents. However, these impressions need to be validated empirically.

Finally, the *First Step* program is currently the focus of two large center grants from the Institute on Education Sciences in which randomized control designs are being used to validate program outcomes, to study implementation fidelity, to evaluate long-term, sustainability processes and results, and to assess teacher and coach characteristics that mediate *First Step* results. We are hopeful that results of these large-scale studies will further establish the scientific integrity of the *First Step* program and its social validity.

GENERAL DISCUSSION

The infusion of child mental health expertise into the normal operations of schooling in order to address behavioral challenges and the social-emotional needs of behaviorally at-risk students continues to be an unfinished agenda. The enormous pressures placed on public schools by the No Child Left Behind Act and the public's demand for accountability, combined with a continuing decline in both fiscal and political support for public schooling, have stressed the enterprise of schooling to extraordinary levels. Behaviorally at-risk students who require specialized accommodations in order to be productive and respond to the normal demands of schooling are viewed by many educators as obstacles to achieving acceptable outcomes at a school level. Concomitant pressures to control, contain, and exclude such students have recently re-emerged as stronger than ever.

Although it is important for BD and mental health professionals to continue advocating for adoption of promising and proven practices for use with marginalized student populations (Gerber, 2001), we need to recognize that the primary mission of schools is about the academic achievement and development of the general student population. The authors have argued in past forums that schooling should adopt the twin goals of academic and social development, but school personnel view social and emotional development as, at best, an artifact of the schooling process rather than as a primary goal. However, a targeted intervention that conserves allocated instructional time or that positively impacts the classroom climate are likely to be much more acceptable to educators than one which is limited in its impact to social or emotional functioning that does not impact academic performance (Adelman & Taylor, 2003).

REFERENCES

Adelman, H., & Taylor, L. (2003). On sustainability of project innovations as systemic change. *Journal of Educational and Psychological Consultation, 14*, 1–25.

Barnett, W. (1985a). Benefit–cost analysis of the Perry Preschool Program and its policy implications. *Educational Evaluation and Policy Analysis, 7*(4), 333–342.

Barnett, W. (1985b). *The Perry Preschool Program and its long-term effects: A benefit–cost analysis*. Ypsilanti, MI: High/Scope Press.

Bingham, F. (2001). Editorial. *Behavioral Disorders, 27*(1), 5–7.

Burns, B., & Hoagwood, K. (2002). *Community treatment for youth: Evidence-based interventions for severe emotional and behavioral disorders.* New York: Oxford University Press.

Domitrovich, C., & Greenberg, M. (2000). The study of implementation: Current findings from effective programs that prevent mental disorders in school-aged children. *Journal of Educational and Psychological Consultation, 11*(2), 193–221.

Fantuzzo, J., McWayne, C., & Bulotsky, R. (2003). Forging strategic partnerships to advance mental health science and practice for vulnerable children. *School Psychology Review, 32,* 17–37.

Gerber, M. (2001), The essential social science of behavioral disorders, *Behavioral Disorders, 27,* 12–20.

Hawkins, D., Catalano, R., Kosterman, R., Abbott, R., & Hill, K. (1999). Preventing adolescent health risk behaviors by strengthening protection during childhood. *Archives of Pediatric and Adolescent Medicine, 153,* 226–234,

Hoagwood, K. (2001). Evidence-based practice in child and adolescent mental health: What do we know? Why aren't we putting it to use? *Emotional & Behavioral Disorders in Youth, 1,* 84–87.

Hoagwood, K. (2003/2004). Evidence-based practice in child and adolescent mental health: Its meaning, application and limitations. *Emotional & Behavioral Disorders in Youth, 4,* 7–8.

Hoagwood, K., & Johnson, J. (2003). School psychology: A public health framework I: From evidence-based practices to evidence-based policies. *Journal of School Psychology, 41,* 3–21.

Horner, R., Sugai, G., Lewis-Palmer, T., & Todd, A. (2001). Teaching school-wide behavioral expectations. *Emotional and Behavioral Disorders in Youth, 1*(4), 77–80.

Katsiyannis, A., & Yell, M. (2004). Critical issues and trends in the education of students with emotional or behavioral disorders. *Behavioral Disorders, 29*(3), 209–211.

Kauffman, J. M. (1993). How we might achieve the radical reform of special education. *Exceptional Children, 60,* 6–16

Kauffman, J. M. (1996). Research to practice issues. *Behavioral Disorders, 22,* 55–60.

Kauffman, J. M. (1999). How we prevent the prevention of emotional and behavioral disorders. *Exceptional Children, 65,* 448–468,

Kauffman, J. M. (2002). *Education deform: Bright people sometimes say stupid things about education.* London: Scarecrow Press.

Kauffman, J. M. (2003). Appearances, stigma, and prevention. *Remedial and Special Education, 24,* 195–198.

Kauffman, J. M. (2004). Foreword. In H. M. Walker, E. Ramsey, & F. M. Gresham, *Antisocial behavior in school: Evidence-based practices* (2nd ed., pp. xix–xxi). Belmont, CA: Thompson/Wadsworth.

Kauffman, J. M. (2005). *Characteristics of emotional and behavioral disorders of children and youth.* Columbus, OH: Prentice Hall.

Kellam, S., & Anthony, J. (1998). Targeting early antecedents to prevent to-
bacco smoking: Findings from an epidemiologically based randomized
field trial. *American Journal of Public Health, 88*, 1490–1495.

Kellam, S., Brown, H., Rubin, B., & Ensminger, M. (1983). Paths leading to
teenage psychiatric symptoms and substance abuse: Developmental epi-
demiological studies in Woodlawn. In S. B. Guze, F. Earls, & J. Barrett
(Eds.), *Childhood psychopathology and development* (pp. 17–51). New York:
Raven Press.

Kellam, S., & Langevin, D. (2003). A framework for understanding "evidence" in prevention research and programs. *Prevention Science, 4*(3),
137–153.

Kellam, S., Mayer, L., Rebok, G., & Hawkins, W. (1998). Effects of improving
achievement on aggressive behavior and of improving aggressive behavior on achievement through two preventive interventions: An investigation of causal paths. In B. Dohrenwend, (Ed.), *Adversity, stress, and
psychopathology* (pp. 486–505). London: Oxford University Press.

Kellam, S., & Rebok, G. (1992). Building developmental and etiological
theory through epidemiologically based preventive intervention trials. In J. McCord & R. Trembly (Eds.), *Preventing antisocial behavior: Interventions from birth through adolescence* (pp. 162–195). New York:
Guilford.

Kellam, S., Rebok, G., Ialongo, N., & Mayer, L. (1994). The course and mal-
leability of aggressive behavior from early first grade into middle school:
Results of a developmental epidemiologically-based prevention trial.
Journal of Child Psychology and Psychiatry, 35, 259–282.

Kratochwill, T., & Shernoff, E. (2004). Evidence-based practice: Promoting
evidence-based interventions in School Psychology. *School Psychology Review, 33*(1), 34–48.

Lynch, R. (2004). *Exceptional returns: Economic, fiscal, and social benefits of investment in early childhood development*. Washington, DC: The Economic
Policy Institute.

Patterson, G. R., Reid, J. B., & Dishion, T. J. (1997). *Antisocial boys*. Eugene,
OR: Castalia Publishing.

Perkins-Rowe, K. (2001). Direct and collateral effects of the *First Step to Success* program: Replication and extension of findings. *Dissertation Abstracts
International, 62*(12A), 4058.

Reid, J. B. (1993). Prevention of conduct disorder before and after school
entry: Relating interventions to developmental findings. *Development &
Psychopathology, 5*, 243–262.

Reid, J. B., Patterson, G., & Snyder, J. (2002). *Antisocial behavior in children
and adolescents: A developmental analysis and the Oregon model for intervention*. Washington, DC: American Psychological Association.

Rogers, E. (1995). *Diffusion of innovation*. New York: The Free Press.

Schoenwald, S., & Hoagwood, K. (2001). Effectiveness, transportabililty,
and dissemination of interventions. What matters when? *Psychiatric Services, 52*, 1190–1197.

Schoenwald, S., & Rowland, M. (2002). Multisystemic therapy. In B. Burns & K. Hoagwood (Eds.), *Community treatment for youth: Evidence-based interventions for severe emotional and behavioral disorders* (pp. 91–116). New York: Oxford University Press.

Sprague, J. & Golly, A. (2005). *Best behavior: Building positive behavior support in schools.* Longmont, CO: Sopris West Educational Services.

Stichter, J., & Conroy, M. (2004). Measurement, validity, and science: A call for elucidating precision and rigor in EBD research. *Behavioral Disorders, 30*(1), 5–6.

Strain, P. (2001). Empirically based social skill intervention: A case for quality of life improvement. *Behavioral Disorders, 27*(1), 30–37.

Strain, P., & Tim, M. (2001). Remediation and prevention of aggression: An evaluation of the regional intervention program over a quarter century. *Behavioral Disorders, 26*(4), 297–313.

Sugai, G., & Horner, R. (2002). The evolution of discipline practices: School-wide positive behavior supports. *Behavior Psychology in the Schools, 24*, 23–50.

Walker, H. (2004). Commentary: Use of evidence-based interventions in schools. *School Psychology Review, 33*(3), 398–407.

Walker, H., Golly, A., McLane, J., & Kimmich, M. (2005). The Oregon First Step to Success Replication Initiative: Statewide results of an evaluation of the program's impact. *Behavioral Disorders, 13*(3), 163–172.

Walker, H. M., Kavanagh, K., Stiller, B., Golly, A., Severson, H. H., & Feil, E. G. (1997). *First Step to Success: Helping young children overcome antisocial behavior.* Longmont, CO: Sopris West.

Walker, H. M., Kavanagh, K., Stiller, B., Golly, A., Severson, H. H., & Feil, E. G. (1998). First Step to Success: An early intervention approach for preventing school antisocial behavior. *Journal of Emotional and Behavioral Disorders, 6*(2), 66–80.

Walker, H. M., Ramsey, E., & Gresham, F. M. (2004). *Antisocial behavior in school: Evidence-based practices* (2nd ed.). Belmont, CA: Wadsworth/Thomson Learning.

Walker, H., Severson, H., & Feil, E. (1995). *The Early Screening Project.* Eugene, OR: Deschutes Research, Inc.

Weikart, D., Bond, J., & McNeil, J. (1978). The Ypsilanti Perry Preschool Project: Preschool years and longitudinal results through fourth grade. *Monographs of the High/Scope Educational Research Foundation,* (3).

Zigler, E., Taussig, C., & Black, K. (1992). Early childhood intervention: A promising preventative for juvenile delinquency. *American Psychologist, 47*, 997–1006.

Chapter 4

Heeding the Call to Radically Reform Special Education for Students with Emotional/Behavioral Disorders through Science

Timothy J. Lewis
University of Missouri

Joseph H. Wehby
Peabody College of Vanderbilt University

In his article that serves as the backdrop for this collection of chapters, Kauffman (1993) challenged special educators to avoid two extremes in considering the present and future state of our field. As Kauffman, a keen student of history points out, "special education should and will be reshaped. The central question is this: How will it change?" (p. 6). On the one hand, complacency and the continuance of doing business as usual will certainly fail to achieve desired outcomes for students with disabilities. At the other extreme, fanaticism and calls for the abandonment of what we know in favor of proposed new ways of knowing will also, given the lack of evidence to date, certainly fail to lead to better student outcomes. Embracing Kauffman's advice, as well as the advice of other leaders in our field, we propose that the "radical reform" will be a long slow process, not a revolution. The "radical" in the reform is the notion that the field of special education will change to improve the lives of students with disabilities based on the field's whole scale adoption of the idea that first and foremost, *empirical science* must guide decision making and that special education continues to be specially designed instruction to achieve individual student educational outcomes. In particular, this chapter focuses on the current state and proposed reform of special education for children and youth with Emotional/Behavioral Disorders (EBD).

Embracing an empirical research-based approach to framing the reform of special education, we must first operationally define the problem we are attempting to solve. The problem, as Kauffman posited, "is that too many students are poorly served by special education because their programs are not really special—no more appropriate than the programs they would receive in general education" (p. 7). This is especially true for students with EBD who continue to have the poorest post-secondary outcomes among all disability groups served by the Individuals with Disabilities Education Act (IDEA; Wagner, Kutash, Duchnowski, & Epstein, 2005). One long-term strategy proposed by Kauffman to achieve the reform of special education is the disaggregating of special education populations. In other words, if we are to address the unique needs of students with EBD, as well as unique variations within the larger group of students with disabilities, we must acknowledge that among the population of school-age students, some children have disabilities that will require specialized instruction. By definition, children and youth qualify for special education services under IDEA because they are not educationally benefitting from instruction in the general education classroom due to their disability. Although the concept seems simple enough, the field has at times eschewed this basic premise and called for the elimination of special education as a separate field (e.g., Gartner & Lipskey, 1989).

The long-term goal, acknowledging that children and youth with disabilities will require special education also, as Kauffman indicates, requires three immediate tasks. First, we must "keep place in perspective." Special education is not a place, it is specialized instruction and related services designed to lead to educational benefit for children and youth with disabilities. Second, we must "choose idea over image." As indicated, this will require the field to rely on science not slogans to solve problems. Finally, we must "avoid fanaticism." Kauffman challenges us to keep the purpose and intent of special education in perspective; to provide an education that is grounded in empirically-based practices for children and youth with disabilities.

Given the basic premise that special education is and should be different than general education, an additional necessary component in operationally defining the problem, is to define what makes special education "special." We propose a three-prong definition. First, an essential component of special education is *advocacy* for children and youth with disabilities and their families. IDEA is a unique piece of federal legislation in that it is both an entitlement and civil rights act. IDEA entitles children and youth ages 0–21 a free and appropriate public education with no exceptions. Along with other statutes, such as the Americans with Disabilities Act and Section 504 of the Rehabilitation Act of 1973, IDEA also provides safeguards to insure that children and youth with disabilities have due process under the law to protect their rights as a class of citizens. Both require special educators to act as advocates on the behalf of children and youth with disabilities. Second, special education, as mandated by IDEA is a *set of policies* guided by federal and state regulations and shaped by case law. In an effort to translate the entitlement and advocacy role of special education, a set of minimal features are set within policy. Finally, special education is *specialized instruction and related services* designed to achieve educational outcomes for those who have not responded positively to the instruction provided to the majority of children in this country.

In our opinion, the basic premise to reform special education through science equally applies to each of the three facets. IDEA is an educational law and was passed to protect students' with disabilities right to a public education. Without knowing how to best achieve educational outcomes, how can the field advocate for children and their families regarding school programs or design policies and procedures that will lead to implementation of effective educational practices? We acknowledge that the issues of civil rights and federal and state policies are complex and we are suggesting what some may term a simplistic or narrow solution. However, if we as a field do not embrace sound empirically based strategies to promote educational outcomes for children and youth with disabilities, the field will continue to be shaped by attorneys, judges, and politicians, and not educators working in concert with families in proactive ways to develop and evaluate effective practices.

Although all three are essential to defining what makes special education "special," for purposes of this chapter we focus on the third component, instruction. A necessary step in disaggregating special education is identifying a separate technology of instruction and supports that will lead to educational benefits for children and youth with EBD. Related to this step is the determination that the specialized technology of instruction and supports is effective and efficient in achieving educational outcomes for students with disabilities. Finally, if a separate technology of instruction and supports does exist and is effective in achieving educational outcomes for students, the need remains to effectively embed proven practices within and across the current education system. Unfortunately, the "final answer" to each of these next steps is beyond the scope of this chapter, and quite frankly, simply does not exist at this time. Instead, we embrace the basic premise posited by Kauffman that students must be disaggregated from the general education population for purposes of achieving the intended outcome of IDEA (i.e., access to specialized instruction and supports that will result in educational outcomes) and explore progress to date, and propose how adopting science as the problem solving framework offers the best hope of achieving the "radical reform" of special education.

ACHIEVING REFORM FOR STUDENTS WITH EBD

Historically, research focusing on instruction and related supports to achieve improved educational outcomes for students' with EBD has addressed one fundamental question; Is there a separate technology of instruction for this group of students and is it effective in achieving educational outcomes? In 1991, a group of leading scholars in the field of EBD summarized the research to date and proposed several instructional practices that had been proven effective and the necessary systems that must be in place within special education programming to reach similar outcomes (Peacock Hill Working Group, 1991). In spite of these recommendations, outcomes for students with EBD who are served by special education continue to paint a bleak picture. Students with EBD are more likely to drop out of school, fail to graduate with a diploma, fail to be gainfully employed, to be arrested at higher rates, and to display higher rates of mental and social problems well into adulthood as compared to both other students with disabilities and the general population (Wagner et al., 2005). Did the authors of the Peacock Hill Working Group get it wrong? Has science let the field down? Is a separate technology of special education a myth?

What has happened since 1991 is the field's failure to consistently implement the necessary *systemic* components to increase the likelihood that specialized practices will impact students. The reasons for the failure to adopt both research-based practices and systemic supports are myriad and have been discussed repeatedly in the literature examining the break down between research and practice (Carnine, 1997; Kauffman, 1996). Kauffman underscores the importance of addressing necessary systems to adopt empirically validated practices in his call for reform. In paraphrasing Sarason (1990), Kauffman (1996) states

> attempts to reform education will make little difference until reformers understand that schools must exist as much for teachers as for students. Put another way, schools will be successful in nurturing the intellectual, social, and moral development of children only to the extent that they also nurture such development of teachers. (p. 7)

Recent work in bridging the research to practice gap by carefully attending to systemic features and what support adults need in school environments to implement and sustain use of best practices through building school-wide positive behavior support (PBS) systems has demonstrated that educators can and will use empirically validated practices in addressing problem behavior (Horner, Sugai, Todd, & Lewis-Palmer, 2005). School-wide PBS has also demonstrated the need to build a continuum of supports based on the premise that some students will need more or differentiated supports to lead to success (i.e., disaggregating students based on educational need). The essential components of school-wide PBS teach educators to (a) use data to guide decision making, (b) select research-based practices to address the problem, and (c) build the necessary system supports to insure school staff can implement the selected practice with fidelity (Sugai et al., 2000). By focusing both on student need (i.e., practices) and adult needs (i.e., systems), schools can begin to achieve reform.

The basic logic of school-wide PBS is teaching educators to effectively problem solve and build solutions using research-based practices. In applying this logic to reforming the field as a whole, Kauffman again provides us with a blueprint:

> special educators will approach problems successfully only if they use the same problem-solving strategies that they recommend for students: careful logical analysis of problems and proposed solutions, meticulous evaluation of data, recognition and appreciation of complexity, tolerance of necessary ambiguity, mindfulness of history, clear communication of ideas, and devotion to ethical decision making. (p. 7)

Building on the premise that research is the key to achieving reform, an examination of instructional strategies and supports for students with EBD is needed.

Careful Logical Analysis of Problems and Proposed Solutions

Based on Kauffman's call to disaggregate special education, we define the problem as one of clearly identifying the essential components of instruction and related supports and the educational systems that are needed to adopt best practices in order to achieve educational outcomes for students with EBD. The proposed solution is to carefully examine research to date and identify needed future research to address weaknesses. As just outlined, the issues of advocacy and proposed policy, although essential features in defining special education, should be kept separate at this point in order to allow the field to avoid complacency through debate about written and unwritten policies (e.g., "that is what the state says to do") or the often times fanatical debates linked to advocacy (e.g., "to insure that all children are educated in the general education classroom we must eliminate special education").

Meticulous Evaluation of Data

It is incumbent on the field to reach consensus on what constitutes data, the research methods that generate data, and how much data under what conditions is sufficient to brand an instructional strategy or support "research-based." In essence, this is the cornerstone of achieving reform in special education and developing a technology of instruction and support to meet the unique needs of students with EBD. To this end, we and others who have written on this topic call for the use of objectivist, empirical methodology to create the "gold standard" for determining what is "research-based" within our field (e.g., Brigham & Polsgrove, 1998; Kauffman, 2002; Lewis, Hudson, Richter, & Johnson, 2004; Mostert, Kauffman, & Kavale, 2003; Wehby, Symons, Canale, & Go, 1998). Fortunately, like other fields such as mental health (e.g., Burns, Hoagwood, & Mrazek, 1999; National Institute of Mental Health, 2001; Rones & Hoagwood, 2000), a set of guidelines have been recently developed to determine rigor within and across studies using methodology common to the field of special education (Odom et al., 2005). Recently Horner, Carr, et al., (2005) on behalf of the Division of Research within the Council for Exceptional Children, established criteria for single subject research to determine what practices should be branded "research-based." Hudson (2006), using this criteria, completed an intensive review of instructional strategies for students with problem behavior. The evaluation was limited to single subject studies that focused on academic outcomes for children and youth with behavioral disorders. Results of Hudson's study indicated there is a single "well-established" research-validated instructional strategy: peer tutoring. Probably efficacious practices included constant time delay although promising practices, those not meeting minimal level of criteria proposed by Horner, include academic interventions such as cover, copy and compare, self-monitoring, and strategy instruction. Within her discussion, Hudson indicates that several other practices were reviewed and individual studies were completed with high rigor; however, many were missing one or two elements proposed by Horner and colleagues (e.g., no social validity measure) or sufficient replications across sites were not completed. In casting a wider net to include all research methodologies without counts of replication at the level proposed by Horner and colleagues, several other instructional strategies have been noted as effective including phonological awareness, academic strategy training, direct instruction in academic subjects, social skill instruction, increasing opportunities to respond, and praise/positive performance feedback (e.g., Dunlap & Childs, 1996; Lewis et al., 2004; Strong, Wehby, Lane, & Falk, 2004).

Although we may not, and should not, be happy with the limited number of practices in our field that can be branded as research-based using high rigor within and minimal numbers across studies, we must continue to use good science to address the challenges that face us with respect to instruction and educational outcomes. In addition, the field needs to examine the proposed criteria to provide minimums to identify research-based practices, including a weighting of key variables. The ideal would be to identify several key research questions with respect to instruction and support for students with EBD, develop a long-term funding stream at the national level, and fund individual research centers that would examine one or more aspects of the issue in depth and over time while working collectively to insure proposed benchmarks to determine "research-based" are followed.

Recognition and Appreciation of Complexity

One of the criticisms leveled against adopting an objective empirical research agenda to reform special education instructional practices is the failure to "see the forest for the trees." By focusing "narrowly" on one or two variables at time, research fails to account for the overall interactive effect of all variables. Unfortunately, advocates who are in favor of abandoning empirical research practices for yet unproven methodology have proposed instead broad or highly idiosyncratic interpretations that prevent educators from identifying and replicating essential features. They are the ones failing to recognize the complexity of the forest, that it is made up of a collection of individual trees. The research agenda within special education should focus on both specific practices as well as the systems necessary to implement and sustain. By focusing on both, research can begin to address and appreciate the complexity of implementing effective instruction. Recent research and proposed methodologies that examine the complex interaction of instructional variables not only allow the field to identify essential features of instruction, but also the conditions within learning environments that will maximize instructional benefit (e.g., Conroy & Stichter, 2003; Gunter & Denny, 1998; Wehby, Lane, & Falk, 2003; Wehby, Symons, & Shores, 1995; Wehby, Tally, & Falk, 2004).

In a previous chapter in this volume, Walker and Sprague call on the field to implement practices with empirically demonstrated efficacy and effectiveness. In other words, empirical research has not failed to identify what works; rather, sufficient research examining systems within schools allowing adoption and sustained use is only now emerging (Gresham, Sugai, & Horner, 2001; Wehby, Lane, & Falk, 2003). Over the last several years, there has been considerable focus on developing effective systems within schools. This work needs to continue; however, specific efforts need to focus on the required magnitude of system support needed for the implementation and maintenance of effective instructional practices in classrooms.

As previously mentioned, the number of practices in the EBD field that meet rigorous evidence-based standards is limited, but evidence also shows that these "proven" methods are rarely implemented in many classrooms serving this population of students. Therefore, as research continues toward developing a set of effective instructional practices for students with EBD, efforts are needed to understand how to transfer and keep these in classrooms.

The field has begun work on two critical steps to insure effective implementation within complex environments. The first is the development of data-decision rules that allow educators to match treatment to presenting problem and modify instruction if treatment fails to achieve the desired outcome (e.g., see chap. 2 by Boardman and Vaughn in this volume). The second is building school environments that foster a culture in which research-based practices are adopted and provide educators with the knowledge, skills, and ongoing supports they need to implement research-based practices (e.g., Sugai et al., 2000).

Tolerance of Necessary Ambiguity

No other disability category presents the same evaluation challenge as EBD. There are few standardized assessments, the category includes students who display externalizing and internalizing behavioral patterns, there is no set of common checkpoints in making a determination, and the field has yet to determine a unified approach for separating the impact of culture and other exclusion factors in the evaluation process. Likewise, as just outlined, ambiguity continues, in determining what research is and what research-based practices are. Whereas society, to some degree, has always dealt with disability, federally mandated special education is a relatively recent phenomenon and the limited extent of research-based practices for students with EBD, as just discussed, underscores the relative recency of the influence of policy on the field post P.L. 94–142. Nevertheless, despite these and other ambiguities, we are able to identify students with EBD and provide them with appropriate services.

The continued reliance on a medical definition to guide evaluation for services, the infancy of our field with respect to a distinct line of research separate from other related disciplines, the lack of systemic support for the adoption of research-based practices, and the need to serve students today forces the field to tolerate some ambiguity. However, it does not require the field to abandon progress made to date in favor of unproven directions lead by fanaticism or that show no promise in identifying instructional strategies and related supports for students with EBD and other disabilities (Kauffman, 2002).

Rather, the ambiguity should further strengthen our resolve to adopt proven scientific methodology to reduce these sources of ambiguity. Likewise, clearly defining the problems—advocacy, policy or practice—will also assist in reducing ambiguity. Finally, attention to building school-wide and program-wide systems in which a culture of giving priority to research-based practices is developed will also allow the field to tolerate ambiguity while moving toward proven methods. Given the limited range of research-based practices to date, in is understandable that educators turn to "promising practices." However, the idea of "promising practices" further underscores the need for a stronger research focus within the field. If educators and their school/program systems adopt promising practices with caution and collect evaluative data, they can begin to achieve radical reform of special education.

Mindfulness of History

Societies have recognized and responded to people with disabilities since the beginning of civilization. The earliest writings found in ancient civilizations make reference to abnormal behavior and physical impairments. Anthropologists speculate that even prehistoric humans attempted to medically intervene on those who were thought to be displaying aberrant behavior (e.g., trephining, the drilling of a hole in the skull, was thought to be an attempt to release evil spirits creating aberrant behavior). Across the centuries, several attempts at classifying, understanding, and treating disabilities have been recorded.

This perspective on history is important in developing an appreciation and understanding of how we define our current field. Although we must be mindful of our history in totality, all the prior threads come together in one of the most significant events, the passage of P.L. 94–142, the Education for All Handicapped Children Act (EAHCA). The EAHCA (and its current version, IDEA) exist primarily due to one important and essential fact: the failure of general education to provide a free and appropriate public education to children and youth with disabilities.

Case law leading up to the passage of PL 94–142 recount several instances in which general education acknowledges it had no means to identify and educate children and youth with disabilities (e.g., *PARC v. Pennsylvania*, 1972, *Mills v. Board of Education*, 1972). One of the most defining moments in our history clearly dictates that children and youth with disabilities must be disaggregated from the larger population of students and receive specialized instruction to address the failure of general education.

As we have just discussed, the field at this point does not have a complete, unambiguous technology to identify and effectively serve all students with disabilities. The field does have several research-based practices and an increasing sophistication in building necessary program systems to implement and sustain adoption of best practices. The field has also demonstrated that the current empirical research paradigm can and will continue to define the technology of specialized instruction and supports for students with EBD.

And yet, there are is a vocal minority who are calling for the abandonment of the current work in favor of a yet unrealized new way of knowing (e.g., Danforth, 2002; Gallagher, 1998). Although certainly not as sexy as a string of adverbs to incite the field to move in new directions in response to a yet to be defined "crisis" in the field, we support Kauffman's call to reform special education through the slow deliberate process of science.

Related to research, history tells us problems are solved through slow, incremental changes that are built on prior solutions (Kuhn, 1996). One of the favorite devices in building a rationale for the "postmodern" abandonment of objectivist empirical methodology is to cite Kuhn's historical examination of science. As Kuhn points out, changes in scientific paradigms, at least among the physical sciences, came about from a crisis created when the current paradigm, after exhausting all attempts, could not solve the problem under investigation. To date, those promoting a "postmodern" paradigm have yet to clearly define "the crisis." Likewise, they have yet to prove that the nonobjective methodology for which they advocate has lead to any instructional strategies and related student outcomes among children and youth with EBD. Beyond pointing out current short-comings in the field, what we have seen are illogical rhetorical loops and selected quotes from Kuhn to promote an agenda that has neither been clearly defined nor provided any methods to truly improve educational outcomes for children and youth (see Kauffman, 2002). If these critics have developed an *evidenced-based* practice that improves the lives of children and youth with EBD, we strongly encourage them to share this information with our field. Until then, we call on the field to continue to be mindful of history and expand the knowledge-base of instructional practices and supports by carefully building on past knowledge and using proven research methodology.

Clear Communication of Ideas

The value of any research-based practice will ultimately lie in its effective use among practitioners. Unfortunately, the field is replete with examples of educators not using best practices, creating a "research to practice gap" (Carnine, 1997; Kauffman, 1996). Landrum (1997) outlined five reasons why educators fail to consult the research base to drive what they do in the classroom, including such things as there is too much data, and that "good" and "bad" data are often indiscernible leading Landrum to conclude that, among practitioners, data are simply not valued.

In an attempt to outline remedies to address the barriers Landrum and others have noted, Carnine (1995, 1997) put forth a call that special education research should attend to three critical elements. First, research must be trustworthy and adhere to sound empirical methodology. Second, research must be accessible to practitioners. Accessibility has since been discussed in terms of both ease of locating research and translating research into "lay" terms. Third, Carnine indicates research must be usable. Usable is defined as addressing presenting problems, exploring interactions between variables, and translating research findings into policy. Kauffman (1996) extends Carnine's framework and adds that research must (a) pose minimal risk of harm, (b) be practical and sustainable, (c) be believable and socially valid, (d) be implemented with a high degree of fidelity, and (e) be accompanied by systematic training.

All of the recommended strategies targeting the research to practice gap, to varying degrees, were addressed within the original Peacock Hill paper. The field has developed standards to discern "good" and "bad" data. There are several instructional strategies and supports that have demonstrated clinical and social significance. There are a myriad of journals reporting research outcomes organized by disability, age of the student, severity of disability, and instructional focus as well as periodicals translating research into lay terms and policy. Every special educator who receives a degree within the discipline at some point in their training had to support their practice with references to the professional literature. So why 15 years after Peacock Hill are we still not implementing research-based practices at the level we should (Landrum, Tankersley, & Kauffman, 2003; Lewis et al., 2004)? In addressing the complexity within the research to practice gap issue, Malouf and Schiller (1995) reached the following simple conclusion: "In sum, teachers' work environments are not conducive to the implementation of research knowledge" (p. 418). The answer to bridging the research to practice gap is not the abandonment of the current research paradigm or the "dumbing down" of research for consumer use; rather, as Kauffman (1996) asks, how can the research and educational community at large "construct a culture of support for research-based practices in education?" (p. 59).

In order to develop a path for clear two-way communication between researcher and practitioners, schools and programs must create effective systems to promote the implementation and sustained use of research-based practices. Likewise, researchers should continue to address the problems of practice as posited by practitioners. Both should work in partnership to identify the necessary systems needed to insure effective implementation. As stated at the outset of this chapter, in order to achieve the whole scale adoption of research as driving practice, we must understand what maintains both student and *teacher* behavior. In addition, we must prepare educators and families of children with disabilities to become "good consumers" of research.

In discussing the establishment of an educational community that values research, comparisons are often made to the medical community. The comparison typically underscores the importance of research to guide practice within medicine such as a doctor prescribing a specific dosage of antibiotics that has undergone rigorous evaluation demonstrating its effectiveness to treat a specific condition. We offer the comparison should extend further by (a) funding educational research at the same fiscal level as that of medical research; (b) establishing longitudinal research centers that examine basic research, clinical trials, and then multisite experimental studies, in some cases over the course of decades, prior to recommending intervention; (c) acculturating educators to value research through information, incentives, and ongoing systemic support; and (d) disseminating research information to the public at large through proactive dissemination similar to the current public health campaigns around smoking, substance abuse, or HIV.

Devotion to Ethical Decision Making

The multifaceted definition of special education proposed in the introduction of this chapter requires special educators to assume many roles: advocate, policy maker, and educator. However, all three should be guided by the central premise of IDEA: to provide specialized instruction to children and youth with EBD that lead to improved educational outcomes. Continuing the focus on the instructional aspect of special education, the selection and implementation of specialized instruction should be guided by empirical research. To choose otherwise is simply unethical.

For example, direct instruction has over three decades of research demonstrating that it can lead to improved educational outcomes among children and youth with disabilities as well as typically developing children. However, teachers routinely choose not to use direct instruction based on false perceptions that it limits their "creativity" (Kauffman, 1996). Following a clear sequence of steps to performing a heart transplant probably limits a physician's creativity as well; thankfully the issue has not been raised, and the procedure is followed as prescribed by research.

Failing to implement research validated practices can lead to irreparable outcomes for children and is tantamount to unethical practice. In a study examining the cumulative impact of poor instruction during elementary school years on later educational development and outcomes, Sanders and Rivers (1996) present a bleak picture. In comparing elementary school students who had three consecutive years of ineffective instruction versus those who had three consecutively effective teachers, differences in student achievement of 50 percentile points were observed. In addition, it appears that many of the children never overcame such a deficit in later schooling regardless of supports in place. In charging the field to adopt research validated practices, Kauffman (1996) provided us with a caveat to consider: what is the risk of not intervening? Ethically, we are obligated to advocate for those practices research has demonstrated effective. Ethically, we are obligated to develop the necessary supports within our educational systems to allow educators to effectively implement best practice. Ethically, we are obligated to continue to challenge what we know through sound research and continue to strive toward the development of efficacious and effective intervention.

CONCLUSION

In this chapter, we have attempted to outline how we might achieve the radical reform of special education through the deliberate use of science to determine specialized instruction and supports for children and youth with EBD. A logical first step, as offered by Kauffman

(2003), is to start with the basic premise that children and youth with disabilities will require differentiated instruction from students without disabilities. Building on this basic premise, we defined what makes special education "special" are three inter-related components; advocacy, policy, and specialized instruction and related supports and focused on the later for purposes of discussion. To date, research has provided the field with a technology of specialized instruction and support that will lead to educational outcomes for children and youth with EBD. Even under the highest level of scrutiny, strategies can be branded as research-based. However, the gap between the knowledge base and implementation remains. The solution we propose to address this is not the abandonment of empirical research in favor of unproven methodologies, rather, we encourage the field to turn our research attention to (a) analysis of the complex interaction of variables that occur in classrooms and (b) the systems that are necessary to implement and sustain use of best practice within schools.

One of the ongoing complaints of the educational community at large is that we are not viewed as a profession of esteem, like law, medicine, or the basic sciences by the general public. And yet, we continue to present ourselves as a field that is fraught with turf battles, lacking a clear direction, and unable to establish a "science" of education. Educators routinely make headlines in local papers for poor or questionable decision making often related to policy or instruction that is not research-based. Given the absence of a clear and respected knowledge base to prepare teachers in education and pedagogy, pundits in the press and politics have gone so far as to call for the dissolution of colleges of education, proposing simply to prepare teachers within the disciplines they will teach. Not only is it incumbent on the field of education to embrace empirical research as the tool to guide decision making to place the field on par with other professions, it is the best hope to impact the children and youth we are charged with serving.

REFERENCES

Brigham, F. J., & Polsgrove, L. (1998). A rumor of paradigm shift in the field of children's emotional and behavioral disorders. *Behavioral Disorders, 23*, 166–170.

Burns, B. J., Hoagwood, K., & Mrazek, P. (1999). Effective treatment for mental disorders in children and adolescents. *Clinical Child and Family Psychology Review, 2,* 199–254.

Carnine, D. W. (1995). The professional context for collaboration and collaborative research. *Remedial and Special Education, 16,* 368–371.

Carnine, D. W. (1997). Bridging the research-to-practice gap. In J. W. Lloyd, E. J. Kameenui, & D. Chard (Eds.), *Issues in educating students with disabilities* (pp. 363–373). Mahwah, NJ: Lawrence Erlbaum Associates.

Conroy, M. A., & Stichter, J. P. (2003). The application of antecedents in the functional assessment process: Existing research, issues, and recommendations. *Journal of Special Education, 37*(1), 15–25.

Danforth, S. (2002). On what basis hope? Modern progress and postmodern possibilities. In M. A. Byrnes (Ed.), *Taking sides: Clashing views on controversial issues in special education* (pp. 2–13). Guilford, CT: McGraw Hill.

Dunlap, G., & Childs, K. E. (1996). Intervention research in emotional and behavioral disorders: An analysis of studies from 1980–1993. *Behavioral Disorders, 21,* 125–136.

Gallagher, D. J. (1998). The scientific knowledge base of special education: Do we know what we think we know? *Exceptional Children, 64,* 493–502.

Gartner, A., & Lipskey, D. K. (1989). *The yoke of special education: How to break it.* Rochester, NY: National Center on Education and the Economy.

Gresham, F. M., Sugai, G., & Horner, R. H. (2001). Interpreting outcomes of social skill training for students with high incidence disabilities. *Exceptional Children, 67,* 331–344.

Gunter, P. L., & Denny, R. K. (1998). Trends and issues in research regarding academic instruction of students with emotional and behavioral issues. *Behavioral Disorders, 24,* 44–50.

Horner, R. H., Carr, E. G., Halle, J., McGee, G., Odom, S., & Wolery, M. (2005). The use of single subject design research to identify evidence-based practices in special education. *Exceptional Children, 71,* 165–179.

Horner, R. H., Sugai, G., Todd, A. W., & Lewis-Palmer, T. (2005). School-wide positive behavior support: An alternative approach to discipline in schools. In L. Bambara & L. Kern (Eds.), *Individualized supports for students with problem behaviors: Designing positive behavior plans* (pp. 359–390). New York: Guilford Press.

Hudson, S. S. (2006). *Identification and teacher perceptions of academic practices: Initial results of quality indicators and a three-tiered classification framework.* Unpublished Dissertation, University of Missouri, Columbia.

Kauffman, J. M. (1993). How we might achieve the radical reform of special education. *Exceptional Children, 60,* 6–16.

Kauffman, J. M. (1996). Research to practice issues. *Behavioral Disorders, 22,* 55–60.

Kauffman, J. M. (2002). *Education deform: Bright people sometimes say stupid things about education.* Lanham, MD: The Scarecrow Press.

Kuhn, T. S. (1996). *The structure of scientific revolutions* (3rd ed.). Chicago: The University of Chicago Press.

Landrum, T. (1997). Why data don't matter. *Journal of Behavioral Education*, 7, 123–129.

Landrum, T. J., Tankersley, M., & Kauffman, J. M. (2003). What is special about special education for students with emotional or behavioral disorders? *The Journal of Special Education, 37*, 148–156.

Lewis, T. J., Hudson, S., Richter, M., & Johnson, N. (2004). Scientifically supported practices in emotional and behavioral disorders: A proposed approach and brief review of current practices. *Behavioral Disorders, 29*, 247–259.

Malouf, D. B., & Schiller, E. P. (1995). Practice and research in special education. *Exceptional Children, 61*, 414–424.

Mills v. Board of Education, 348 F. Supp. 866 (D. D. C. 1972).

Mostert, M. P., Kauffman, J. M., & Kavale, K. A. (2003). Truth and consequences. *Behavioral Disorders, 28*, 333–347.

National Institute of Mental Health. (2001). *Blueprint for change: Research on child and adolescent mental health*. Rockville, MD: Author.

Odom, S. L., Brantlinger, E., Gersten, R., Horner, R., Thompson, B., & Harris, K. (2005). Research in special education: Scientific methods and evidence-based practices. *Exceptional Children, 71*, 137–148.

Peacock Hill Working Group. (1991). Problems and promises in special education and related services for children and youth with emotional and behavioral disorders. *Behavioral Disorders, 16*, 299–313.

Pennsylvania Association of Retarded Citizens v. Commonwealth of Pennsylvania, 343 F. Supp. 279 (E. D. Pa. 1972).

Rones, M., & Hoagwood, K. (2000). School-based mental health services: A research review. *Clinical Child and Family Psychology Review,3*(4), 223–241.

Sanders, W. L., & Rivers, J. C. (1996). *Cumulative and residual effects of teachers on future student academic achievement*. Research Progress Report. Knoxville: University of Tennessee Value-Added Research and Assessment Center.

Sarason, S. B. (1990). *The predictable failure of education reform: Can we change course before it's too late?* San Francisco: Jossey-Bass.

Strong, A., Wehby, J. H., Falk, K. B., & Lane, K. L. (2004). The impact of a structured reading curriculum and repeated reading on the achievement of junior high students with emotional and behavioral disorders. *School Psychology Review, 33*, 561–581.

Sugai, G., Horner, R. H., Dunlap, G., Hieneman, M., Lewis, T. J., Nelson, C. M., et al. (2000). *Applying positive behavioral support and functional behavioral assessment in schools*. Washington, DC: OSEP Center of Positive Behavioral Interventions and Supports.

Wagner, M., Kutash, K., Duchnowski, A. J., & Epstein, M. H. (2005). The special education elementary longitudinal study and the national longitudinal study: Study designs and implications for children and youth with emotional disturbance. *Journal of Emotional and Behavioral Disorders*, 13, 25–41.

Wehby, J. H., Lane, K. L., & Falk, K. B. (2003). Academic instruction for students with emotional and behavioral disorders. *Journal of Emotional and Behavioral Disorders, 11,* 194–197.

Wehby, J. H., Symons, F. J., Canale, J. A., & Go, F. J. (1998). Teaching practices in classrooms for students with emotional and behavioral disorders. *Behavioral Disorders, 24,* 51–56.

Wehby, J. H., Symons, F. J., & Shores, R. E. (1995). A descriptive analysis of aggressive behavior in classrooms for children with emotional and behavioral disorders. *Behavioral Disorders, 20,* 87–105.

Wehby, J. H., Tally, B. B., & Falk, K. B. (2004). Identifying the relation between the function of problem behavior and teacher instructional behavior. *Assessment for Effective Instruction, 30,* 41–51.

Part II

REPAIRING AND ELABORATING SPECIAL EDUCATION'S CONCEPTUAL FOUNDATIONS

In Atlanta, Georgia, on May 27, 2006, James M. Kauffman accepted an award for the *Effective Presentation of Behavior Analysis in the Mass Media* from the Society for the Advancement of Behavior Analysis for his 2002 publication *Education Deform: Bright People Sometimes Say Stupid Things about Education.* In this award-winning text, Kauffman reveals his characteristic candor in calling down folly and in calling for all of us to make sense about education if we want it to improve.

> Here, I think, is a "hard" reality: Poorly thought out statements de-form education, whether their nonsense is postmodern or political or both and even if they're based on poorly done science. Our most helpful strategy is to keep a good head on our shoulders—to think at least as logically and systematically as we expect our students to think. Probably we will be modeling for our students what we expect of them if we refuse to give up the quest for improvement—just as we seek simplicity, if we're smart—but distrust it. (Kauffman, 2002, p. 39)

Throughout his career James Kauffman has been an articulate advocate for the education of children and youth with disabilities, and a vocal critic of nonsense that masquerades as special education reform. Serving as "the conscience for the field on critical issues" (Polloway, 2000, p. 323), he has written extensively for academic publications and communicated effectively with wider audiences. The challenge in portraying Kauffman's deep concern with misguided approaches to special education is selecting from among the many powerful examples he has used to convey what he argues are predictable problems in public policy. Those of us familiar with his scholarship and with his comments in the popular press remember Kauffman's (1994) remarks, criticizing funding cuts for short-changing education and the full inclusion movement for emphasizing the site over the soundness of instruction, saying that "no one is facing up to the desperation of special education children and teachers. Special education is like a train that's headed for a wreck because it's on the wrong track"(para 1).

No less candid today than yesterday, Kauffman continues to speak truth to power by challenging contemporary reform agendas that presume to apply to all students without accounting for the extraordinary problems of students who have extreme difficulty in learning the general education curriculum. In his resolute pursuit of sense-making, Kauffman takes issue with what he calls the senseless rhetoric of the No Child Left Behind Act of 2001 (NCLB), and his message is clear: "When someone suggests that all children will be able to perform at ____ (> 0) level, that all children will succeed, or that no child will be left behind, he or she is contributing to needless and unhelpful silly-talk about schools and schooling" (Kauffman & Konold, in press). His arguments are persuasive that current policies purport to improve special instruction for students with disabilities, as they undermine the individualized focus of special education, making it easier to exclude students from school, especially students with emotional and behavioral disorders (Kauffman & Landrum, 2006).

In more than 30 years of teaching, writing, and speaking about the education of children and youth with disabilities Kauffman has defended the foundational premise that special education is driven by an instructional mission. Themes that permeate his scholarship, such as making a difference in people's lives by improving instruction and making decisions about special education by relying on reason, also permeate the chapters in this section. Mark Mostert celebrates the personal and professional legacy bequeathed to special educators by their progenitors; Barbara Bateman follows the evolution of special education law that serves both to reflect and to shape the field's foundations; and Naomi Zigmond proposes a re-formation of the role and responsibilities of special educators in contemporary schools. Gary Sasso in conclusion addresses the philosophical underpinnings of special education, sharing as he does Kauffman's quest for truth, reason, objectivity, and confidence through the incremental pursuit of knowledge through rational inquiry.

REFERENCES

Kauffman, J. M. (1994). Special education gets poor grades. *USA Today Magazine*, New York: The Society for the Advancement of Education. Retrieved June 15, 2006, from www.findarticles.com/p/articles/mi_m1272/is_n2587_122/ai_15173069.

Kauffman, J. M. (2002). *Education deform: Bright people sometimes say stupid things about education.* Lanham, MD: Scarecrow Press.

Kauffman, J. M., & Landrum, T. J. (2006). *Children and youth with emotional and behavioral disorders: A history of their education.* Austin, TX: PRO-ED.

Kauffman, J. M., & Konold, T. (in press). Making sense in education: Pretense (including NCLB) and realities in rhetoric about schools and schooling. *Exceptionality.*

Polloway, E. (2000). Influential people in the development of the field of special education. *Remedial and Special Education, 21*(6), 322–324.

Chapter 5

James Milton Kauffman:
A Legacy of Special Education's
Unheralded Historical Distinctives

Mark P. Mostert
Regent University

How uneasily, although I am sure humbly, they now must sleep. Their legacies unselfishly hard-fought lie blind beside them. Still, if we would only pause, even momentarily, we would hear them. Faint echoes cling to the hope that we might turn the yellowing pages of their unsparing lives. Perhaps they watch us, willing to assist, but the Rubicon, swollen by other times and events, flows too swiftly by.

No matter. Their daguerreotyped words wait patiently to teach, again, faded truths that now perplex us to willful ignorance or unsubtle re-invention. Individuals all, they afford us the pillars of humanhood to assuage those who were formerly called imbeciles, gimps, pinheads, 'tardos, crazy; now called other, more familiar, and somewhat less harsh names. Names usually chosen matter-of-factly, markers for a perplexing child, a sightless woman, or, perhaps, for poor souls raving their lives away. Each moniker was dragged, reluctantly, from its neutral dwelling and, buffeted alike by the storms of prejudice and the warm rays of fealty, leaves behind a restless miasma that almost randomly comforts or condemns.

83

No matter. We are compelled to grasp Those-With-Names by their souls. Perhaps it is that those-who-sleep badger us on: *Do not forsake them,* they say; *We did not toil in vain. We bequeathed to you an ancestry of good. Good women. Good men. Noble peers who looked beyond the gnarly bonds of their contexts and dared to embrace what others shunned.*

If we dare to dwell in the edifice of our past, we find it hallowed ground, its robust pillars explaining the legacy of love for the different and undefended.

COMMUNITY

What of community? One way to explain what we mean by community is a group of people with shared distinctives setting them together as well as apart. Setting apart for togetherness is often useful, perhaps even essential to craft a discernable communal face. However, communities' idiosyncratic markers are also pregnant with the divisive seed of tyranny, which, once delivered, will seek to maim and destroy:

> Fellow citizens, much can be done for them; instead of condemning the poor blind man to stand at the corner of the street, and ask for charity; or to remain cooped up within the walls of an alms-house, or to sit and mope away his solitary existence among his happier friends, alike a burden to them and himself—you may give to him the means of becoming an enlightened, happy and useful member of society; you may give him and his fellow-blind the means of earning their own livelihood, or at least of doing much towards it; you may light the lamp of knowledge within them, you may enable them to read the Scriptures themselves.

Thus wrote Edward Brooks, Horace Mann, and S. C. Phillips in their public trustee's report of the New England Institution for the Education of the Blind (Brooks, Mann, & Phillips, 1833).

VIRTUE

What then, shall we say of virtue? It is an ongoing state of goodness, a panoply of intimately considerate reflexive outlooks matching conviction and action strength for strength. Virtue-making, we might say, is an invisible spinning of existential silver threads acknowledging and engaging aliveness into a glittering web free to shine or tarnish. It is a decent rectitude, inward looking, outwardly directed:

> Cover your eyes for a short time, and you shut out this world of beauty. Close your ears, and you exclude this world of sounds. Refrain from speaking, and you cease to hold communion with the world of intelligence. Yet, were it in your power to continue thus for hours, even for days, you still have within your minds a treasury of knowledge to which she can never resort. You can not picture to yourselves, the utter desolation of one, whose limited acquirements are made at the expense of such toil, and with the hazard of such continual error. Never, therefore, forget to be grateful for the talents which you are endowed. For every new idea which you add to the mental storehouse, praise Him, who gives you with unveiled senses, to taste the luxury of knowledge. When the smile of your parents and companions makes your heart glad, or when you look at the bright flowers and fair skies of summer, think with compassion of her, who must never see the face of her fellow creatures, nor the beauty of the earth and sky. When you hear the melody of music, of the kind voice of your teachers; strive to value and improve your privileges; and while you pour forth all the emotions of your souls in the varieties of language, forget not a prayer of pity for her who dwells in perpetual silence; a prayer of gratitude to Him who has caused you to differ from her.

Here, a glimpse of virtue in Lyman Cobb's *Juvenile Reader;* the story "The deaf, dumb, and blind girl" (Cobb, 1834, pp. 98–99).

BENEVOLENCE

What of benevolence? We might say that benevolence exemplifies the truly guileless goodness of the heart and mind; a spiritually bright compulsion, perhaps, to do good without resentment or manifest self-interest. Benevolence looks outward, seeking others who might benefit from its warm expressions; unhesitating, it exudes gentle compassion to the bereft, comfort for hurting souls and twisted limbs:

> … distant from the poorhouse a few rods, was a small wooden building, constructed of plank, affording a single room; this was unfurnished, save with a bundle of straw. The occupant of this comfortless abode was a young man, declared to be incurably insane. He was chained, and could move but a little space to and fro; the chain was connected to the floor by a heavy staple at one end-the other was

attached to an *iron collar which invested his neck*—the device, it seemed, of a former keeper. In summer the door was thrown open, but during winter it was closed, and the room was in darkness. Some months after I saw this poor patient, and after several individuals also had witnessed his sufferings, the authorities who directed the affairs of the poorhouse reluctantly consented that he should be placed under the care of Dr. Bell. The man who was charged to convey the patient the distance of rather more than forty miles, having bound and chained him, (I have the impression that, by the aid of a blacksmith, he was released at this time from the torturing iron ring,) conveyed him as far as East Cambridge, arriving at dusk. Instead of proceeding with the patient at once to the hospital, which was distant less than a mile, in Somerville, he chained him for the night to a post in the stable. After breakfast he was released and carried to the hospital in a state of much exhaustion. While the careful attendants and humane physician were busied in removing the strong bands which chafed his limbs, and lacerated the flesh in many places, he continually endeavored to express his gratitude—embracing them, weeping, and exclaiming, "Good men! Kind men! Ah, good, kind men, keep me here."

So wrote Dorothea Dix to the Congress of the United States regarding the state of the insane (Dix, 1850, para. 96).

STEADFASTNESS

Steadfastness—a sometimes uncomfortable idea. No matter, it is the granite sense of unwavering, not being persuaded from a resolute steadiness, and a sure foundation for withstanding the arduous journey from idea to outcome; a fatal foe of wan timidity and febrile irrationality:

In a previous letter I think I wrote you that "mug" and "milk" had given Helen more trouble than all the rest. She confused the nouns with the verb "drink." She didn't know the word for "drink," but went through the pantomime of drinking whenever she spelled "mug" or "milk." This morning, while she was washing, she wanted to know the name for "water." When she wants to know the name of anything, she points to it and pats my hand. I spelled "w-a-t-e-r" and thought no more about it until after breakfast. Then it occurred to me that with the help of this new word I might succeed in straightening out the "milk-mug" difficulty. We went out to the pump-house, and I made Helen hold her mug under the spout while I pumped. As the cold water gushed forth, filling the mug, I spelled "w-a-t-e-r" in Helen's free hand. The word coming so close upon the sensation of cold water rushing over her hand seemed to startle her. She dropped the mug and stood as one transfixed. A new light came into her face.

A joyous Anne Sullivan, on April 5, 1887, to her friend Sophia C. Hopkins, about her student, Helen Keller (Macy, 1903, p. 316).

RESTORATION

How might we regard restoration? It is the putting-right of the broken; that is, it is the regeneration of the damaged and the imperfect to where there is no recrimination for things left undone. Restoration inhabits the cheerfulness of perfection but acknowledges the gloom of the unachievable:

> Though handicapped, he outdid himself and reached his limits. The Wild Boy belongs not to the history of genius but to the history of the species itself. He is the other prodigal, who did not squander his inheritance but, to a remarkable degree, recovered it after it had been taken from him. Helped and loved by Itard and Madame Guerin, the boy in his own modest way met the challenge expressed in Hamlet's lines ... "What is a man If his chief good and market of his time be but to sleep and feed? A beast, no more." (Shattuck 1994, p 183)

A beast no more, indeed.

DILIGENCE

What shall we say of diligence? Perhaps it is a quality that is more of the will than the heart, an often solemn undertaking, given its patina of doggedness. A habitual effort pressing energy toward an enterprise deserving of persistence. Attentive, vigilant, unwavering, as steady as morning follows night:

> A little ball which I have in our museum of children's work I am inclined to consider the most valuable thing in the whole collection. The boy who made it was almost of the lowest grade of mentality. His hand against every man, he fancied every man's against him. Always under close custodial care that he might harm neither himself nor others, he would vent his spleen in tearing his clothing. His teacher, a woman of rare patience and devotedness, one day sat beside him tearing strips of old linen and laying them in order. "See, Willie, let us make some pretty strips and lay them so." His wonder grew at seeing

her doing what he had been scolded for doing, and at once there was a bond of sympathy. She was playing his game—the only one, poor little fellow, that he was capable of—and he joined in. "Now we will draw out the pretty threads and lay them in rows." For weeks the child found quiet pastime in this occupation and the violent nature grew quieter in proportion. One day the teacher said: "Let us tie these threads together and make a long string." It took him months to learn to tie those knots, but meanwhile his attendants were having a breathing space. "Now we will wind this into a pretty ball and I will cover all you make for the boys to play with," and a new occupation was added to his list. The next link in this curious chain of development was a lesson in knitting. Through months of patient teaching it was at last accomplished, and the boy to the day of his death found his life happiness in knitting caps for the children, in place of tearing both them and their clothes. (Barr, 1899, p. 205)

So wrote Martin W. Barr of the emotionally disturbed.

COMPASSION

Can we explain compassion? Perhaps we might consider it a deeply held, if somewhat mysterious responsiveness to the abject misfortune of others. We might more narrowly embrace this loving refuge as a ministry that seeks out suffering in the hope, vainly, perhaps, of relieving it:

O how much better you will be to get a good schooling don't you think so. mother donit fore the best, so hurry & learn so you can be a clark some day & I will be so glad to see that day come. (Dulberger, 1996, frontispiece)

So bravely wrote a late-19th century destitute mother to her son, having placed him in the Albany Orphan Asylum in upstate New York in desperate hopes of him having a better life than she could offer.

CONSOLATION

We must necessarily consider consolation. It is a cherished act, gifting soothing reassurances to the afflicted, encouraging them and binding their souls. But, above all, consolation confers the precious legacy of hope:

The deformity which I am now exhibiting was caused by my mother being frightened by an Elephant; my mother was going along the street when a procession of Animals were passing by, there was a terrible crush of people to see them, and unfortunately she was pushed under the Elephant's feet, which frightened her very much; this occurring during a time of pregnancy was the cause of my deformity.

The measurement around my head is 36 inches, there is a large substance of flesh at the back as large as a breakfast cup, the other part in a manner of speaking is like hills and valleys, all lumped together, while the face is such a sight that no one could describe it. The right hand is almost the size and shape of an Elephant's foreleg, measuring 12 inches round the wrist and 5 inches round one of the fingers; the other hand and arm is no larger than that of a girl ten years of age, although it is well proportioned. My feet and legs are covered with thick lumpy skin, also my body, like that of an Elephant, and almost the same color, in fact, no one would believe until they saw it, that such a thing could exist … [M]y deformity had grown to such an extent, so that I could not move about the town without having a crowd of people gather around me. I then went into the infirmary at Leicester, where I remained for two or three years, when I had to undergo an operation on my face, having three or four ounces of flesh cut away; so thought I, I'll get my living by being exhibited about the country … in fact I may say I am as comfortable now as I was uncomfortable before. (Merrick, n.d., para. 1, 2)

Joseph Carey Merrick, the "Elephant Man," in his own words.

LIBERATION

Liberation also beckons. Liberation looses the bonds of possibility, freeing to the sky the human as it soars over its now-rusting chains. It may be pure or, achieved for its own sake and not for the liberated, reveal a cesspool of putrid and boundless selfishness:

I got used to the silence and darkness that surrounded me until she became my teacher-who was to set my spirit free … Some one was drawing water and my teacher placed my hand under the spout. As the cool stream gushed over one hand she spelled into the other the word water, first slowly, then rapidly. I stood still, my whole attention fixed upon the motions of her fingers. Suddenly I felt a misty consciousness as of something forgotten—a thrill of returning thought; and the mystery of language was revealed to me. I knew then that w-a-t-e-r meant the wonderful cool something that was flowing over my hand. That living word awakened my soul, gave it light, hope, joy, set it free. (Keller, 1967/1905, pp. 34–35)

So reminisced the blind and deaf Helen Keller in *The Story of My Life*.

TEMPERANCE

Temperance? Here, another task of the will. We might perhaps see temperance as a necessary skill of willful self-restraint born from a commitment to eschewing excesses of judgment; a reflective moderation for decision-making, for weighing in the balance, and not found to be wanting:

> But although advocating their claim to special advantages in the matter of education, and to certain social privileges, as matters of right and justice, not of pity or indulgence, it has sometimes been my duty to express opinions concerning the blind as a class, which jostle and offend that peculiar sensitiveness and large self-esteem which are unduly developed in many of them by mistaken kindness. I have been constrained to speak of them as they have ever been, and ever must be, as one of the *defective* classes of society; to show that their lack of one important sense does necessarily, and in spite of compensations, imply bodily inferiority, which is almost necessarily followed by deficiencies in the force and variety of mental faculties and capacities. (Richards, 1909, p. 18)

So wrote Samuel Gridley Howe of the reality of blindness.

OBLIGATION

On we go to obligation. We might opine that it is a person's honorable covenant steadfastly connecting, above all, their own actions to an external moral or social benchmark. It is a covenant compelling the transformation of the conscience to the will:

> Independence, this goal of human existence, comes in a broad spectrum and may mean for the most severely retarded no more than the painstakingly acquired ability to raise one's hand to bring food to the mouth, and for the more advanced individual the privilege of moving about freely in the community. In between these two poles there lies a multitude of opportunity for us to enrich the life of the older mental retardate, and to support his natural tendency to seek gratification, however limited, of his desire toward greater independence. (Dybwad, 1860, para. 18)

So spoke Gunnar Dybwad, reminding us that the retarded grow old, too.

JUSTIFICATION

Why justification? It is more than a simple excuse. Rather, we might believe it to be an overt engagement in the condition of making the case for what we see as true, as just. It must be a strong apology that refutes condemnation, negating the shoals of bigotry and derision for the enveloping depths of considered rationality:

> Twenty years ago, when my sister entered an institution, it was most unusual for anyone to discuss this problem in terms of hope. But the weary fatalism of those days is no longer justified. The years of indifference and neglect are drawing to a close, and the years of research and experiment, faithful study, and sustained advance are upon us. To transform promise to reality, the mentally retarded must have champions of their cause, the more so because they are unable to provide their own. (Shriver, 1962, p. 74)

This was Eunice Kennedy Shriver's wistful take on Rose, her sister with mental retardation.

ENCOURAGEMENT

Why encouragement? We may embrace it to be a form of support, and even perhaps, approval, given to those we know are disheartened and betrayed. It is a helpful and guided solace that sees beyond the hedgerow of the immediate to the green meadows of the future:

> There is a part of a child's soul that has always been unknown but which must be known. With a spirit of sacrifice and enthusiasm we must go in search like those who travel to foreign lands and tear up mountains in their search for hidden gold. This is what the adults must do who seeks [sic] the unknown factor that lies hidden in the depths of a child's soul. This is a labor in which all must share, without distinction of nation, race, or social standing since it means the bringing forth of an indispensable element for the moral progress of mankind. (p. 15)

These were the encouraging words of Maria Montessori (1972).

This is a legacy created by those who need to be remembered for what they learned, for what they taught, for who they are.

KAUFFMAN

So, what of James Milton Kauffman?

A faithful man, one who has bequeathed a fine example of recognizing and building what we are about. A man who will, I'll wager, unselfishly (but stubbornly) refuse to claim what he so clearly is: The progenitor of an honored legacy that has led where we, his students, have respectfully followed.

Kauffman's gifted historical understandings enshrine him in our heads, but, much more importantly, his smile can never leave our hearts.

REFERENCES

Barr, M. W. (1899). The how, the why, and the wherefore of the training of feeble-minded children. *Journal of Psycho-asthenics, 4,* 204–212.

Brooks, E., Mann, H., & Phillips, S. C. (1833). *Address of the trustees of the New England Institution for the Education of the Blind for the public.* Retrieved January 23, 2006, from http://www.disabilitymuseum.org/lib/docs/1926.htm.

Cobb, L. (1834). The deaf, dumb, and blind girl. In L. Cobb (Ed.), *Cobb's new sequel to the juvenile readers, or fourth reading book* (pp. 67–72). New York: Caleb Bartlett.

Dix, D. L. (1850, August 8). *Memorial of Miss D. L. Dix to the Senate and House of Representatives of the United States: 33rd Congress, 1st session, Senate report no. 57.* Retrieved January 23, 2006, from http://www.disabilitymuseum.org/lib/docs/1239.htm.

Dulberger, J. A. (1996). *"Mother donit fore the best": Correspondence of a nineteenth-century orphan asylum.* Syracuse, NY: Syracuse University Press.

Dybwad, G. (1960, May). *Developing patterns for aid to the aging retarded and their families.* Speech presented at a conference on The Outlook for the Adult Retarded, Langhorne, PA. Retrieved January 23, 2006, from http://www.disabilitymuseum.org/lib/docs/2232card.htm.

Keller, H. (1967). *The story of my life.* New York: Scholastic Book Services. (Original work published 1905.)

Macy, J. A. (Ed.). (1903). *The story of my life by Helen Keller, with her letters and a supplementary account of her education, including passages from the reports and letters of her teacher, Anne Mansfield Sullivan.* New York: Doubleday, Page, & Co.

Merrick, J. C. (n.d.). *Autobiography.* Retrieved January 23, 2006, from http://www.josephmerrick.com/.

Montessori, M. (1972). *The secret of childhood* (M. J. Costelloe, Trans.). New York: Ballantine.

Richards, L. E. (1909). *Letters and journals of Samuel Gridley Howe: The servant of humanity.* Boston: Dana Estes & Co.

Shattuck, R. (1994). *The forbidden experiment: The story of the wild boy of Averyon.* New York: Kodansha International.

Shriver, E. K. (1962, September 22). Hope for retarded children. *Saturday Evening Post,* pp. 71–74.

Chapter 6

Law and the Conceptual Foundations of Special Education Practice

Barbara Bateman
University of Oregon

Special education practice and research have not always converged. Practice sometimes operates independently from research whereas research does not always address concerns central to practice. Now the Individuals with Disabilities Education Act[1] (IDEA, 2004) mandates that practice must be based on peer-reviewed research to the extent practicable. How this will be interpreted by special education practitioners and the legal system remains to be seen, but there is now a mandated, as well as a logical connection between research and practice.

Law may provide insights into the foundations of practice and into the connection between practice and research, but it does not provide a foundation for research. Law sets boundaries for certain research activities, based on the same principles of due process that

---

[1]As of the 2004 reauthorization the title is the Individuals with Disabilities Education Improvement Act. However, the acronym IDEA is so widely used, we retain it. We also use IDEA to encompass the original Education for all Handicapped Children Act of 1975.

now govern special education practice. Beyond that, principles of science rather than law must provide the conceptual foundations for research. Therefore, this discussion deals only with the legal foundations of special education practice.

In 1975, the combined efforts of leading special educators, special education professional organizations, dedicated parents and elected officials created the Education for all Handicapped Children Act of 1975, which was renamed the Individuals with Disabilities Education Act in 1990 (IDEA, 1990, 1997, 2004). Arguably, IDEA reflected a combination of the conceptual foundations of special education practice as they were then and as the law's architects believed they should be. This discussion explores these conceptual foundations of special education practice as they have appeared in federal law from 1975 to the present.

LAW AS A POSSIBLE ILLUMINATOR OF SPECIAL EDUCATION'S CONCEPTUAL FOUNDATIONS

Law not only reflects conceptual foundations but it also significantly influences them. Within law we know that legislation results in litigation which in turn affects new legislation which again results in litigation—this cycle is unending. In special education law many of the conceptual foundations of special education were imbedded in IDEA in 1975, influencing both practice and research and thereby modifying the conceptual underpinnings of the field. Each time Congress amended IDEA—in 1986, 1990, 1997, and 2004—the changes in the law reflected and then affected research, practice and the conceptual foundations of the field.

Just as importantly, these interactive, proactive, and reactive components of special education—law, practice, research, and conceptual foundations—are all imbedded in a complex cultural milieu, which affects, responds to, and is made up of diverse beliefs, values, traditions, goals, and more. Perhaps the true wonder is not that special education is now divided, contentious, disputatious, and worse, but that it has survived at all as an identifiable (or nearly so) endeavor.

Any proposition—real or ideal—that is offered as a foundational notion or a basic premise of special education has probably been or soon will be disputed and vigorously attacked from within special education, as well as from without. This having been said, the intent of this discussion after a bit more ground-laying is to examine special education law to see if it, in fact, it sheds any light on today's conceptual foundations of special education.

In the United States, it was historically the province of states to provide or not provide special education, as they chose. In the late 1960s and early 1970s this laissez-faire attitude gave way to the federal civil rights movement and the recognition that children with disabilities actually have an entitlement to education, just as do nondisabled children. Support for making education available to all children, including those with disabilities, was found in the federal and state constitutions, in the economics of increased self-sufficiency, and in a growing societal awareness of the moral and social rightness of including more and more of us in "We the People" of this country. In a very real sense, the history of the United States is the story of expanding our recognition of basic and full human rights beyond the white, male property owners who originally laid claim to those rights.

Unlike race, disability has not been recognized by the courts as a suspect class deserving special consideration for purposes of constitutional equal protection under the 14th Amendment. Nevertheless, the entitlement of persons with disabilities to be free from discrimination is now well established by statute.

As part of the expanding civil rights movement the Rehabilitation Act (1973) prohibited discrimination solely on the basis of disability by agencies or organizations that received federal dollars. Two decades later the Americans with Disabilities Act (ADA, 1990) extended that nondiscrimination protection for disabled persons and even reached into the private sector, regardless of funding sources. The nondiscrimination mandates of the Rehabilitation Act and ADA are legally grounded in the U.S. Constitution and are parallel in form and function to other civil rights laws, which prevent discrimination based on characteristics such as race, sex, or age.

This entitlement of persons with disabilities to full and equal rights under the law is a cornerstone in the conceptual foundation of special education. Over the past 35 years, these rights of persons with disabilities have been so firmly established in the law that it is

unthinkable that our society would now significantly backtrack or re-
nege on this premise. Law evolves. Seldom does it revolve.

In 1975, two years after the anti-discrimination provisions of the
Rehabilitation Act were enacted, the best guidance then available for
special education practice was incorporated into the IDEA. Careful
examination of the IDEA reveals the conceptual foundations central
to the thinking of those who designed and influenced the law. At that
time, as now, the law was leading practice. This gap between law and
practice is arguably a result of the sophistication and foresight of the
designers of IDEA.

IDEA is an affirmative action rather than a nondiscrimination law.
The Rehabilitation Act and ADA declare that discrimination based
solely on disabilities must not occur; IDEA specifies what must be included in special education practice. For this reason, the discussion
of legal sources for conceptual foundations of special education
practice focuses primarily on IDEA.

The conceptual foundations of special education are reflected and
created in far more places than law. Nevertheless, an examination of
special education law, here and now, seems a reasonable and possibly fruitful way to look for major conceptual foundations of the field
in addition to the already mentioned cornerstone of full and equal
legal rights for people who have disabilities.

THE DISABILITY CONCEPT

Special education law is premised on the concept that some students have disabilities and that some of those students need and are
entitled to special education. Both prongs of this premise are currently challenged by some. Nevertheless, the reality of disabilities
(whether called impairments, differences, variations, or other
names) and unique educational needs resulting from them are fundamental conceptual underpinnings of special education. Without
them, special education would collapse, exactly as some wish. The
premise that some children have disabilities requiring special education is seen in special education law's *child find* mandate and as-
sessment/evaluation procedures for eligibility determination and
needs identification.

Child Find

The *child find* legal requirement of IDEA is a straightforward, affirmative duty placed on each state to identify, locate, and evaluate all children with disabilities who reside in the state, regardless of the nature or severity of the disabilities. Prior to the IDEA, many children with disabilities were never known to public agencies, and especially not to public schools. An implicit underpinning of the concept that students who have disabilities are entitled to special education is that federal and state governments are responsible for insuring that those students have the opportunity to receive their entitlement.

Assessment, Eligibility, and Needs

Imbedded in *child find* is the duty of the state to evaluate all children within the state who have a disability. This assessment has two purposes, each highlighting a fundamental premise of special education. The first purpose is to determine whether the child has a qualifying disability, that is, is eligible for the benefits of IDEA and/or the protection of the Rehabilitation Act and the ADA. All three laws are premised on the propositions that disabilities exist, can be identified, and should be identified. If these basic foundation stones are rejected, special education and any discussion of it are ended. To believe that the child whose leg was amputated should not be identified as needing instruction in using a prosthesis or that the child with the cochlear implant should not be assisted in benefitting from it, is too absurd and irrational to merit consideration. Whatever those who would abolish special education mean by abolition, they cannot mean that.

The second purpose of IDEA's mandated assessment is to identify all of the child's unique educational and functional needs, thus laying the essential foundation for that child's education program. The word *unique* has special significance, as do many words in a statute. *Unique* in this context denotes that children identified as having a disability may have some educational needs that are substantially unusual and different from the needs of otherwise similar but nondisabled children. These unique needs will, or should, be the centerpiece of the child's program of special education. And yet, as

Kauffman (1993) pointed out, some critics argue (e.g., Ysseldyke, Algozzine, & Thurlow, 1992) that the different practices used with special education students must be replaced with school experiences exactly like those used with nondisabled regular students.

If IDEA's premises are correct—that disability exists, can be identified, and may result in *unique* educational needs—then to deny students with disabilities the different, special practices they need is illegal and wrong.

PROGRAM DEVELOPMENT

As Zigmond (1997) has so accurately observed

> Special education is, first and foremost, instruction focused on individual need. It is carefully planned. It is intensive, urgent, relentless, and goal directed. It is empirically supported practice, drawn from research. To provide special education means to set priorities and select carefully what needs to be taught. It means teaching something special and teaching it in a special way … [It means] defining the special education curriculum appropriate for each student that will be designated on the annual IEP. To provide special education means monitoring each student's progress … and taking responsibility for changing instruction when the monitoring data indicate that sufficient progress is not being made. (p. 385)

Much, if not almost all, of what is labeled *special education* today is not recognizable as the specialized, intensive, individualized services of the 1950s, 1960s, and 1970s. IDEA defines special education as specially designed instruction to meet the child's unique needs. Do these activities fit that definition—a history test being read to a child, students completing worksheets independently while the resource teacher works with a small group, an aide walking behind a child going to another room or two regular education teachers discussing a child's behavior plan?

At the heart of IDEA and of special education, as it once was, lies each child's individualized education program (IEP). Unique educational needs require individualized services. In today's world, special education has become so large and so much like regular education, that its traditional focus on individualized and individual teaching has been all but replaced by the group focus that is necessarily at the core of regular education. This failure to tailor each program precisely to fit the child's unique needs is undoubtedly responsible for much that is said to be wrong with special education. The numbers of children being served in special education has grown so rapidly over the past 30 years that the numbers of qualified, experienced special educators available to serve them has not kept up. Hence caseloads have become overwhelming and IEPs too often reflect ongoing programs, not children's individual needs and services.

This failure to individualize programs as we once did has been greatly exacerbated by a parallel failure in assessment. Instead of conducting a truly individualized diagnostic investigation of each child's performance we began to rely on a "canned" combination of a tiny handful of standardized tools. Clinical expertise in making informal assessments, observations, analyses of work samples, and more has seemingly been replaced by computer-generated test results/reports. One cannot plan a program from a WISC Full Scale IQ of 85 and a Woodcock-Johnson standard score of 92. One of the pioneers of modern-day special education, Samuel Kirk, was passionate in his quest for diagnostic procedures that led directly to educational programming and his Illinois Test of Psycholinguistic Abilities (Kirk & McCarthy, 1961/1968) was a major step in that direction. Ironically, now that the technical inadequacies which led to the demise of the original ITPA have been overcome in ITPA-3 (Hammill, Mather, & Roberts, 2001) the field has seemingly lost interest in diagnosis for teaching. Perhaps part of the problem is that the discipline of school psychology has grown, just as special education has, and it has all but taken over the entire assessment process. Time was when the special educator was responsible, prior to and along with teaching, for whatever diagnostic assessment was done. This separation that has occurred between assessment and teaching has also contributed substantially to the perceived inadequacies of special education services.

Although special education needs to return to genuine individualization of services based on a thorough diagnosis of unique needs, it is also true, as Kauffman has observed, that there is a role for recognizing categories of disability in planning and implementing special education. In our fervor to abolish labels we must not fail to recognize that in some situations the type of disability at issue is important.

From funding consequences to profound cultural implications the category of disability, for example, deafness, can be pivotal. Insistence on true individualization does not and should not mean that we ignore the fact that these may be significant similarities across those who share a type of disability.

Intensity of Special Services

The needed special education services, including their duration and frequency, are to be determined by the IEP team and they are to be made available by the school district. Conceptually, this is a reasonable plan. In reality, a perceived lack of adequate funds plus insufficient and inadequately trained staff often result in services that are not nearly intensive enough to be effective. An additional factor, sadly important here, is the resistance in many quarters to adopting research-proven, effective practices.

In disabilities as different from each other as dyslexia and autism, far more is now known than is usually implemented about effective, intensive interventions. For example, Shaywitz (2003), a leading dyslexia expert, notes that a child who has a reading disability may require 150–300 hours of intensive instruction, that is, 90 minutes a day for 1 to 3 years. Additionally, the later the effective instruction is begun the more time is required for remediation. Rare is the reading program that provides sufficient early, intensive remediation.

For young autistic children, 25–40 or more hours a week of one-to-one intervention with 50–100 learning opportunities per hour using discrete trial, incidental teaching, and other behavior analytic techniques has been found to be effective, whereas less intensive and/or eclectic interventions are less so (Eikeseth, Smith, Jahr, & Eldevile, 2002; Howard, Sparkman, Cohen, Green, & Stanislaw, 2005). Again, only a small but growing number of public school programs for autistic children provide this intensity of appropriate intervention unless required to do so by a court or hearing order.

IDEA now requires that to the extent practicable special education and related services must be based on peer-reviewed research. It remains to be seen whether this legal provision will be enthusiastically implemented and/or rigorously enforced. Regardless, law has now articulated the principle of employing data-based special education interventions. Similarly, the No Child Left Behind Act (2001)

Reading First Program grants require schools to use reading methods and materials that have been proven effective in scientific research. Numerous special educators have urged for decades that the field's practices follow the data ever more closely. Now their pleas are bolstered by law. If special education law is the conceptual beacon some of us believe it to be, it is natural to wonder why this requirement for research-based practices was not made part of the special education legal fabric until 2004. Might lawmakers have previously assumed educators did base practice on the best research available and therefore didn't need a mandate to do so?

Benefit

What is success in special education? What is the result that allows us to say an intervention was effective? For regular education the issue is much simpler. Norms reflect what students do, and in turn, success is when students "meet" the norms, that is, when they do what they do. That, of course, is an oversimplification, but the point is that norms of almost any and every sort provide standards against which most students' performance can be evaluated and a degree of success assigned.

For many special education students, the normative approach is not helpful. We have instead looked to statistics on dropout rates, graduation rates, after-school employment, welfare applications, and so on. However, as the special education population changes and both resources and expectations fluctuate, these figures can become difficult to interpret.

In legal terms, success in providing special education is providing a free appropriate public education (FAPE). *Free* means at no cost to the parents, *public* means to State public school standards and *education* includes developmental and functional skills as well as academics. And, of course, developmental and functional skills include social, emotional, physical, and vocational development, and more. The difficult piece of FAPE and the one of major interest in this discussion is *appropriate*. What does the law teach us about the meaning of *appropriate*? Is *appropriate* in fact a useful concept for defining success in providing special education?

The term *appropriate* was partially defined by statute and regulation in the original IDEA and has been carried through into the reauthorization of 2004. However, then as now, that definition provided little real guidance in deciding whether an individual education program did or did not rise to the level of appropriate. So, in the famous, now two-decades old case of *Board of Education v. Rowley* (1982) the U.S. Supreme Court defined an appropriate education as an individualized program, which is reasonably calculated to allow the student to receive educational benefit. However, with one exception, the *Rowley* court sidestepped the critical question of *how much educational benefit* is required for a special education program to be deemed appropriate or successful. The court spoke only to the situation of mainstreamed students and declared that such students must be provided all the services necessary to allow them to pass regular examinations and to truly progress from grade to grade. The Supreme Court naively believed that only children like Amy Rowley, who outperform nondisabled peers and are fully capable of making genuine year-for-year academic progress, are mainstreamed alongside their nondisabled peers.

Since the *Rowley* decision, the federal circuit courts of appeal have had to develop their own standards for determining how much benefit is required to be deemed appropriate in all the non-Rowley cases. The majority of the circuits have used language like "meaningful" and "more than trivial" to describe the benefit required to rise to the level of appropriate. The 11th Circuit, however, stands alone in having held that making measurable gains in the classroom is sufficient, even if the gains are not generalized across settings (*J.S.K. v. Hendry*, 1991). The other circuits are also in agreement with each other that any determination of the adequacy of benefit must consider the abilities of the individual child (e.g., see *Hall v. Vance*, 1985), whereas the 11th Circuit looks to the needs rather than to the abilities of the child.

Parental Participation

Mandating parental participation in a child's special education program is clearly not possible. What is mandated by IDEA is the *opportunity* for full and equal parent participation in all the major decisions about the child's special education. Some practitioners may observe that involving parents at every stage can be a bit cumbersome at times, but clearly we all recognize in the long run that parental participation and partnership are in the best interests of children and of the special education profession. The legal requirements regarding parental participation are more detailed and demanding (some might say nitpicky) than many would like, especially in the prior written notice, progress reporting, and procedural safeguards requirements. However, in retrospect it seems fair to note that most of these requirements came about because in the past too many of us failed to always deal appropriately with all parents in these matters. Be that as it may, IDEA now lays down explicit rules for relating to parents of special education students. And the law leaves no doubt that the conceptual foundation underpinning the special education parent–professional relationship is the entitlement of parents to be full and equal participants in their child's educational process.

PLACEMENT

No one has contributed more than Kauffman (e.g., 1994, 1995, 1999–2000; Kauffman & Hallahan, 1993, 1997, 2005) to our understanding of the role, appropriate and inappropriate, of place in special education. To try to shed any further or different light on what he has said so pointedly, articulately, and accurately would be foolish and unnecessary. An examination of the basic concepts of IDEA related to placement simply underscores what Kauffman has long recognized and forcefully advocated.

The conceptual underpinning of the law concerning placement is that a special education student's placement must be no more *restrictive* than is necessary to allow fulfillment of the primary purpose of IDEA to ensure an appropriate education. Inclusion of children who have disabilities with nondisabled children is a preference of the law when that inclusion is consistent with offering an appropriate education, and only then. So, the first piece of the law's conceptual foundation of placement is that program appropriateness is primary and the restrictiveness of the environment is secondary.

To discuss the relative importance of appropriateness of program and restrictiveness of environment even in this most basic way is to assume that we know what *restrictiveness* means. As Crockett and Kauffman (2001) provocatively asked, the least restrictive environment

(LRE) is least restrictive of what? Many talk as if they know the answer to that all-important question, but few ever share the answer. The legal concept of LRE was used in lawsuits of the early 1960s when institutionalized persons were being kept in situations/places far more restrictive of physical liberty than were necessitated by their conditions.[2] Physical liberty is seldom an issue in public schools, so we must ask again, LRE is least restrictive of *what*? Perhaps, someone might suggest, the answer is restrictive of social liberty, that is, of the right to be with nondisabled persons during the academic part of the school day. This academic part of a school day constitutes approximately 8% of a calendar year, (180 school days × 4 academic hours = 720 hrs = 8% of the 8,960 hours in a year), leaving more than 90% of the year for other matters including social contact with whomever the family wishes. Although the 8% is relatively small, it is nonetheless true that that particular 8% devoted to structured education is critical. School is an especially important part of children's and families' lives, no doubt. However, important as it is, is it consistent with our own experience to want always to be with those who perform at levels significantly different from our own? Does the elderly, out of condition matron in sweats choose to join an aerobics group with slim, 20ish, spandex-suited models? When you go out to dinner, do you or do you not go with "birds of a feather" with whom you share interests and experiences? Some of us seek groups where our performance level is average—sometimes relatively strong, other times not so strong. Some of us may prefer to be near the top rung of the ladder most of the time. However, few of us prefer to perform always near the bottom rung of the ladder, relative to our companions. Yet this is what inclusion means, academically and often socially, for many students who have disabilities.

Science may not yet be able to definitively sort out the effect of the 8% (or less) of the included child's year that is spent in school with higher performing companions. Common sense says that when a specialized setting, rather than a regular classroom, provides the appropriate education program, then the benefits of being with nondisabled children can be arranged during the rest of the year the child is not in the special setting.

---

[2]The concept that government may not unduly restrict us or use more drastic measures than necessary to accomplish its legitimate purpose goes back to the due process clause of the 14th Amendment and permeates constitutional law.

An unfortunate misreading of *Brown v. Board of Education* (1954) has led some to believe that LRE means that disabled children have a legal right under the equal protection clause to be educated with nondisabled children. In fact, *Brown* does not stand for that proposition because (a) it dealt solely with race, which is a suspect class, that is, one having greater legal protection from discrimination than nonsuspect classes such as disabled (*Cleburne v. Cleburne Living Center*, 1985) and (b) unlike disability, race is not relevant to grouping for educational purposes.

Colker (2006) has provided an in-depth, insightful, legal analysis of special education's integration presumption erroneously derived from *Brown* (1954). Colker begins with the observation that *Brown* disallowed total racial segregation in public schools, giving rise to a legal presumption favoring racial integration. This integration presumption, Colker argues, was borrowed by special education from the racial civil rights movement without a legal mandate or empirical justification. She also demonstrates with persuasive historical detail that Congress included the integration presumption (LRE) in IDEA to close inhumane, disability-only institutions and not to require full inclusion for school children with disabilities.

IDEA now, as from its beginning, requires that a child be placed in other than the regular classroom only when education there (in the regular class) cannot be achieved satisfactorily. Although the Supreme Court has not yet ruled on a placement case, it has given us at least two clear previews of its position as to what "achieved satisfactorily" means. In *Rowley* (1982) the court said that when a child is being mainstreamed the system itself monitors progress:

> Regular examinations are administered, grades are awarded and yearly advancement to higher grade levels is permitted for those children who attain an adequate knowledge of the course material ... children who graduate from our public school systems are considered by our society to have been "educated" at least to the grade level they have completed ... [therefore,] if the child is being educated in the regular classrooms of the public education system, [the IEP] should be reasonably calculated to enable the child to achieve passing marks and advance from grade to grade. (at 3049)

Rowley thus defines who should be educated in the regular classroom—those who, with adequate support, can truly do the regular work, participate in the curriculum, and graduate with performance at the completed grade level.

The Supreme Court has also provided a preview of the other side of the coin, that is, those who should *not* be mainstreamed. The Supreme Court has said very directly

> the Education of the Handicapped Act [now IDEA] requires an "appropriate" education, not one that is equal in all respects to the education of nonretarded children; clearly, admission to a class that exceeded the abilities of a retarded child would not be appropriate. (*Cleburne, supra* at 445)

In addition to the principle that restrictiveness of placement is subordinate to appropriateness of program, IDEA also requires that every placement decision be individualized, be made by a team, be based on the child's completed IEP (program) and be selected from a continuum of available alternative placements. Obviously, if all children were to be educated in a regular classroom, as full inclusionists would have it, it would be patently foolish for IDEA to require the full continuum of placements from resource rooms through special classes, special schools, residential placements, and more. One placement size does not fit all children and IDEA recognizes this. In sum, the law of special education placement is that the team must make an individualized placement decision based on a full continuum of alternate placements and should select the LRE placement in which education can be achieved satisfactorily.

FUNDING

A safe wager is that the overwhelming majority of us can not even rank order, let alone assign actual dollar values, to the annual U.S. expenditures for war, cosmetics, alcoholic beverages, pre-school education, repair to interstate highways, research to prevent/cure cancer, or space exploration, and on and on. Numbers the magnitude of national expenditures frequently leave us somewhere between befuddled and numb. So, it may not be truly meaningful to try to analyze or even discuss intelligently the relationships between funding and the conceptual foundations of special education. What is crucial is that our society, through its elected federal officials, has made a decision to provide a free, appropriate public, education to every child who has a disability, regardless of the nature or severity of that disability.

We know that (a) the federal contribution to the cost of special education is far less than the originally promised 40% of excess (above the cost of regular education) costs; (b) local school districts believe they need more dollars for special education than they have; (c) IDEA and case law do not allow a school district or a state to use lack of funds as a legal defense for failure to provide FAPE to a student; (d) many special education front-line personnel believe they must not seek services, materials or equipment for special education students beyond that which is readily available, for fear of jeopardizing their jobs; (e) special education public relations have not convincingly shown the public that dollars spent in special education are cost-effective in the long term; and (f) thus there is a backlash in many quarters against special education spending.

The most fundamental funding issue is exactly where on this society's prioritized spending list effective special education falls. The political process and the legal system have interacted to result in the IDEA mandate that every eligible child with a disability is entitled to a FAPE, that is, an appropriate public education at no cost to the parents. The courts have embraced the homespun saying that an appropriate program is neither a shiny Cadillac nor a rusted-out Volkswagen; rather it is a running Chevrolet. And lawyers have enjoyed distinguishing one car from the "tuther."

Parents and special educators alike are shocked, often appalled, when they learn of the cost to taxpayers' in some special education cases. In one California case (*Sacramento v. Holland,* 1994) the final tab was nearly two million dollars and the outcome was that a child who had mental retardation was entitled to be placed in a regular education setting. Although that case was not typical, it is also not unusual for special education cases to exceed several hundred thousand dollars cost to taxpayers. A common and reasonable estimate of the cost of a hearing (prior to court action) is $10,000 a day. In an unpublished case the writer was involved in many years ago, the school district spent about 100,000 taxpayer dollars in a legal battle to avoid settling with the family for the 2,000 dollars they were seeking from the district for partial reimbursement of the air transportation costs for their daughter's private special education schooling. In addition to that $100,000 for legal expenses, the district taxpayers were also required by the court to pay the full expenses of the girl's private schooling for several more years. The good news is that the young woman is now a caring, competent special education teacher.

Three things are certain about special education funding: (a) Every child who has a disability is entitled to an appropriate education at public expense; (b) the cost of appropriate education for disabled children averages more than for nondisabled children; and (c) huge amounts of resources—money, time, energy and good will—are drained out of special education by legal disputes, record keeping, and bureaucratic incompetence and nonsense.

The fundamental conceptual and legal foundations of special education funding are similar—children who have disabilities are entitled to a publicly funded appropriate education. It seems unlikely there will be changes to this basic premise. However, priorities and passions may continue to nibble away at the edges of the entitlement.

PERSONNEL PREPARATION

Support for personnel preparation is included in IDEA. There can be no doubt this is in recognition of the critical importance of having sufficient highly trained special education personnel who can effectively employ research-based interventions. The need for specially trained special educators is directly related to the fact that many children who have disabilities have unique needs. The law presumes special training is required, a presumption that was not challenged until the 1980s. The merit of the challenge has yet to be shown and for now the law recognizes and reinforces the concept that special education professionals require specialized training to meet the unique, heterogeneous needs of children who have disabilities.

DUE PROCESS

The legal concept of constitutional due process can be complex, but it can also be understood at a basic level as *fundamental fairness* in how the government deals with us. Public schools, of course, are government agencies and so they are required by the U.S. Constitution to deal fairly with those touched by them, including children who have disabilities. The roots of the procedural safeguards granted to parents and children in special education law are found in constitutional due process.

One might wonder whether legal, procedural safeguards are a necessary or proper part of the conceptual underpinnings of special education. The procedural safeguards—records access and privacy, participation in meetings, independent evaluations, stay-put, prior written notice, and hearing and appeal rights—resulted from special education practices of the 1960s and earlier when school (government) personnel, including special educators, often dealt heavy-handedly with parents. Even if legal procedural principles are not conceptual foundations per se, they are and should remain a bedrock part of special education practice.

The due process principles required by both special education law and by professionalism include (a) recognizing parents as true participating partners in their child's education (records access, evaluation input, IEP and placement decision making); (b) informing parents, timely and fully, about the school's proposed plans regarding the child (prior written notice, stay-put); and (c) ensuring impartial dispute resolution procedures.

SUMMARY

Special education law embodies basic premises that both reflect and shape the conceptual foundations of special education practice. Among those discussed are these:

1. Persons with disabilities may not be discriminated against solely on the basis of disability.
2. Children with disabilities are entitled to education, as are nondisabled children.

3. Disabilities exist, can be identified and sometimes require specially designed instruction and other services to meet unique needs.
4. Children who have disabilities need individualized special education programs, often intensive and specialized. They are entitled to individualized special education and related-services sufficient to allow them to receive educational benefit, which is meaningful and commensurate with their abilities.[3]
5. Special education practice should be guided by research; research should be responsive to practice issues, among others.
6. Parents should have the opportunity to participate fully and meaningfully in decisions about their children's special education services and placement.
7. Placement decisions should be individualized and selected from a full continuum of alternative placements; the integration presumption should be empirically re-evaluated.
8. Every child who has a disability is entitled to a publicly funded appropriate education, just as are children who do not have a disability.
9. Specialized training is required to work most effectively with children who have disabilities.
10. Public schools are government agencies and as such are required by the U.S. Constitution to deal with children who have disabilities and their parents in a fundamentally fair way—that is, to observe the basic procedural safeguards of IDEA in letter and spirit.

Law is obviously not the only framework from which conceptual foundations of a discipline can be discerned. It may not even be a particularly excellent one. However, it does reveal some incredibly basic, fundamental premises on which special education stands at the beginning of the 21st century. As we move further into the 21st century we can all hope that special education practice moves ever closer to the legal precepts that govern it and that it follows ever more closely the research that guides it.

---

[3]Except in the 11th Circuit where the legal entitlement is less and is based on need rather than ability.

REFERENCES

Americans with Disabilities Act, 42 U.S.C. §12132 *et seq.* (1990).

Board of Education of Hendrick Hudson School District v. Rowley, 458 U.S. 176, 102 S. Ct. 3034 (1982).

Brown v. Board of Education, 347 U.S. 483 (1954).

Cleburne v. Cleburne Living Center, 473 U.S. 432 (1985).

Colker, R. (2006). The disability integration presumption: Thirty years later. *University of Pennslyvania Law Review, 154,* 789–862.

Crockett. J. B., & Kauffman, J. M. (2001). The concept of the least restrictive environment and learning disabilities: Least restrictive of what? Reflections on Cruickshank's 1977 Guest Editorial for the *Journal of Learning Disabilities.* In D. P. Hallahan & B. K. Keogh (Eds.), *Research and global perspectives in learning disabilities: Essays in honor of William M. Cruickshank* (pp. 147–166). Mahwah, NJ: Lawrence Erlbaum Associates.

Eikeseth, S., Smith, T., Jahr, E., & Eldevile, S. (2002). Intensive behavioral treatment at school for 4–7 year-old children with autism: A 1-year comparison controlled study. *Behavior Modification, 26,* 49–68.

Hall v. Vance, 744 F.2d 629 (4th Cir. 1985).

Hammill, D. D., Mather, N., & Roberts, R. (2001). *Illinois Test of Psycholinguistic Abilities* (3rd ed). Austin, TX: PRO-ED.

Howard, J. S., Sparkman, C. R., Cohen, H. G., Green, G., & Stanislaw, H. (2005). A comparison of intensive behavior analytic and eclectic treatments for young children with autism. *Research in Developmental Disabilities, 26,* 359–383.

Individuals with Disabilities Education Act, 20 U.S.C. §1400 *et seq.* (1990, 1997, 2004).

J. S. K. v. Hendry, 941 F.2d 1563 (11th Cir. 1991).

Kauffman, J. M. (1993). How we might achieve the radical reform of special education. *Exceptional Children, 60,* 6–16.

Kauffman, J. M. (1994). Places of change: Special education's power and identity in an era of educational reform. *Journal of Learning Disabilities, 27,* 610–618.

Kauffman, J. M. (1995). Why we must celebrate a diversity of restrictive environments. *Learning Disabilities Research & Practice, 10,* 225–232.

Kauffman, J. M. (1999–2000). The special education story: Obituary, accident, report, conversion, experience, reincarnation, or none of the above? *Exceptionality,* 8 (1), 61–71.

Kauffman, J. M., & Hallahan, D. P. (1993). Toward a comprehensive delivery system for special education. In J. I. Goodlad & I. C. Lovitt (Eds.), *Integrating general and special education* (pp. 73–102). New York: Macmillan.

Kauffman, J. M., & Hallahan, D. P. (1997). A diversity of restrictive environments: Placement as a problem of social ecology. In J. W. Lloyd, E. J. Kame'enui, & D. Chard (Eds.), *Issues in educating students with disabilities* (pp. 325–342). Mahwah, NJ: Lawrence Erlbaum Associates.

Kauffman, J. M., & Hallahan, D. P. (Eds.). (2005). *The illusion of full inclusion: A comprehensive critique of a current special education bandwagon*. Austin, TX: PRO-ED.

Kirk, S. A., & McCarthy, J. J. (1961/1968). *Illinois Test of Psycholinguistic Abilities (ITPA)*. Urbana, IL: University of Illinois Press.

No Child Left Behind Act, 20 U.S.C. §6301 *et seq.* (2001).

Rehabilitation Act, 29 U.S.C. §794 (1973).

Sacramento Board of Education v. Holland, 14 F.3d 1398 (9th Cir. 1994).

Shaywitz, S. (2003). *Overcoming dyslexia*. New York: Knopf.

Ysseldyke, J. E., Algozzine, B., & Thurlow, M. (1992). *Critical issues in special education* (2nd ed.). Boston: Houghton Mifflin.

Zigmond, N. (1997). Educating students with disabilities: The future of special education. In J. W. Lloyd, E. J. Kame'enui, & D. Chard (Eds.), *Issues in educating students with disabilities* (pp. 325–342). Mahwah, NJ: Lawrence Erlbaum Associates.

Chapter 7

Delivering Special Education Is a Two-Person Job: A Call for Unconventional Thinking

Naomi Zigmond
University of Pittsburgh

These are difficult times for special education teachers. As districts move toward greater inclusion of students with learning and behavior disorders (L/BD; McLeskey, Henry, & Axelrod, 1999; McLeskey, Hoppey, Williamson, & Rents, 2004), it is increasingly difficult for special education teachers to understand the goals of their special education programs, the roles they should assume, the priorities they should establish, and the ways in which they should organize their activities and spend their time (Billingsley, 2004). Many new special education teachers are finding that they have been "prepared for jobs that no longer exist and that they are not equipped for the jobs they face" (CEC, 2000, p. 19). The changes in their role "threaten a loss of tradition, status, influence, and the very core of what makes special education special" (Ferguson & Ralph, 1996, p. 49). Prolonged, excessive, and competing role problems are likely to result in greater stress, less job satisfaction, less commitment, and greater intent to leave the profession (Billingsley, 2004) at a time

115

when the demand for special education teachers is strong and expected to increase substantially (U.S. Department of Labor, 2006).

There are no simple solutions to the difficulties special educators face. There is no body of research in special education from which to extract validated directions and definitions. Solutions generalized from research in general education have sometimes led us down wrong paths. Perhaps it is time for some unconventional thinking. In celebration of the career of Jim Kauffman, and as I pass my 40th year as a professor of special education, I offer some alternative groundings for the practice of special education today.

Before getting started, however, two clarifications are in order. First, I have focused this chapter on the roles and responsibilities of the *special education teacher*, and deliberately not on the *teacher of students with disabilities*. I believe strongly in the imperative that students with learning and behavior disorders (L/BD) be educated in general education classrooms by general education teachers to the maximum extent appropriate. I believe strongly that general education teachers, whether they are certified in elementary education or a secondary content subject, have an obligation to teach well *all* of the students who appear in their classes, to accept students with disabilities (and others with diverse interests, needs, and characteristics) into the fold and teach them the prescribed general education curriculum (or as much of it as the students are capable of learning). I believe strongly that preservice and in-service courses should equip general education teachers to do that. But these general education teachers are not the educators I am concerned with in this chapter. My focus is on the roles and responsibilities of *the special education teacher*—the teacher with a special certification who is specially trained to do special things with special students.

Second, my focus is on the teachers who teach students with L/BD—classified as students with learning disabilities, behavior disorders/emotional disturbance, and mild mental retardation. These students account for about 68% of the students with IEPs and about 7.5% of the resident school-age population nationwide (U.S. Department of Education, 2003).

So, "out of love for the truth and the desire to bring it to light" (Luther, 1517, p. 29) here are the nine theses (happily not 95) I wish to nail on the schoolhouse door (see Table 7.1). It is my hope that these proposals for the qualifications, roles, and responsibilities of

TABLE 7.1

Nine Unconventional Propositions

Nine Theses to Nail on the Schoolhouse Door

1. "Highly qualified" in a special educator should be defined by pedagogical expertise and deep knowledge of, and skill in, differentiated instruction.

2. Consistent with the commitment to LRE and inclusion, and to having "core content" taught by content experts, *all* content instruction for students with L/BD should be taught by a content specialist certified in general education.

3. Co-teaching is not a good use of the expertise of the special education teacher.

4. Co-teaching may be "satisfying" to both special education teachers and general education teachers but it is counterproductive in terms of building capacity in general education.

5. Because general education teachers are likely to have minimal training in special education, reinvent the special education "consulting teacher" role to help build capacity in general education. This is Job Number One.

6. In the amount of time generally allocated to a content subject, students with L/BD cannot be expected to learn the entire curriculum; priorities need to be established.

7. If we want special education students to master a core academic subject, they, and their teachers, will have to work longer and harder.

8. The IEP should NOT be aligned with the general education curriculum; rather it should specify those curricular elements that need to be learned that are NOT covered in the general education curriculum. Delivering this curriculum is Job Number Two.

9. The quality of the special education program (as defined in the IEP and carried out in the Resource Room) should be judged by the extent to which it facilitates students' learning of unique and important skills and knowledge and not by the extent to which it is aligned with the general education curriculum.

---

the special education teacher will stimulate debate and clarify policy in educating students with L/BD in the first half of the 21st century.

PROPOSITION 1

"Highly qualified" in a special educator should be defined by pedagogical expertise and deep knowledge of and skill in differentiated instruction.

In general education, research in schools and classrooms peopled primarily by students without disabilities, "highly qualified teachers" have been found to significantly increase student performance (Darling-Hammond & Youngs, 2002; Sanders & Horn, 1998; Wilson, Floden, & Ferrini-Mundy, 2002). In those schools and classrooms, the quality of the teacher contributed more to student achievement than any other factor, including student background, class size, or class composition (Sanders & Horn, 1998) and teacher quality was generally equated with teacher content knowledge and content-specific pedagogical expertise (NCTQ, 2004; Rice, 2003)). Building on that research, reform efforts in elementary and secondary teacher education programs in colleges and universities around the nation have focused on content knowledge and content course-taking among prospective teachers (Darling-Hammond, 2000). Alternative routes to teacher certification have encouraged individuals with content specializations to become teachers and learn how to teach on-the-job (NCEI, 2006).

Because the No Child Left Behind Act (NCLB) defines a highly qualified teacher as one who is competent in core content knowledge, and the Individuals with Disabilities Education Act (IDEA, 1997, 2004) places so high a priority on having students with disabilities master the general education curriculum, the focus on content knowledge as an indicator of quality has been extended to cover special education teachers as well. In some states that is not a problem; special education has always been an add-on certificate and special education teachers have always had to carry dual certifications. In other states, however, in which it is possible to obtain a first certification in special education only, the message being heard is that you cannot be a highly qualified special educator unless you are certified in something else! Earning at least a bachelor's degree, being prepared to teach students with disabilities, and passing the state licensure examination in special education is only the beginning; special education teachers of any students who will participate in statewide assessments that will be judged against grade-level standards (which includes the vast majority of students with L/BD) must demonstrate competence in the core subject areas in which they might teach by taking courses, passing state content examinations, or by completing a teacher certification program in general education (see American Federation of Teachers, 2005; National Education Association/National Association of State Directors of Special Education, 2005).

I do not take issue with the possibility that as a profession, we should require that special education be a second certificate that adds specializations to the general training provided to general education teachers at the elementary or secondary levels (on the medical model of the general practitioner who then specializes). What is insulting is the order in which appropriate preparation is prioritized (see NEA/NASDSE, 2005), the disproportionate value placed on content vs. pedagogy in the professional activities of the special education teacher, and the dictate from Congress rather than from thoughtful special educators or our national organizations that dual certification is appropriate and should be required.

PROPOSITION 2

Consistent with the commitment to LRE and inclusion, and to having "core content" taught by content experts, all content instruction for students with L/BD should be taught by a content specialist certified in general education.

IDEA 1997 introduced, and IDEA 2004 reiterated, the notion that all students with disabilities should have access to the general education curriculum. Whether taught in a general education classroom or in a special self-contained classroom or school, students with disabilities are to be exposed to the same curricular content as students who do not have disabilities (i.e., the curriculum set by state or school district guidelines) and they are to be held to the same achievement standards as students who do not have disabilities. This mandate, coupled with the long-standing commitment to educating students with disabilities in the least restrictive environment, has compelled school districts to return students with L/BD to their home schools and regular classrooms (or to not remove them from those environments in the first place; McLeskey et al., 2004).

It makes perfectly good sense. Content should be taught by a content specialist. Students with L/BD in regular schools should be in general education elementary classrooms or in secondary math classes, science classes, social studies classes, and so on, taught by teachers who are "highly qualified" in the content. In a special school, or if a special class is warranted, instruction in math, science, social studies, and so on, should be delivered by a certified content specialist or a teacher dually certified in the content and in special education.

PROPOSITION 3

Co-teaching is not a good use of the expertise of the special education teacher.

To help make the LRE placement more palatable to general education teachers, special education teachers, and parents of students with disabilities, and following the lead of prominent inclusion advocates (Cook & Friend, 1996; McLeskey & Waldron, 1995; Roach, Salisbury, & McGregor, 2002) more and more school districts are placing the special education teacher into the general education classroom, along with his or her students, to work side-by-side with the general educator. According to the National Center on Educational Restructuring and Inclusion (NCERI, 1995), this kind of co-teaching arrangement is the collaborative model used most often by schools.

Co-teaching is a special education service delivery model in which two certified teachers, one general educator and one special educator, share responsibility for planning, delivering, and evaluating instruction for a diverse group of students, some of whom are students with disabilities. Co-teaching, theoretically, draws on the strengths of both the general educator who understands the structure, content, and pacing of the general education curriculum and the special educator who can identify unique learning needs of individual students and enhance curriculum and instruction to match these needs. Co-teaching accomplishes two objectives: to have the students with disabilities taught the general education curriculum by a general education content specialist, and to have special education ideas and practices readily available to the students with L/BD in that class and to their general education teacher by having the special education teacher available in the room to provide help (Thousand & Villa, 1989).

Most of the published literature on co-teaching focuses on logistics, generally emphasizing that co-teaching is hard to do well without careful planning, ongoing co-planning, enthusiastic pairs of teachers compatible in teaching philosophy (as well as temperament and personality), and strong administrative (principal) support (see Bauwens, Hourcade, & Friend, 1989; Cook & Friend, 1995; Gately & Gately, 2001; Reeve & Hallahan, 1994; Vaughn, Schumm, & Arguelles, 1997; Walther-Thomas, Korinek, McLaughlin, & Williams, 2000). Some articles provide rich descriptions of co-teaching implemented in elementary, middle school, or high school classrooms (see Baker & Zigmond, 1995; Walther-Thomas, 1997; Weiss & Lloyd, 2002), often concluding that teachers adopt a particular arrangement (usually the "one teach/one assist" arrangement, sometimes the team teaching arrangement) and use it exclusively.

Research on the effectiveness of co-teaching is still in its infancy (Weiss & Brigham, 2000; Zigmond, 2003) and data on achievement outcomes for students with disabilities in co-taught classes have been particularly elusive. Recent data, however, suggest that co-teaching does not create an educational environment in which students with L/BD are likely to make achievement gains. In a quantitative classroom observation study, Magiera & Zigmond (2004) explored whether co-teaching changed the instructional experience for middle school students with disabilities in ways that would likely enhance achievement (e.g., producing smaller instructional groups, more time on task, more teacher–student interactions, and greater student participation); they found that it did not. These results were replicated in a study of co-teaching in 14 secondary schools in science classes (Zigmond, 2004) and social studies classes (Zigmond, 2006).

Furthermore, a qualitative study of the role and contribution of the special education teacher in co-taught secondary school classes characterized the special education teacher as,

> a nice addition, an occasional relief for the GET [general education teacher], and more attention to students when class is organized for small group (team) or independent seatwork. But none of what we

saw would make it more likely that the students with disabilities in the class would master the material. We did not hear the SETs [special education teachers] chime in with carefully worded elaborative explanations. We rarely heard SETs rephrase something already said to make the explanation clearer. We virtually never saw the SET provide explicit strategic instruction to facilitate learning or memory of the content material. (Zigmond & Matta, 2005, p. 73)

Zigmond and Matta (2005) hypothesized that if students with disabilities were mastering the content and earning passing grades in these high school courses, it was not because of something special the special education co-teacher was doing. If students with disabilities were not mastering the content and not earning passing grades, the kinds of coaching and team teaching they saw was not likely to make much difference in academic achievement. The special education teachers shared the instructional burden but did not make a unique contribution. When students were organized into teams or small groups, or given independent seat-work assignments, the special education teacher was there to answer a question or help with a solution. But there was no sustained instruction for students having particular difficulties, no reteaching for students who had not reached mastery, and no strategic instruction for students who tend to need explicit instruction in strategies. The special education teachers provided *support* rather than strategic, intensive, relentless instruction to students with disabilities in inclusion classes and they did so without much thoughtfulness or preplanning.

PROPOSITION 4

Co-teaching may be "satisfying" to both special education teachers and general education teachers, but it is counterproductive in terms of building capacity in general education.

Several researchers have reported, in the main, high levels of satisfaction among all constituents once a co-teaching model has been implemented (see Pugach & Johnson, 1995; Purkey & Smith, 1985; Voltz, Elliot, & Cobb, 1994). General education teachers, often initially skeptical about sharing their classroom space, generally come to enjoy having a second adult in the room who can not only provide assistance but also adult conversation. Special education teachers feel liberated from the confines of the special education resource room and feel good about reaching more students.

But in the long run, co-teaching as a routine service delivery model is not only an inefficient use of resources (teaching a content class is typically not a two-person job), it is counterproductive at least in part because it fails to build capacity among general education teachers. A "highly qualified" general education teacher should not only be expert in the content being taught, but also expert in content-specific pedagogy that reaches a very diverse student body. None of the advocates for co-teaching (e.g., Bauwens & Hourcade, 1995; Cook & Friend, 1996; Vaughn et al., 1997; Walther-Thomas et al., 2000) have proposed that it is an intermediate service delivery model, a vehicle for teaching general education teachers how to instruct students with disabilities effectively on their own. Special education teachers as co-teachers relieve the burden from the general education content specialist of developing and implementing adaptations and modifications appropriate to individual students with disabilities but doing it *for* them is not the same as teaching them to do it themselves.

PROPOSITION 5

Because general education teachers are likely to have minimal training in special education, reinvent the special education "consulting teacher" role to help build capacity in general education. This is Job Number One.

A more effective way of serving students with L/BD (and their general education teachers) would be for one special educator in a school building to provide "indirect" services, to be a "consulting teacher" (see Graden, Casey, & Bonstrom, 1985; Laurie, Buchwach, Silverman, & Zigmond, 1978; Polsgrove & McNeil, 1989; West & Idol, 1987). Instead of assuming a direct instructional role with students with disabilities, these individuals would serve students with disabilities *indirectly* by working collaboratively with students' general education content teachers. They would work in various contexts throughout the school as needed, rather than being scheduled routinely into particular classrooms. They would work almost exclusively with other adults (i.e., regular education teachers, administrators) rather than with students, although they may occasionally model teaching strategies in a classroom or assist with student assessments. This role is not new—it was very popular three decades ago when the field first explored ways to facilitate mainstreaming of students with disabilities into general education learning environments (see Johnson, Pugach, & Hammitte, 1988; Polsgrove & McNeil, 1989; Zigmond, 1978). But special education was ahead of its time, and teacher-as-coach had not yet been accepted as a legitimate role. Now, the "consulting teacher" role (Idol, 1988; Idol & West, 1988) has been rediscovered (or reinvented), has been renamed "coach," and is being promoted as a way to provide job-embedded staff development to teachers of reading or mathematics (Neufeld & Roper, 2003; Staub & West, 2003; West, 2002). The role, as a full-time job, has been legitimized in the Reading First initiative as critical to improving the capacity of teachers in elementary schools to teach reading effectively to diverse learners (IRA, 2004; Sparks & Hirsh, 1997).

Coaches work with teachers to change their attitudes, expectations, and teaching and testing styles. A special education-teacher-as-coach could provide the job-embedded staff development that would help general education teachers learn how to appropriately modify learning environments and instructional strategies to effectively provide differentiated instruction for the individuals with exceptional learning needs in their classrooms (CEC, 2005; Deshler, Ellis, & Lenz, 1996; Mastropieri & Scruggs, 2007; Wood, 1998). In a consulting teacher service delivery model, performance of students with L/BD on high stakes tests would not be seen as an accountability measure of special education. The success (or failure) of students with L/BD to master the core academic content would not be attributed to special education (as it still is in most co-teaching arrangements) because special education teachers would not have had any direct responsibility for instruction in those subjects. Perhaps until responsibility is placed squarely on the shoulders of general educators, we cannot expect them to take seriously their role in teaching *all* the students in their classes.

PROPOSITION 6

In the amount of time generally allocated to a content subject, students with L/BD cannot be expected to learn the entire curriculum; priorities need to be established.

The school year is a fixed commodity. Those who plan courses of study use logic and experience to determine how much can be accomplished in one grading period, one semester, or one school year and organize/pace instruction so that most students can learn what they need to learn, in the time they have to learn it. Students with L/BD generally start each school year knowing less than their age-mates, have more to learn, and take longer to learn it (Zigmond, 1996). They cannot cover the same ground in the same amount of time as their nondisabled peers. Progress monitoring data have shown that with enormous effort on the part of both teacher and students, they can learn at the same rate as their peers (Fuchs, Fuchs, & Fernstrom, 1993; Fuchs, Fuchs, & Hamlett, 1989) but even in those circumstances the students with L/BD would end the year as far behind their age-mates as they started. Two things would need to happen before we could expect students with L/BD to "catch up." First, we, the adults and experts, would need to set priorities within the general education curriculum, deciding which parts of each curriculum are essential and need to be mastered, and which could be omitted without jeopardizing a student's progress the following year. The curriculum for students with L/BD has already narrowed (as it has for most students) to concentrate on what will be assessed on the statewide accountability test. For students who are hard to teach (or find it hard to learn) the curriculum would need to be narrowed even more. Second ...

PROPOSITION 7

If we want special education students to master a core academic subject, they, and their teachers, will have to work longer and harder.

Even after curriculum objectives have been prioritized (and the number to be mastered reduced somewhat), in order to learn what needs to be learned, students with L/BD would need to work longer and harder than students without L/BD. This could be accomplished by lengthening the school day and the school year, or by rethinking the schedule within the school day to provide more opportunities for instructional time and guided practice on critical curricula. Some content would have to be eliminated for twice (or three times) as much time to be allocated to prioritized areas like reading, or math or science. Students might also have to give up extracurricular activities and free time on Saturdays or holidays. This was the strategy used to accomplish the "calculus miracle" dramatized in the film *Stand and Deliver* and in Mathews' (1988) biography of *Escalante: The Best Teacher in America*. What is clear in both the film and the book is that we cannot assume that students are incapable of mastering a content subject if we do not provide ample opportunity for them to receive the needed instruction.

PROPOSITION 8

The IEP should NOT be aligned with the general education curriculum; rather it should specify those curricular elements that need to be learned that are NOT covered in the general education curriculum. Delivering this curriculum is Job Number Two.

Historically, school districts (or states) developed planned courses, defining the what (the curriculum objectives), and the how (the textbooks and materials and even, sometimes, the orientation to instruction—hands-on, constructivist, direct instruction) of each course to be taught. Historically, in special education, the IEP team had the right, even the obligation, to determine what unique skills and knowledge a particular student needed to be taught in lieu of or in addition to the general curriculum, and to suggest the locale and the specially designed instruction that would accomplish that need. This unique curriculum might have included basic academic skills, language and communication skills, social skills, motor skills, and/or perceptual skills taught in a resource room or in a self-contained class. Some skills were selected because they were thought to be prerequisite to the acquisition and mastery of reading, writing, spelling or arithmetic; some were selected because parents or teachers believed those were the most important skills for that student to learn that year. In either case, the special education teacher sought to teach "special stuff" and not what everyone else was learning (i.e., *not* the general education curriculum). The IEP team was assigned responsibility for making individual decisions about what each student should learn, how each student should be taught, and where that instruction should take place.

This approach to IEP planning lost favor in 1997 when the IDEA reauthorization and regulations expressed distinct preferences. In relation to *what*, the preference was to learn the general education curriculum. In relation to *how*, the preference was for research-validated practices. In relation to *where*, the preference was in a seat next to a student without disabilities, in a general education classroom in the neighborhood school. Although these were preferences, and not limitations on the decisions the IEP team was invested in making, the preferences strongly influenced the range of choices considered by IEP teams and helped to redefine the role of the special education teacher as someone who supported students in learning the general education curriculum, not someone who taught something unique. It is time to reconsider that path. "Supporting" students in their learning of the general education curriculum does not utilize fully the specialized skills in assessment and differentiated instruction that are the hallmarks of an expert special education teacher.

Many students may be capable of intuiting the relationships between letters and sounds, the meanings of words, the strategies for taking a test, the most efficient ways to understand and remember complex material that has been read. But students with learning and behavioral disorders don't intuit well! They generally need direct, explicit instruction to master what other students might be expected to "pick up on their own." The job of the special education teacher should be to find the time and resources to teach students with L/BD all the skills NOT taught in the general education curriculum.

Students with L/BD are often overwhelmed, disorganized, and frustrated in school. They often have inadequate prior knowledge, significant difficulties with both short-term and long-term memory, poor study skills, and problems maintaining attention, To be more efficient and effective learners, they need to become strategic learners, deliberate in their use of strategies and techniques. Learning strategies are "techniques, principles, or rules that facilitate the acquisition, manipulation, integration, storage and retrieval of information across situations and setting" (Alley & Deshler, 1979, p. 13). Strategies are the "tools and techniques we use to help ourselves understand and learn new material or skills; integrate this new information with what we already know in a way that makes sense; and recall the information or skill later, even in a different situation or place" (Pierangelo & Giuliani, 2006, p. 164). Over the course of their schooling, many students figure out on their own their strengths and weaknesses in learning situations and what strategies and techniques they naturally tend to use when learning something new; students with L/BD tend not to figure this out. They do not develop on their own efficient, effective, and organized steps and procedures to use when learning, remembering, or performing academic or social tasks. Special education teachers can be enormously helpful in this regard. They can introduce students to specific strategies for reading, learning, remembering, and test taking. They can demonstrate when and how the strategies are used. They can provide opportunities for students to discuss, reflect on, and practice strategies, giving feedback to help students refine their strategy use and learn to monitor their own usage (Rosenshine & Stevens, 1986). Direct and explicit strategy instruction for students with L/BD carries the additional benefit of promoting independence in acquiring and performing academic tasks (Ellis, Deshler, Lenz, Schumaker, & Clark, 1991).

Other unique curricular elements that should be taught by the special education teacher include "teacher-pleasing behaviors" and "behavior control skills" developed and validated by Zigmond and colleagues as a "school survival skills curriculum" (Kerr & Zigmond, 1986; Silverman, Zigmond, & Sansone, 1981). Special education teachers might also provide direct, explicit instruction in social skills to improve students' perceptions and understandings of social situations; research tells us that if social skills training is to be effective, it must be systematic, prolonged, based on a field-tested curriculum, and combined with effective instruction to address the academic failure that may contribute to low self-esteem, peer rejection, and inadequate social skills (Hallahan Lloyd, Kauffman, Weiss, & Martinez, 2005; Vaughn et al., 2003).

For adolescents, transition planning is important. Students with L/BD need school time to think about and talk about what they might do with their lives, what they might be, and what schooling and work training it takes to be that. This kind of transition planning has to be not only comprehensive but also individualized, "based on personal needs, interests and preferences" (Shapiro & Rich, 1999, p. 142). And an important part of that transition training involves learning to be a self-advocate (Durlak, Rose, & Bursuck, 1994; Scanlon & Mellard, 2002). According to Skinner (1998), "students become self advocates when they (a) demonstrate understanding of their disability, (b) are aware of their legal rights, and (c) demonstrate competence in communicating rights and needs to those in positions of authority" (p. 279). Teaching students how to talk about their disability, to identify effective accommodations, and to suggest strategies for implementing them takes extended, protected time and teaching strategies that involve modeling, reinforcing, shaping, and practice (Durlak et al., 1994).

This (and other unique skills; see Fuchs & Fuchs, 1995) would be the stuff of special education—all the things that students with L/BD are expected to know or be able to do that no one in general education will take the time or resources to teach explicitly. Planning and delivering instruction in unique disability-specific skills is not a new idea. It is clearly articulated in the calls for teachers of students with visual impairment to teach an "expanded core curriculum" (Corn, Hatlen, Huebner, Ryan, & Siller, 1995; Hatlen, 1996; Koenig & Holbrook, 2000). Special education teachers of students with L/BD in Job Number Two would spend some time devoted to modifying instruction and materials for general education teachers who are teaching the core curriculum common to all students (English, mathematics, science, health and physical education, fine arts, social studies and history, economics and business education, and vocational education). But they would spend most of their time preparing and delivering instruction in unique skills that are specific to the needs of their individual students.

PROPOSITION 9

The quality of the special education program (as defined in the IEP and carried out in the Resource Room) should be judged by the extent to which it facilitates students' learning of unique and important skills and knowledge and not by the extent to which it is aligned with the general education curriculum.

In the model I am proposing, it is likely that much of the curriculum and instruction delivered in the special education resource room would not be intricately coordinated with the rest of the curriculum being delivered by general education teachers. But that's OK. Science teachers have a curriculum to teach. So do music teachers, and art teachers, and social studies teachers, and math teachers. In most schools, the science curriculum is not coordinated with the math curriculum, or the English curriculum is not synchronized with the social studies curriculum. By the same token, a special education

curriculum uniquely designed to teach each student things not covered in the general education curriculum need not be coordinated
and synchronized with the rest of the students' school day. Of course,
to the extent possible, students would be taught to apply the skills
and strategies learned in special education to real life situations encountered throughout the school day. But like most other teachers of
specialized content, the special education teachers would be "able to
teach what she wanted and did not have to 'worry' about what they
were doing in the GE classroom" (Klingner & Vaughn, 2002, p. 27).

CONCLUDING COMMENTS

My aim in this chapter is to challenge conventional wisdom in special
education and offer new ways of serving students with learning and
behavior disorders in this first half of the 21st century. I propose that
general education certified content teachers teach content—to
whomever is supposed to learn it—and that elementary and secondary teacher preparation programs include sufficient exposure and
practice in pedagogical alternatives that these teachers can successfully adapt and modify curricula to meet diverse student needs. I
propose that for curricula considered essential, more than the usual
amount of school time be allocated to instruction and practice, because students with L/BD learn more slowly and need more practice
to master the required content. I propose that a "special education
coach" be assigned to each school building to provide consultation
and job-embedded staff development that helps build capacity
among general education teachers for meeting the needs of diverse
learners in their content classes. I further propose that this role, Job
Number One, take the place of the special education co-teacher for a
more productive use of professional resources.

I believe that the most popular service delivery model, co-teaching, cannot provide sufficient opportunities for individualized, intensive, instruction for students with L/BD. Changes in service
delivery models, in the time allocated to instruction on the content
of the accountability assessment, and in the instructional practices of
teachers responsible for prioritizing and "covering" the content
might very well lead to greater numbers of students becoming
proficient.

I propose that special education teachers be judged as "highly qualified" by their expertise in teaching specialized and individualized curricula to students with disabilities. I propose that the IEP specify the unique curricular needs of each individual student with L/BD, and teaching that curriculum be the responsibility of the special education teacher in Job Number Two. I propose that to the extent appropriate, these unique curricula be related to the curricula taught by general education teachers, but that the quality of the IEP be judged not by the extent of that relationship but by the extent to which it meets the individual needs of a particular student.

I have not discussed the need for instruction based on research-validated procedures and strategies. Nor have I discussed the importance of "response-contingent instruction" (Zigmond, Vallecorsa, & Silverman, 1983) and the necessity of monitoring student progress and adjusting instruction to ensure growth. These I have assumed are "givens." I have also not assigned to the special education teacher responsibility for teaching reading and language arts. I confess I have always considered relentless instruction in reading to be the appropriate domain of special education teachers of students with L/BD. I don't now. If eligibility for special education services comes more and more to be defined by a lack of responsiveness to interventions focused on having the student learn the general education curriculum, this role for the special education teacher seems to make less and less sense. After a student has failed to learn to read the first time around, then failed to profit from a targeted intervention, and then failed to improve with an appropriate research-based tertiary intervention, is it appropriate to recommend that the special education teacher focus time and energy teaching this student to read a fourth time?

What I have focused on, instead, is the need for special education to return to being special, and the need for special education teachers to teach special stuff in a special way to their students and to other teachers. I acknowledge that to include "special stuff" in the curriculum of students with L/BD and at the same time allocate more-than-the-usual amount of time to content subjects for which there is a state accountability assessment will require eliminating some parts of the regular education curriculum that currently fill students' days. It will mean acknowledging that students with L/BD have different needs that should be celebrated and addressed, and not hidden and ignored. It will mean being honest with students and their parent and teachers about how much harder and longer these students will have to work to achieve goals that come easily to other students. It will mean getting back to the idea that some students need something special and to get that special something for them is not only doable but our obligation and responsibility. It sees delivery of special education as a two-person job. It means a re-formation of special education.

REFERENCES

Alley, G., & Deshler, D. (1979). *Teaching the learning disabled adolescent: Strategies and methods.* Denver, CO: Love.

American Federation of Teachers. (2005). *Comparison of highly qualified teacher requirements for special education teachers under NCLB and IDEA.* Retrieved June 15, 2006 from www.aft.org/topics/nclb/downloads/HQTforspecialed.pdf.

Baker, J., & Zigmond, N. (1995). The meaning and practice of inclusion for students with learning disabilities. *The Journal of Special Education, 29,* 163–180.

Bauwens, J., & Hourcade, J. J. (1995). *Cooperative teaching: Rebuilding the schoolhouse for all students.* Austin Texas: PRO-ED.

Bauwens, J., Hourcade, J., & Friend, M. (1989). Cooperative teaching: A model for general and special education integration. *Remedial and Special Education, 10,* 17–22.

Billingsley, B. (2004). Promoting teacher quality and retention in special education. *Journal of Learning Disabilities, 37*(5), 370–376.

Cook, L., & Friend, M. (1995). Co-teaching: Guidelines for creating effective practices. *Focus on Exceptional Children, 28,* 1–16.

Cook, L., & Friend, M. (1996). Co-teaching: Guidelines for creating effective practices. *Focus on Exceptional Children, 28,* 1–16.

Corn, A. L., Hatlen, P., Huebner, K. M., Ryan, F., & Siller, M. A. (1995). *The national agenda for the education of children and youths with visual impairments including those with multiple disabilities.* New York: American Foundation for the Blind Press.

Council for Exceptional Children. (2000). *Bright futures for exceptional learners: An action to achieve quality conditions for teaching and learning.* Reston, VA: Author.

Council for Exceptional Children. (2005). *Resources on "highly qualified" requirements for special educators.* Arlington, VA: Author.

Darling-Hammond, L. (2000). Teacher quality and student achievement: A review of state policy evidence. *Education Policy Analysis Archives,8*(1). Retrieved February 8, 2006, from http://epaa.asu.edu/epaa/v8n1.

Darling-Hammond. L., & Youngs, P. (2002). Defining "highly qualified teachers": What does "scientifically-based research" actually tell us? *Educational Researcher, 31*(9), 1–13.

Deshler, D. D., Ellis, E. S., & Lenz, B. (1996). *Teaching adolescents with learning disabilities: Strategies and methods.* Denver, CO: Love.

Durlak, C. M., Rose, E., & Bursuck, W. D. (1994). Preparing high school students with learning disabilities for the transition to postsecondary education: Teaching the skills of self-determination. *Journal of Learning Disabilities, 27*(1), 51–59.

Ellis, E., Deshler, D., Lenz, B., Schumaker, J., & Clark, F. (1991). An instructional model for teaching learning strategies. *Focus on Exceptional Children, 23*(6), 1–23.

Ferguson, D. L., & Ralph, G. R. (1996). The changing role of special educators: A development waiting for a trend. *Contemporary Education, 68,* 49–51.

Fuchs, D., & Fuchs, L. (1995). What's special about special education? *Phi Delta Kappan, 76,* 522–530.

Fuchs, D., Fuchs, L., & Fernstrom, P. (1993). A conservative approach to special education reform: Mainstreaming through transenvironmental programming and curriculum-based measurement. *American Education Research Journal, 30,* 149–178.

Fuchs, L., Fuchs, D., & Hamlett, C. (1989). Effects of instructional use of curriculum-based measurement to enhance instructional programs. *Remedial and Special Education, 10,* 43–52.

Gately, S., & Gately, F. Jr. (2001). Understanding co-teaching components. *Teaching Exceptional Children, 33*(4), 40–47.

Graden, J. L., Casey, A., & Bonstrom, O. (1985). Implementing a prereferral intervention system: Part 2. The data. *Exceptional Children, 51,* 487–496.

Hallahan, D. P., Lloyd, J. W., Kauffman, J. M., Weiss, M. P., & Martinez, E. A. (2005). *Learning disabilities: Foundations, characteristics and effective teaching* (3rd ed.). Boston, MA: Pearson.

Hatlen, P. (1996). *The core curriculum for blind and visually impaired students, including those with additional disabilities.* Austin, TX: Texas School for the Blind and Visually Impaired. Retrieved April 20, 2002, from http://www.tsbvi.edu/agenda/corecurric.htm.

Idol, L. (1988). A rationale and guidelines for establishing special education consultation programs. *Remedial and Special Education, 9,* 48–58.

Idol, L., & West, J. F. (1988). Consultation in special education (Part II): Training and practice. *Journal of Learning Disabilities, 20,* 474–494.

Individuals with Disabilities Education Act (IDEA). (1997). *Public Law 105–17.* Washington, DC: U.S. Government Printing Office.

Individuals with Disabilities Education Improvement Act. (2004). *Public Law 108–446.* Washington, DC: U.S. Government Printing Office.

International Reading Association. (2004). *The role and qualifications of the reading coach in the United States.* Newark, DE: Author.

Johnson, L. J., Pugach, M. C., & Hammitte, D. J. (1988). Barriers to effective special education consultation. *Remedial and Special Education, 9,* 41–47.

Kerr, M. M., & Zigmond, N. (1986). What do high school teachers want? A study of expectations and standards. *Education & Treatment of Children, 9*(3), 239–249.

Klingner, J. K., & Vaughn, S. (2002) .The changing roles and responsibilities of an LD specialist. *Learning Disabilities Quarterly, 25,* 19–31.

Koenig, A. J., & Holbrook, M. C. (2000). Planning instruction in unique skills. In A. J. Koenig & M. C.Holbrook (Eds.), *Foundations of education: Instructional strategies for teaching children and youths with visual impairments* (2nd ed., pp 196–220). New York: American Foundations for the Blind Press.

Laurie, T., Buchwach, L., Silverman, R. & Zigmond, N. (1978). Teaching secondary learning disabled students in the mainstream. *Learning Disability Quarterly, 1*(4), 62–72.

Luther, M. (1517). Ninety-five theses. In A. Spaeth, L. D. Reed, H. Eyster Jacobs, et al. (Trans. & Eds.), *Disputation of Doctor Martin Luther on the power and efficacy of indulgences* (Vol. 1; pp. 29–38). Philadelphia: A. J. Holman Company.

Magiera, K., & Zigmond, N. (2004). Co-teaching in middle school classrooms under routine conditions: Does the instructional experience differ for student with disabilities in co-taught and solo-taught classes? *Learning Disabilities Research and Practice, 20,* 79–85.

Mastropieri, M., & Scruggs, T. (2007). *The inclusive classroom: Strategies for effective instruction* (3rd ed.). Upper Saddle River, NJ: Pearson.

Mathews, J. (1988). *Escalante: The best teacher in America,* New York: Holt.

McLeskey, J., Henry, D., & Axelrod, N. M. (1999). Inclusion of students with LD: An examination of data from *Reports to Congress. Exceptional Children, 31,* 55–66.

McLeskey, J., Hoppey, D., Williamson, P., & Rents, T. (2004). Is inclusion an illusion? An examination of national and state trends toward the education of students with learning disabilities in general education classrooms. *Learning Disabilities Research and Practice, 19*(2), 109–115.

McLeskey, J., & Waldron, N. (1995). Inclusive elementary programs: Must they cure students with learning disabilities to be effective? *Phi Delta Kappan, 77,* 300–303.

NCEI. (2006). *Alternative teacher certification: A state-by-state analysis.* Washington, DC: National Center for Education Information.

NCERI. (1995). *National study of inclusive education* (2nd ed.). New York: National Center on Educational Restructuring and Inclusion, The Graduate Center, CUNY.

NCTQ. (2004). *Searching the attic: How states are responding to the nation's goal of placing a highly qualified teacher in every classroom.* Washington, DC: National Council on Teacher Quality.

National Education Association/National Association of State Directors of Special Education. (2005). *What constitutes a highly qualified special education teacher under the Individuals with Disabilities Education Improvement Act of 2004 (P.L. 108–446.).* Retrieved June 15, 2006, from www.nea.org/specialed/images/ideahqtchart.pdf.

Neufeld, B., & Roper, D. (June 2003). *Coaching: A strategy for development of instructional capacity.* Providence, RI: Annenberg Institute for School Reform.

Pierangelo, R. & Giuliani, G. (2006). *Learning disabilities: A practical approach to foundations, assessment, diagnosis and teaching.* Boston, MA: Pearson.

Polsgrove L., & McNeil, M. (1989). The consultation process: Research and practice. *Remedial and Special Education, 10*(1), 6–13.

Pugach, M. C., & Johnson, L. J. (1995). *Collaborative practitioners: Collaborative schools.* Denver, CO: Love.

Purkey, S. C., & Smith, M. S. (1985), School reform: The district policy implications of the effective schools literature. *Elementary School Journal, 85,* 353–389.

Reeve, P., & Hallahan, D. (1994). Practical questions about collaboration between general and special educators. *Focus on Exceptional Children, 26*(7), 1–12.

Rice, J. K. (2003) *Teacher quality: Understanding the Effectiveness of teacher attributes.* Washington, DC: Economic Policy Institute.

Roach, V., Salisbury, C., & McGregor, G. (2002). Applications of a policy framework to evaluate and promote large scale change. *Exceptional Children, 68,* 451–464.

Rosenshine, B., & Stevens, R. (1986). The use of scaffolds for teaching higher level cognitive strategies. *Educational Leadership, 49,* 26–33.

Sanders, W., & Horn., S. (1998). Research findings from the Tennessee Value-Added Assessment System (TVAAS) database: Implications for educational evaluation and research. *Journal of Personnel Evaluation in Education. 12,* 247–256.

Scanlon, D., & Mellard, D. F. (2002). Academic and participation profiles of school age dropouts with and without disabilities. *Exceptional Children, 68,* 239–258.

Shapiro, J., & Rich, R. (1999). *Facing learning disabilities in the adult years.* New York: Oxford University Press.

Silverman, R., Zigmond, N., & Sansone, J. (1981). Teaching coping skills: A school survival skills curriculum for adolescents with learning disabilities. *Focus on Exceptional Children, 13*(6), 1–20.

Skinner, M. E. (1998). Promoting self-advocacy among college students with learning disabilities. *Intervention in School and Clinic, 33,* 278–283.

Sparks, D., & Hirsh, S., (1997). *A new vision of staff development.* Alexandria, VA: Association for Supervision and Curriculum Development.

Staub, F., & West, L. (2003). *Content focused coaching: Transforming mathematics lessons.* Portsmouth, NH: Heinemann.

Thousand, J. S., & Villa, R. A. (1990). Strategies for educating learners with severe disabilities within their home schools and communities. *Focus on Exceptional Children, 23,* 1–24.

U.S. Department of Education. (2003). *To assure the free appropriate public education of all children with disabilities. Twenty-fifth annual report to Congress on the implementation of the Individuals with Disabilities Education Act.* Washington, DC: Office of Special Education Programs, U.S. Government Printing Office.

U.S. Department of Labor, Bureau of Labor Statistics. (2006). *Teachers—special education.* Retrieved April 28, 2006, from www.bis.bov/oco/ocos070.htm.

Vaughn, S., Schumm, J. S., & Arguelles, M. E. (1997). The ABCDE's of co-teaching. *Teaching Exceptional Children, 30,* 4–10.

Vaughn, S., Kim, A., Sloan, C. V. M., Hughes, M. T., Elbaum, B., & Sridhar, D. (2003). Social skills intervention for young children with disabilities: A synthesis of group design studies. *Remedial and Special Education, 24,* 2–15.

Voltz, D. L., Elliot, R. N., Jr., & Cobb, H. B. (1994). Collaborative teacher roles: Special and general educators. *Journal of Learning Disabilities 27*(8), 527–535.

Walther-Thomas, C. S. (1997). Co-teaching experiences: The benefits and problems that teachers and principals report over time. *Journal of Learning Disabilities, 30,* 395–407.

Walther-Thomas, C., Korinek, L., McLaughlin, V., & Williams, B. (2000). *Collaboration for inclusive education: Developing successful programs.* Needham Heights, MA: Allyn & Bacon.

Weiss, M., & Lloyd, J. (2002). Congruence between roles and actions of secondary special educators in co-taught and special education settings. *The Journal of Special Education, 36*(2), 58–68.

Weiss, M. P., & Brigham, F. J. (2000). Co-teaching and the model of shared responsibility: What does the research support? In T. E. Scruggs & M. A. Mastropieri (Eds.), *Advances in learning and behavioral disabilities: Educational interventions* (Vol. 14, pp. 217–245). Stamford, CT: JAI Press.

West, J. F., & Idol, L. (1987). School consultation (Part 1): An interdisciplinary perspective on theory, models and research. *Journal of Learning Disabilities, 20,* 388–408.

West, P. R. (2002). 21st century professional development: The job-embedded, continual learning model. *American Secondary Education, 30*(2), 72–86.

Wilson, S., Floden, R., & Ferrini-Mundy, J. (2002). Teacher preparation research: An insider's view from the outside. *Journal of Teacher Education, 53,* 190–204.

Wood, J. W. (1998). *Adapting instruction to accommodate students in inclusive settings* (3rd ed.). Upper Saddle River, NJ: Merrill.

Zigmond, N. (1978). A prototype of comprehensive services for secondary students with learning disabilities: A preliminary report. *Learning Disability Quarterly, 1*(1), 39–49.

Zigmond, N. (1996). Organization and management of general education classrooms. In D. Speece & B. Keogh (Eds.), *Research on classroom ecologies: Implications for inclusion of children with learning disabilities* (pp. 163–190). Hillsdale, NJ: Lawrence Erlbaum Associates.

Zigmond, N., & Sansone, J. (1986). Designing a program for the learning disabled adolescent. *Remedial and Special Education, 7*(5), 13–17.

Zigmond, N. (2003). Where should students with disabilities receive special education services? Is one place better than another? *Journal of Special Education, 37*(3), 193–199.

Zigmond, N. (2004, April). *Special education co-teachers in secondary school science classrooms: What does it look like? What does it accomplish?* Presentation at the 2004 Council for Exceptional Children Annual Convention, New Orleans, LA.

Zigmond, N. (2006). Reading and writing in co-taught secondary school social studies classrooms: A reality check: *Reading and Writing Quarterly, 22*(3), 249–268.

Zigmond, N., & Matta, D. (2005). Value added of the special education teacher in secondary school co-taught classes. In T. M. Scruggs & M. A. Mastropieri (Eds.), *Advances in learning and behavioral disabilities: Research in secondary schools* (pp. 55–76). Oxford, UK: Elsevier.

Zigmond, N., Vallecorsa, A., & Silverman, R. (1983). *Assessment for instructional planning in special education*. Englewood Cliffs, NJ: Prentice Hall.

Chapter 8

Science and Reason in Special Education: The Legacy of Derrida and Foucault

Gary M. Sasso
University of Iowa

The most informative, dominant, and valuable legacy left to us by previous generations of special educators is the use of rational inquiry and reason to guide both our ethical and practical decisions regarding children with disabilities. James Kauffman would argue that the central question for us is how to sort true beliefs from unsupportable notions in our role as educators. The argument that Kauffman has made throughout his career, one that has been passed down to the rest of us, is that checking each belief through a systematic and public empirical model is the only legitimate way to sort true from false notions. However, in the final decade of the last century, postmodern philosophies that propose a brand of cultural and cognitive relativity began to challenge the basic tenets that have guided our work.

The present chapter is written to support the intellectual bankruptcy of postmodernism by exposing the illogical and often simplistic pronouncements inherent in this philosophy. At the core of postmodernism is an unsupportable belief, that of cultural and

139

cognitive relativity, most fully expressed by two of the continental founders of the postmodern project, Jacques Derrida and Michel Foucault. Therefore, an additional purpose of this chapter, and in the spirit of the work of Kauffman, is to describe how the work of these two philosophers has both guided those who continue to propose relativist arguments and denied them a relevant voice in the lives of children with disabilities.

Criticism of relativism in its current guise as postmodernism began very early with philosophers of science of no particular political persuasion (Laudan, 1990). Then, in the mid-1980s, Ferry and Renaut (1985) foreshadowed the fall of poststructuralism in French intellectual circles with their critique of what they called "French Philosophy of the 60s." They focused on the anti-humanism of four of the most fashionable French writers: Michel Foucault, Jacques Derrida, Pierre Bourdieu, and Jacques Lacan. Ferry and Renaut argued that the main project of these deconstructionists, poststructuralists, and psychoanalysts, "the total critique of the modern world," is permeated by internal inconsistencies and is both logically vacuous and politically irresponsible. In 1987, another French publication, by Victor Farias, cost Foucault, Derrida, and Lacan many of their supporters by revealing that the intellectual mentor to whom all three were indebted, the German existentialist philosopher Martin Heidegger, had been an anti-Semite, a Nazi informer on academic colleagues in the 1930s, and a financial member of the Nazi party. Although Foucault and Derrida thought his work pointed in radical directions, Heidegger himself continued to believe until his death in 1976 that his philosophy confirmed the inner truth and greatness of the Nazi movement. This was followed in 1991 by the work of David Lehman, who showed that the deconstruction project of Derrida and de Man was not value-free but a "program that promotes a reckless disregard of the truth and a propensity for hero-worship" (p. 267). Finally, in 1986, Merquior wrote a brilliant critique of structuralist and poststructuralist thought, suggesting that the deep cultural crisis claimed by postmodernists appears to have been much more eagerly assumed than properly demonstrated, due to postmodernists' interest in being perceived as soul doctors to a sick civilization.

THE POSTMODERN CULTURAL COMMUNITY

It is important to understand that the very concept of disinterested inquiry to which most of us aspire, along with the application of data derived from inquiry to help children with disabilities, are rejected by postmodernists. To them, scholarship is, in most ways, a political project. Instead of the idea of knowledge for its own sake, of letting an argument go wherever the logic leads, without fear or favor, and using that knowledge to guide us in the education of children (Sasso, 2001), the postmodern argument is based on a vision of social justice. It is social justice of an ostensibly leftist variety, although I will argue that the outcome of an adherence to postmodern "justice at any cost" is not justice and, furthermore, leads to decidedly illiberal policies. As these relativist philosophies have become dominant across significant sections of our universities, it has become clear that postmodernists are not, for the most part, experts in a given field. As Tallis (1999) has pointed out, they are instead "Professors of Things in General," who have freed themselves from a specific area of peer-reviewed or otherwise tested expertise and believe they have something worthwhile to say about any area of study. Thus, they are not professors of the humanities, they instead use the humanities to promote a political agenda. They are not professors of education, but attempt to advance their vision of social justice on education. And, sadly, at least partly because of diversity programs that have been instituted in our nation's universities that are based on postmodern notions of multiculturalism, it is why some African Americans have become not Black professionals, but instead *Professional Blacks* (Bernstein, 1994; Sowell, 1999).

Postmodern thinking embraces cultural and cognitive relativity. As such, these relativists reserve their harshest criticism for Enlightenment thinking. Therefore, in order to get at the central fallacies of postmodern relativist arguments, we should re-visit the Enlightenment. Emerging in 17th century Europe, this movement represented a response to the atrocities committed in the name of culture and religion. At the heart of the philosophy of the Enlightenment was a belief in the power of reason informed by empirical experience, with a corresponding rejection of unthinking prejudice and argument from authority. This was not merely an epistemological position; it was also an ethical one. Reason and empirical science are essential elements in the fight against the inequities and iniquities that have added immeasurably to human suffering and blocked the way to progress. The refusal to accept the validity of anything for which one could see neither the reason nor the evidence was also a rejection of the authority of those who have claimed unique possession of the truth. These are the elements of Enlightenment thought: critical individualism hostile to an authority (both in matters of knowledge and power) based on custom and tradition, and a faith in reason and unprejudiced observation, more specifically in its most regulated expression in science. Like science, Enlightenment thought was fundamentally democratic: It presupposed the equality of all men and their equal right to freedom and self-development. It identified two main barriers to human happiness: ignorance, and the obstacles placed in the way of progress by those whose vested interests (whether religious or political) were threatened by the advancement of the poor and the underclass.

The Enlightenment assumption of the importance of reason requires liberation from the control of custom and example, which has been responsible for atrocities far more horrific than any that can be laid at the feet of modernism. The truly rational thinker is an individual using methodological doubt to set aside all the beliefs and superstitions that lead to permanent underclass status. As Gellner (1992) noted:

> That which is collective and customary is nonrational, and the overcoming of unreason and of collective custom are one and the self-same process. ... Error is to be found in culture; and culture is a kind of systematic, communally induced error. It is through community and history that we sink into error, and it is through solitary design and plan that we escape it ... Truth is acquired in a planned orderly manner by an individual, not slowly gathered up by a herd. (p. 3)

The classical liberal view of the Enlightenment sprang up precisely because its adherents recognized the dangers of insisting that individuals have significance only if they are part of a larger whole. These thinkers rebelled against this sort of social determinism. For example, John Locke defined the position of being under the determination of someone other than himself without that individual's consent as a form of tyranny (Tallis, 1999). One of the great blessings of the civilizing process, the Enlightenment concluded, is that it raises humans above that servile status by making them aware of their individual rights, interests, and powers as well as free from irrational passions and fears.

However, throughout history, Enlightenment thought has encountered a Counter-Enlightenment shadow (Tallis, 1999). Whether it was Rousseau's reflections on the loss of the "Noble Savage," Pascal's inability to forgive Descartes for reducing the role of faith and marginalizing God, Kant's *Critique of Pure Reason,* de Maistre's belief in the need for obedience and subjection, or Boas' conceptualization of cultural relativity (Gay, 1967; Goldman, 1973); reason and logic have been attacked from many sources as a system that reduces aesthetic values to cold, hard, value-free knowledge. Thus, there is much in present-day Counter-Enlightenment thought that is not new; for example, the attack on reason as a force within human affairs, either in the public or the private sphere; the denial of universal values; and the critique of science. All of these are familiar enough. What is new in the recent postmodern attack is the level at which these attacks are directed. The current critique can be summarized as an all-out assault on the notion of a disinterested, rational, autonomous, conscious agent. This assault is characterized by a denial of the central role of reasoned action in human life, and this was made possible by two of the French founders of postmodernism, Jacques Derrida and Michel Foucault.

Jacques Derrida

In United States, the postmodern movement can trace its theoretical origins back to the mid-1970s when a number of academics discovered French theory. Initially, the most influential of these was the "Yale School" of literary criticism, which embraced the poststructuralist theories of the Algerian-born French philosopher Jacques Derrida. His brainchild is "deconstruction," a form of criticism that is elusive of definition, but which has its etymological root in Martin Heidegger's concept of *Destruktion*—or more exactly, in Heidegger's call for the destruction of ontology, the branch of metaphysics that studies the nature of being. Academic deconstruction blends together elements of linguistics, literary criticism, and philosophy into a method of analysis that can be used within diverse intellectual disciplines; a stated goal is to dissolve the borders that traditionally separate one discipline from another. Derrida (1976) maintained that deconstruction defies all categories and definitions; that it is so "new" that we can't fit it into existing frames of thought, and so "radical" that it would declare those frames of thought invalid, obsolete, exploded.

Deconstruction insists that intellectual discussion in *any* discipline must include a discussion of linguistics. And, although it is difficult to pin down a set of beliefs related to this model, the following appear to be consistent with its central claims (Derrida, 1976, 1978, 1979):

- Nothing exists ahead of language or outside it; there are no things or ideas except in words. But, words are severed from their meanings; the linguistic intention is severed from the linguistic event.
- There are no facts, only interpretations, and no truths, only expedient fictions.
- Words speak us; we are not in control of our words, but they control us.
- Presence is absent; or, an absolute ground for truth is indispensable and that in its absence, no moral judgments can be made.
- Language, not knowledge, is power.

Deconstructionists like putting things, as they say, *sous rature* ("under erasure"). A typical ploy is to print certain words or phrases in cancelled form, with slash marks running through them, as though to include and exclude them at the same time. Words for Derrida are "signs," ciphers signifying nothing. Although ostensibly about literature, deconstruction in its purer forms doesn't want to be a party to anything so reactionary as the clarification of literature. The aim is not to elucidate but to expose and unmask, to demystify and dismantle—to deconstruct—and you can deconstruct just about anything. In deconstruction, everything is equally "literature"—not in the sense that it is good writing, but in the sense that its meaning is a function of interpretation. As Lehman (1991) has suggested, a "sign" is a metaphor for a larger enterprise: the workings of a theory that revels in extreme doubt, boasts of its own rebellious stance, asserts ideas without necessarily subscribing to them, and regards moments of self-contradiction as critically important.

The whole deconstructive method appears to entail a kind of devil's advocacy taken to the point of bad faith (Lilla, 2001; Merquior, 1986). Deconstructionists have the knack of exempting themselves from their own strictures, expecting to be understood even as they insist that all messages are unintelligible. For this and other reasons, a debate with a disciple of Derrida is a difficult proposition. It is hard to argue with someone who inhabits an alternative universe—a realm of discourse in which opposites unite, black can mean white, a stop sign can mean go, the defense attorney can be counted on to hang his own client, and the teacher can be counted on to do her worst for the student. A postmodernist says that the laws of physics are merely social conventions, like traffic laws. However, as Lehman (1995) commented "to deconstruct *that* position you would need only to cross the street against the flow of rushing traffic" (p. 26).

As a critical methodology, deconstruction places its emphasis on tearing down a concept or a clause—on "putting in question" or "problematizing" it, to use the approved jargon. Deconstruction attempts to destroy the conceptions of the Enlightenment, presumably so that the culture can evolve in new directions. Deconstruction itself offers no model for this evolution, only a method of taking things apart. In this, deconstructionists are like members of a terrorist sect, and they seem to enjoy being characterized as embattled outsiders fighting the good fight (although most often from the safety and comfort of their campus offices). This terrorist analogy can be seen in the deconstructive shift of attention from the content of a person's ideas to his or her hidden motives; you don't read a book, you *interrogate* it. An idea subjected to deconstruction is an idea whose legitimacy is permanently cast in doubt. If one follows this line of reasoning, it is less important to pay attention to *what* someone says than to determine *who* he is, in order to know what he is really saying. The content of speech, then, is replaced by the person speaking and the determination of his or her "real motives." The very word *deconstruction* is meant to undermine the either/or logic of the opposition construction/destruction. Using deconstructive logic you can undermine the ground rules that make debate—by "proving," for example that what your adversary says is not what it appears to be. Thus, you need not contest the premises or dispute the conclusions of your opponent's argument; instead, you reject your opponent altogether as either a dupe or a mouthpiece for a set of "hidden articulations." As this method of criticism has evolved across disciplines and topics, a distinct pattern has emerged. As long as the manuscript (or argument) makes the right noises, the content almost seems to be beside the point. A set of recurring code words needs to be inserted into the text, and, armed with their jargon and a sort of boilerplate outline, the clever deconstructionist can criticize most anything. Lehman (1995) provides a template:

> The first sentence should feature *hegemony*; the second *itinerary;* the third *foregrounding;* the fourth, *privilege* used as a verb (for example, "the retrograde critic privileges the author"). There should be plenty of *de-* or *dis-* prefixes, beginning with *deconstruction* and *dismantling,* and as many *–ize* suffixes, such as *problematize, valorize, contextualize, totalize.* A good way to begin your *discourse* (you must always call it that) is with a nod toward Derrida, an allusion to de Man, and a determination to call into question some *binary opposition* or other. You are going to deconstruct the dichotomy of your choice: *male* and *female, nature* and *culture, center* and *periphery, speech* and *writing, presence* and *absence.* … Your task is to dismantle hierarchies and you do this by showing that the first term in any such set is implicitly—and unjustly—endorsed ("privileged") in Western philosophy. You don't call it Western philosophy, of course; you refer knowingly to "the metaphysics of presence." It would probably be a good idea to mention "the prisonhouse of language," too. You must remind your readers periodically that no escape from language is possible. Language has humanity in thrall; textuality is all. (pp. 83–84)

In deconstructionist writing in general and Derrida in particular, there is a tendency to employ a rhetorical effect that can be described as the move from the exciting to the banal and back again (Searle, 1998). This is the way it is done: Derrida (or one of his disciples) advances some astounding thesis, for example, writing came before speaking, nothing exists outside of texts, meanings are undecidable. When challenged, they say, "You have misunderstood me, I only meant such and such," where such and such is some well-known cliché. Then, when the cliché is acknowledged, they assume that its acknowledgement constitutes an acceptance of the original exciting thesis. For example, Derrida claims that writing comes before speech, that written language precedes spoken language; "I shall try to show that there is no linguistic sign before writing," he states (Derrida, 1976, p. 14). But the claim that writing precedes speaking is obviously false, as any classical linguist can attest. Of course, Derrida does not mean this. What he means in large part is that many of the features of written speech are also features of spoken language. Once this banality is acknowledged, he then supposes that he has demonstrated the original thesis. From the exciting to the banal and back again. As Wolin (2004) said, "There's the bit where you say it and the bit where you take it back" (p. 232).

Although deconstruction was roundly criticized as a philosophy that provides a direct path to a number of unsavory political notions throughout the 1980s, it was the news of Heideggar and de Man's Nazi wartime collaboration and the deconstructionist response to those revelations late in that decade that exposed deconstruction as an ideology that can produce effects eerily similar to those of the "big lie" in propaganda. The plain message of de Man's "The Jews in Contemporary Literature" in 1941 (de Man, 1989) is there for all to see. But, in his deconstruction of de Man's anti-Semitic essay, Derrida (1989) made a major blunder. As Lehman (1995) stated:

> … here was Derrida suggesting, then insinuating, then implying, then not denying, then all but saying—in that maddening round-about way of his—that de Man's piece subverted its own intentions and led the reader to an aporia, or a terminal ambiguity, with the effect that "The Jews in Contemporary History," was, no matter what it seemed to say, really a critique of "vulgar Anti-Semitism." … In one breath Derrida pardoned de Man for his pro-Nazi writings, and in the next he accused the journalists writing about de Man of employing Nazi tactics. It was, by twisted logic, they who were guilty of "the exterminating gesture." The world of deconstruction was a topsy-turvy one, all right. (p. 139)

Following the de Man affair, Derrida turned his attention to politics. His aim appeared to be to show that the entire Western tradition of thinking about politics has been distorted by the concept of identity. From his point of view, then, it would seem that all Western political ideologies—fascism, conservatism, liberalism, socialism, communism—would be equally unacceptable. That is the logical implication of Derrida's attack on logocentrism. (Note that the Greek term *logos* means word or language, but it can also mean reason or principle, an equation of speech with intentionality that Derrida considered impossible.)

Readers of his work, therefore, assume that he believes there can be no escape from language, and therefore no escape from deconstruction for any of our concepts. But in his work in the 1990s, Derrida changed his mind. It turns out that there is a concept, though only one, resilient enough to withstand the critique of deconstruction, and that concept is "justice" (Derrida, 1994). Now it turns out, according to Derrida, that justice is beyond understanding through nature or reason, leaving only one possible means of access to its meaning: revelation. However, as Lilla (1998) has noted, Derrida's turn to this topic bears all the signs of intellectual desperation. He clearly wants deconstruction to serve some political program, and to give hope to the Left. Yet the logic of his philosophy does not allow him to do this without the distinct appearance of hypocrisy. He cannot find a way of specifying the nature of the justice to be sought through left-wing politics without opening himself to the very deconstruction he so happily applies to others. Unless, of course, he places the "idea of justice" in the eternal, messianic beyond where it cannot be reached by argument, and assumes that his ideologically sympathetic readers won't ask too many questions (Lilla, 1998).

Michel Foucault

Foucault deserves special mention in any discussion of postmodern ideas because his arguments insisting that psychiatric laws and treatment are weapons that modern societies wield in order to enforce their own definitions of normality and to punish those who do not conform contributes greatly to a current negative view of special education. To his supporters he is often regarded as a patron saint of poststructuralism. To his critics, he is an ape of Nietzsche, but one that Nietzsche warned about; a type of decadent Romantic who lives too much and thinks too little (Nietzsche, 1974). However, Foucault has been very influential by reviving Nietzschian ideology in France in the 1960s, and in spreading it to academia in the United States in the 1970s and 1980s.

Foucault, who died in 1984, is, like Derrida, a French import to academia in the United States. But, where deconstructionists specialize in the idea that language refers only to itself, Foucault's focus was "power." His greatest claim was that every institution, no matter how benign it seems, is really a scene of domination and subjugation; that efforts at enlightened reform—of asylums, of prisons, of society at large—have been little more than alibis for extending state power; that human relationships are, underneath it all, struggles for mastery and control; that truth itself is merely a coefficient of coercion.

Foucault's writings include *Madness and Civilization* (1961), which is a history of the growth of psychiatry; *The Birth of the Clinic* (1963), a study of medicine in the 18th and 19th centuries; *The Order of Things* (1966), and *The Archaeology of Knowledge* (1982), both on the history of ideas; *Discipline and Punish* (1975), a book regarding the origins of prisons in the 19th century; a three-volume work entitled *The History of Sexuality* (1976–1979); a volume about a 19th-century triple murderer, and one about a 19th-century hermaphrodite. He also wrote a number of articles on the methodology of studying human affairs, and later in his life published many of his views in the form of interviews.

Foucault's appeal appears to have derived from his stance as a radical non-Marxist. As it became difficult for even the most progressive liberals to believe that Marxism could offer a plausible political alternative in the 1980s, Foucault's popularity grew (Ferry & Renaut, 1985). As a historian, he held that the main revolutionary struggle was not against political or economic institutions. Instead, the real radicals were those who challenged the major Western philosophies or "systems of thought." This is radicalism perfectly compatible with more sedentary practice in the academic realm of classrooms and conferences. For professors who read and absorb the lessons of Foucault, it becomes clear that there is no longer any need to do anything as concrete or practical as working for political parties, actively supporting legislation, or demonstrating in the streets. Instead, followers of Foucault can spend their time reading, debating, and writing their criticisms of the academic disciplines of philosophy, history, sociology, criminology, education, and psychiatry. None of this, Foucault argued, was a less practical or inferior variety of politics. Theory, in this view, does not express, translate, or serve to apply practice; it *is* practice, it *creates* knowledge (Tallis, 1999).

It is important, before going any further into the work of Foucault, to discuss how the term "theory" doesn't mean the same thing to postmodernists as it does to the rest of the special education community. For most of us, the scientific method is not radically different from the rational attitude in everyday life (Sokal & Bricmont, 1998). Indeed, even postmodernists use methods of induction, deduction, and assessment of evidence to assist them in determining everything from the cheapest flight to get them to the Modern Language Association conference to determining if they have enough publications to warrant a positive tenure decision. Objective research tries to carry out these operations in a more careful and systematic way, by using controls and statistical tests, insisting on replication, deliberately attempting to falsify a theory, and so on, and any conflict is generally found at the level of conclusions, not the basic approach. The main reason that we believe the best-verified scientific theories is that they more fully explain the coherence of our experience and they successfully solve problems. This agreement between theory and experiment (or controlled observation), when combined with thousands of other similar ones, would be a miracle if science said nothing at least approximately true about the world (Pinker, 1997; Sokal & Bricmont, 1998).

In contrast, the postmodern approach to theory is one in which large-scale generalizations about human society or human conduct are taken as given before either research or writing starts. These generalizations, or laws, then provide a framework from which deductions about the subject can be drawn. They then search for instances that confirm what they already believe, overlooking or explaining away any instances that may disconfirm the theory. Information is used as long as it fits the theory, the (circular) reasoning being that because it fits the theory, it must be factually correct. This is such an elementary cognitive error that it has been very difficult for the rest of us to believe that it occurs in individuals who write in flowery prose and who appear to be otherwise intelligent people (Kauffman, 2002).

In *The Order of Things* (1966), Foucault insisted that his philosophy is anti-humanist. It was in this book that he posited "The death of man," by which he meant that the humanist philosophy of the Enlightenment had been overthrown. Humanists have long shared a commitment to the idea that the human subject, understood as consciousness and will, is the originator of human actions and understanding. The notions of individual freedom and individual responsibility, and the philosophies that support them, have long been based on it. However, according to Foucault, this movement had run its course and was no longer applicable, with the humanism of the modern era supplanted by the anti-humanism of the postmodern.

One of Foucault's central anti-humanist claims is that humanism's belief in the autonomy of the subject is an illusion. The two concepts that come under sharpest criticism are *free will* and *consciousness* (and, as a result, the rationalist philosophical stance). The humanist perspective states that the individual is a free agent who normally weighs issues confronting him and makes his own, rational decision about what to do. Foucault rejects this as naïve because it omits the unconscious. This concept of the unconscious, which originated in mid-nineteenth century German philosophy, has allowed anti-humanists to proclaim that the entire humanist tradition has been wrong to assign to the conscious mind the central role in the functioning of a human being. Like Freud and later Lacan, they believe that the unconscious is the dominant influence on behavior and thought, that we must abandon the assumption that purposeful action is consciously directed. Thus, we must reject our belief in the autonomy of the individual (Shattuck, 1999).

Foucault also claimed that we need to abandon the common sense assumption that there is a real world outside ourselves and that we can have knowledge about it. He believed that our minds are confined to the realm of our language. Foucault took this "primacy of language" thesis straight from Nietzsche, who believed that humans impose their own arbitrary constructions of meaning on what would otherwise be nothing but chaos, that our language is not reflective of anything real. Thus, we should not think that language reflects reality in any way, or that the words we use correspond in some direct sense to objects in the world. From this perspective, those who are influential enough to define the concepts of an era consequently define the sense of reality held by their fellow human beings.

In the 1970s, as Foucault emerged as a critic not only of modern philosophy but of modern society, he developed the term *geneology.* He derived his conception of this word again from Nietzsche, who believed that the idea of objectivity in science is false, that there is "only a perspective seeing, only a perspective knowing." Foucault combined this idea with another of Nietzsche's (1967), "the will to power," to argue that not only was all scientific knowledge subjective but that it was a tool of power in the hands of those who formulated it. The task, according to Foucault, is to analyze who uses this type of discourse and for what ends. He insists that theories that call themselves scientific are not disinterested but are linked to relations of authority, and further, that knowledge and power are always and necessarily interdependent. In Foucault's world, a place where power is enforced is also a place where knowledge is produced and, conversely, a place from which knowledge is derived is a place where power is exercised. So, instead of referring to "power" and "knowledge" separately, he suggests the term *power/knowledge* (Foucault, 1975).

This cognitive relativism allowed Foucault to claim that there is no accumulation of knowledge; there are instead only inconsistencies. Thus, the thinking of one era is not better, not more knowledgeable than another, only different. This belief appears to be the product of another belief: that there is no progress from one era to another. But, the consequence of rejecting the idea of the growth of knowledge is to be forced to claim that knowledge is relative to particular historic eras. Foucault, therefore, believed that each era devises its own "truths" and its own "knowledges."

Foucault also argued that knowledge is relative not only to historic eras but to social groups as well. Each social group has their own versions of knowledge, even if they are mutually inconsistent. Those in power generate the kind of knowledge needed to maintain their power. And, those who are subject to this power need their own, alternative kinds of knowledge in order to resist. In these beliefs, therefore, are the seeds of some strands of radical multiculturalism and feminism. That is, "Truth" is not something absolute that everyone must acknowledge, but merely what counts as true within a particular "discourse,"[1] ethnic group, or gender.

It is not difficult to show that a relativist conceptualization of truth is untenable. If what is true is always relative to a particular society,

---

[1]Indicates that the term *discourse* corresponds to what we would know as an academic discipline: clinical, medical, economic, educational. But, part of his aim in using this term was to reject the conventional classification that defines academic disciplines into separate categories such as "science," "literature," "philosophy," or "history."

there are no propositions that can be true across all societies. However, this must also mean that Foucault's own claim cannot be true for all societies. It is contradictory. This relativist fallacy also applies to the concept of knowledge. We cannot believe that there are alternative, competing forms of knowledge, as Foucault maintains. Inherent in the concept of knowledge is that of truth (Sasso, 2001). That is, we can only know something if it is true. If something is not true, or even if its truth status is uncertain, we cannot know it (Haack, 1998). To talk, therefore, of opposing knowledges is to hold that there is one set of truths that runs counter to another set of truths. There are perfectly good words for what Foucault is discussing; *beliefs* and *values*. It is certainly possible to talk about beliefs or values that may be held in opposition because neither beliefs nor values necessarily entail truth. But Foucault's idea that there are "knowledges" held by the central powers opposed to the subjugated knowledge of the oppressed is an abuse of both logic and language. Consider Foucault's central contention, that objective truth is a "chimera," that truth is always and everywhere a function of power, of "multiple forms of constraint," and that some version of this claim is propagated as gospel by postmodernists across the country. Is this contention true? Is it in fact the case that truth is always relative to a "regime of truth," that is, to politics? If one says "Yes, it is true," then one is plunged directly into a contradiction. As Wilson (1998) has noted, it is a bit like the saying, "All Cretins are liars; I am a Cretin." This is indeed a paradox, and one that won't be solved until relativists realize the trap they have put themselves in by adopting Foucault as their oracle.

Despite its logical untenability, this genealogical method is very attractive to the followers of Foucault. In debate with "positivists" or "humanists," any question about the facts of a statement is ignored and the focus is directed to a way in which what is said reflects the prevailing "discursive formation" or how it is a form of knowledge that serves the power of the scientific tradition. As Windschuttle (1996) has observed, one of the reasons for Foucault's popularity in the university environment is that he offers such tactics to his followers—tactics that should be regarded as the negation of the traditional aims of the university: the gaining of knowledge and the practice of scholarship. Instead of talk about real issues, all we get is talk about talk. Instead of debates based on evidence and reason, all we get is a retreat to a level of abstraction where enough is assumed to have been said when one has identified the epistemological position of one's opponent.

Madness and Civilization (1961) was Foucault's first major work. In it, he attempted to overturn the traditional stories told about the treatment of insanity and about the wider growth of medicine as a science. Instead of a history of progress and increasing knowledge over the last 200 years, Foucault is interested in a different story. The period covered by this book, the 1650s to the 1790s, was a time, he argues, in which the human sciences developed a new regime of widespread repression.

During what others consider to be the time of the Enlightenment, when rational scientific method replaced religious faith and superstition as the basis of knowledge, Foucault insisted that the elevation of reason meant the denial of madness as part of the human condition. Foucault claims that in the Middle Ages and Renaissance the insane were familiar figures within society, and the concept of madness was accepted as falling within the common parameters of the human experience. However, from 1650 onward, Foucault asserts that European society began "the great confinement." According to his historic account, increasingly larger numbers of people—up to 1% of the population of Paris—were incarcerated in hospitals, institutions, and workhouses that were quickly established across Europe and in England. His main thesis, then, is that the central feature of Western philosophy was its definition of man as a rational being, a creature who reasons. Foucault believed that this was the major failing of the traditional view, because it denied other aspects of humanity such as its unconscious, voluntaristic, orgiastic and self-destructive sides. Therefore, the history of insanity is really the story of the way the concept of reason has suppressed that of madness, and he presents psychiatric laws and treatment of the insane as weapons that modern societies use in order to enforce their own definitions of normality and to punish those who do not accept them. This last charge, updated to the 21st century, forms the basis for the view of special education as punishment rather than as an attempt to serve and assist individuals with disabilities.

As Windschuttle (1996) has shown, Foucault's scholarship in this and his other work is riddled with errors. During the Middle Ages, for example, Foucault contends that the insane supposedly wandered freely from town to town or traveled on a literal Ship of Fools up and down the Rhine. Windschuttle lays out in devastating detail how, in every case, Foucault's account is wildly inaccurate. There was no Ship of Fools as Foucault describes; his dates are often wrong by a century or more; less than one hundredth of 1% of the population of Paris was institutionalized during that time; and as for the treatment of the insane, Windschuttle quotes the historian Andrew Scull (1993):

> Where the mad proved troublesome, they could expect to be beaten or locked up; otherwise they might roam or rot. Either way, the facile contrast between psychiatric oppression and an earlier, almost anarchic toleration is surely illusory. (p. 141)

Foucault is just as unreliable in his account of the response of modern society to the insane. Madness became an issue of public policy with the rise of democratic, egalitarian societies, primarily because these societies accepted the madman not as the "other," or as someone outside humanity, but as another human being, as an individual with the same basic status as everyone else. Any close reading of the history of this age cannot dismiss the strong philanthropic and humanitarian motives that drove Pinel and Tuke to develop a "moral treatment" of the insane that recognizes their humanity. It is, of course, also clear to anyone who has studied the history of institutionalized care (Scull, 1977) that the social experiment represented by asylums largely failed in its aims. It was impossible to exclude the external environment, and the process of insulating clients produced unforeseen problems, including dependency and conformity, and authoritarian internal management. But, despite these problems and failures, the representation of madness provided by the asylum does not accord with Foucault's claim that it was fundamentally repressive. The asylum always treated madness as a contingent and temporary condition of a person whose basic humanity was still legally asserted, which was certainly not the case during the Middle Ages and Renaissance. Even when the insane were deprived of normal human rights because of their condition, they were still subject as citizens to due process of the law, and their rights were always conditionally, not permanently, deprived. Foucault's central claim—that the history of insanity supports Nietzsche's and Heidegger's thesis that the modern era has imposed a repressive concept of humanity by rejecting "the other," cannot be justified or sustained.

It is impossible to discuss Foucault the academic and political persona without discussing his personal life. This is because he, as much as any other public figure in recent memory, acted out his personal life as part of his philosophy. During the 1970s, Foucault's celebration of "transgression" as a way of life and of psychological quest turned toward sadomasochistic eroticism and torture. As Shattuck (1999) vividly points out, Foucault, in his later publications, begins to point toward a figure whose work and thoughts will be shown to be the salvation of mankind. In *The History of Madness*, he refers to "a massive cultural fact that appeared precisely at the end of the 18th century and that constitutes one of the greatest conversions of the occidental imagination ... madness of desire, the insane delight of love and death in the limitless presumption of appetite" (p. 210). Again, at the end of *Madness*, "Through him the West has regained the possibility of surpassing reason through violence." And, at the close of *The Order of Things*, Foucault claims that the knowledge we have gained from this author and the "mutation" he has brought down on us is the only knowledge that "has allowed the figure of man to appear (p. 386). Who is this great thinker that will become our savior? The answer is the Marquis de Sade. As Shattuck notes:

> Readers familiar with Sade's work may perceive the true direction of Foucault's project: to seduce and to pervert, following the doctrine that elevates power above truth. But you would not grasp this project from an uncritical reading of Foucault's abstract, obscurantist prose. (p. 79)

Lest you think that this is overstating either Shattuck's interpretation of Foucault on this matter, or the influence of this drivel on his followers, in recent years professors in colleges of education have begun teaching seminars and including sections in methods courses for teacher trainees related to how the work of the Marquis de Sade can guide us in the enlightened instruction of our children and youth (Sasso, 2002).

Whether some sexual practices or lifestyles are harmful to individuals and society is, of course, a difficult moral question. But one, we insist, that can be informed by logical, disinterested inquiry (e.g., what are the individual and combined effects of such practices on persons, groups, and society?). Foucault's version of postmodern nihilism, on the other hand, provides no assistance in this matter, or any other matter of concern. Like all postmodern theory, its main job is to be disturbing and subversive. Therefore, it must find a prevalent belief to explode. If it cannot, and if it is only viewed as offering one particular suggested alternative to the sins of Western Civilization to be considered along with others, it loses its mystique and is left exposed in its absurdity.

CONCLUSION

The faulty assumptions and careless scholarship of Derrida and Foucault have provided adherents to postmodern/poststructural philosophies with what is, at best, a shaky foundation regarding knowledge claims. As postmodernism was being denounced as an illegitimate philosophical model across Europe in the late 1960s and early 1970s, proponents in the United States were able to preserve it by connecting relativist ideals to progressive political causes. One of the results of this unnatural alliance has been the use of a number illiberal arguments regarding how truth and knowledge are to be decided:

- Egalitarian Principle: All sincere persons' beliefs have equal claim to respect.
- Radical Egalitarian Principle: The beliefs of persons in historically oppressed classes or groups get special consideration.
- Humanitarian Principle: Any method of choosing beliefs will do, with the overriding priority to avoid all hurtful beliefs (Rauch, 1994, p. 6).

Standing in contrast to these principles is a system of empirical science that is more than a way of making things. It is a way of organizing society and a way of behaving. Science does indeed involve the creation of technology, but more than that, it creates verifiable knowledge. It is a model based on skepticism, although not the nihilistic inductive skepticism postulated in 1739 by Hume. It is instead a skepticism that requires us to abide by two central rules: (a) A claim can be established as knowledge only if it can be debunked, in principle, and only insofar as it withstands attempts to debunk it (falsifiability) and (b) a claim to knowledge can be established only insofar as the method used to check it gives the same result regardless of the identity of the investigator (replication). These two rules define a decision-making system that can be used to determine whose opinions are worth believing, and they establish an open "game" in which it does not matter who you are (Pope, philosopher, physician, president, literary theorist), but instead how honest you are. It is a game defined by distinctive characteristics: if you play the game, you can't set the outcome in advance, and you can't exempt any player from the rules, no matter who he happens to be. This model guarantees something vitally important that postmodern thinkers fail to grasp. That is, the empirical model requires us to look for errors in our own thinking, and to change our minds if the tests we use return results that do not coincide with our beliefs (Kauffman & Sasso, 2006).

By their nature, then, these science rules demolish the political legitimacy of intellectual authoritarianism from whatever source. Anyone who claims to be in charge of knowledge (be it a religion, ethnic group, or enlightened moralist) is disqualified from participating in knowledge-making. No one is granted personal authority simply because of who he or she happens to be; the rules apply to everyone. It is true that for most of history (and not just Western history) women, Blacks, and others were denied equal access to the intellectual and scientific establishment, as they were denied equal access to so much else. We do not need postmodernism to be aware of that. But, this fact represents not the failure of liberal science but the failure to embrace it. This model is very different from being an *equal-results* knowledge maker. The empirical model is instead based on the notion that to believe incorrectly is never a crime, but simply to believe is *never* to have knowledge. In other words, a systematic empirical model does not restrict belief, but it does restrict knowledge. It absolutely protects freedom of belief and speech, but it absolutely denies freedom of knowledge. No one has the right to have his or her opinions, however strongly held, taken seriously as knowledge. Instead, the contrary is the rule; a selection process designed to test beliefs and reject the ones that fail the test. If your belief is rejected by a critical empirical assessment, you are free to reject the assessment and keep believing. That is freedom of belief. However, you are not entitled to expect that your belief will be accepted as knowledge by an intellectual establishment.

This model helps to ensure that only ideas that have undergone testing can be counted in the body of knowledge, and this is very important. However, this model is what the followers of Derrida and Foucault are attempting to circumvent by confusing belief with knowledge, and postulating that there is no difference between the two. Often, they will take it a step further, arguing that a critical consensus, a vote, an underrepresented group, or a political body should be able to decide what is and is not knowledge. However, this is a critical error and one that has led to atrocities small and large. A liberal empirical model does not infer intellectual majoritarianism or egalitarianism. People do not have a claim to knowledge because 51% of the public agrees with you, or because your "group" was historically left out. Instead, a person has a claim to knowledge to the extent that his/her opinion survives multiple and rigorous tests. This point applies to both the natural sciences and the social sciences, to what method of reading is more effective in teaching most children or the historical basis of belief. For example, the critical consensus of historians is that many minority groups did not make much of a contribution to the writing of the Constitution. Attempting to find a role for them and install them in the textbooks may make some people feel better. But doing so would betray the community of critical empiricism. That is, it is dishonest. It also leads to factional arguments as other political groups demand their share of history. If, on the grounds of equality, radical Afrocentrists win equal time for their claim that the ancient Egyptians were Black Africans or that the Greeks stole their knowledge from Africa, then creationists, astrologists, Christian Scientists, White supremacists, and all others should be able to have their claims honored as well.

One final legacy of the work of Derrida and Foucault as it has been extended to the academy and to political priorities is the notion of *respect*. It is only after an idea, or model, or technology has survived rigorous checking that it is deserving of respect. We often hear people in our field arguing that all ideas are *at least* worthy of respect. In truth, they have inverted the argument. Respect is the *most*, not the least, that should be afforded someone's idea. If the idea is not verified by public and repeated testing, it is entitled to no respect whatsoever. This is why it is so important that believers in intelligent design, alien watchers, Afrocentrists, and White supremacists be granted every entitlement to speak but no entitlement to have their opinions respected. If they refuse the rules for making knowledge, they should expect instead to have their beliefs rejected; they should expect that, if for any reason they refuse to submit their ideas for checking through an objective empirical model, that their opinions will be ignored or ridiculed—and rightly so. People are entitled to a degree of basic respect by way of being human. However, respect is no opinion's birthright. The statement "We must respect all beliefs" is not innocent or wise. If you agree to require equal time for someone's excluded belief, you are accepting exactly what Foucault railed against; that a belief is only respectable if the politically powerful say it is.

In conjunction with this postmodern notion of respect is the idea that opinions and harsh words are hurtful and offensive, if not to society, then to individuals. Facing up to this argument is difficult, although it is necessary if we are to support an honest knowledge-making enterprise. Seeking and defending knowledge can be painful, for the same reason that it can also be exhilarating. It does not come free, it is often difficult and elusive, and it is rarely a settled matter. Public criticism of empirical work is often merciless and hurtful. So, although we should never go out of our way to be offensive or inflammatory, in order to make knowledge, it is necessary to sometimes be offensive and inflammatory. However (and this is the critical point), in an open, empirical society, to upset people cannot be the same thing as being wrong. Nothing is owed to those who have been offended by objective attempts to create knowledge. The alternative to this, one that has grown out the postmodern, relativist movement, is to reward people for being upset. However, as we have observed countless times, once people learn that they can get something for open displays of pain, they often go into what Rauch (1994) called the business of "professional offendedness" (p. 130). Ideas and words are sometimes very upsetting, but if everyone has the right not to be upset, then all criticism, and therefore all scientific inquiry, is at best morally hazardous and at worst impossible. When faced with this problem, some postmodernists retreat to the position that *some* people (e.g., historically oppressed groups) have a special right not to be upset. But that idea is no better than the original. It relinquishes any checks on knowledge, because it disallows the empirical rule that anyone is allowed to criticize another, regardless of race or ethnic history, or any other variable. Finally, if we adopt this idea, then the only arbiter of what is upsetting is a centralized political authority.

Science is difficult. It is expensive, it often leads down blind alleys, and those who investigate are constantly criticized by their colleagues. Social science is, by most accounts, even harder than the natural sciences, and we have not achieved the same impressive progress as the natural sciences. There are a number of reasons for this. First, as Haack (2003) has correctly pointed out, the public does not respect the social sciences as much because historians, playwrights, and so on, have already taught us so much about the complexities of human nature and human society, making it harder for a psychologist or educator to discover something that seems genuinely new, not already part of our common sense knowledge. Second, we sometimes try to be like the natural sciences in the wrong way, focusing too much on mathematical trappings (see NCLB and "Gold Standard" research) and too little on the underlying demands of well-conducted research. But it is also because, as many others have pointed out, social science is in many ways more difficult and more demanding than the task of the natural sciences. Social science investigates questions about which people have strong personal and political feelings, and we are often under pressure to come up with solutions for social problems for which the public or government demands speedy remedies, making it harder for us to remain free of bias. The objects of our study, human beings, are vastly complex, and can react to claims and predictions made about them as the objects of the natural sciences cannot, making the task of the social science researcher intellectually more difficult. However, it remains the best way of sorting out our problems and coming to possible solutions. The easy cynicism and doubt of the postmodernists, on the other hand, has at last been shown to be self-undermining and unable to adequately address any of our most pressing issues.

REFERENCES

Bernstein, R. (1994). *Dictatorship of virtue*. New York: Random House.

De Man, P. (1989). *Wartime journalism, 1940–1942*. Lincoln, NE: University of Nebraska Press.

Derrida, J. (1976). *Of grammatology*. Baltimore, MD: Johns Hopkins University Press.

Derrida, J. (1978). *Writing and difference*. Chicago: University of Chicago Press.

Derrida, J. (1979). *Deconstruction and criticism*. New York: Seabury.

Derrida, J. (1989). *Like the sound of the sea deep within a shell: Paul de Man's war*. Lincoln, NE: University of Nebraska Press.

Derrida, J. (1994). Force de loi. In D. Cornell & M. Rosenfeld (Eds.), *Deconstruction and the possibility of justice* (pp. 120–141). New York: Routledge.

Farias, V. (1987). *Heideggar and Nazism*. Philadelphia, PA: Temple University Press.

Ferry, L., & Renaut, A. (1985). *French philosophy of the sixties: An essay on antihumanism*. Amherst, MA: The University of Massachusetts Press.

Foucault, M. (1961). *Madness and civilization: A history of insanity in the age of reason*. New York: Vintage Books.

Foucault, M. (1963). *The birth of the clinic: An archaeology of medical perceptions*. New: Vintage Books.

Foucault, M. (1966). *The order of things: An archaeology of the human sciences*. New York: Random House.

Foucault, M. (1975). *Discipline and punish: The birth of the prison*. London: Allen Lane.

Foucault, M. (1979). *The history of sexuality, Volume 1: An introduction*. London: Allen Lane.

Foucault, M. (1982). *The archaeology of knowledge*. New York: Pantheon Books.

Gay, P. (1967). *The Enlightenment: An interpretation*. London: Weidenfeld & Nicolson.

Gellner, E. (1992). *Postmodernism, reason, and religion*. London: Routledge.

Goldman, L. (1973). *The philosophy of the Enlightenment: The Christian burgess and the Enlightenment*. London: Routledge.

Haack, S. (2003). *Defending science—within reason*. Amherst, NY: Prometheus Books.

Kauffman, J. (2002). *Education deform: Bright people sometimes say stupid things about education*. Lanham, MD: Rowman & Littlefield Education.

Kauffman, J., & Sasso, G. M. (2006). Toward ending cultural and cognitive relativism in special education. *Exceptionality, 14*(2), 65–90.

Laudan, L. (1990). *Science and relativism: Some key controversies in the philosophy of science*. Chicago: The University of Chicago Press.

Lehman, D. (1991). *Signs of the times: Deconstruction and the fall of Paul De Man*. London: Poseidon Press.

Lehman, D. (1995). Deconstruction after the fall. In D. Eddins (Ed.), *The emperor redressed: Critiquing critical theory* (pp. 132–149). Tuscaloosa, AL: The University of Alabama Press.

Lilla, M. (2001). *The reckless mind: Intellectuals in politics*. New York: New York Review of Books.

Merquior, J. G. (1986). *From Prague to Paris: A critique of stucturalist and post-structuralist thought*. London: Verso Press.

Nietzsche, F. (1967). *The will to power*. New York: Random House.

Nietzsche, F. (1974). *The gay science*. New York: Vintage Books.

Pinker, S. (1997). *How the mind works*. New York: Norton.

Rauch, J. (1994). *Kindly inquisitions: The new attacks on free thought*. Chicago: The University of Chicago Press.

Sasso, G. M. (2001). The retreat from inquiry and knowledge in special education. *Journal of Special Education*, *34*, 178–193.

Sasso, G. M. (2002, November). *Cognitive relativity in the social sciences*. Keynote presentation to College of Education Faculty at Kent State University, Kent, OH.

Scull, A. (1977). *Decarceration: Community treatment and the deviant: A radical view*. Englewood Cliffs, NJ: Prentice Hall.

Scull, A. (1993). *The most solitary of afflictions: Madness and society in Britain, 1700–1900*. London: Yale University Press.

Searle, J. R. (1998). *Mind, language, and society*. New York: Basic Books.

Shattuck, R. (1999). *Candor and perversion: Literature, education, and the arts*. New York: Norton.

Sohal, A., & Bricmont, J. (1998). *Fashionable nonsense: Postmodern intellectuals' abuse of science*. New York: Picador USA.

Sowell, T. (1999). *The quest for cosmic justice*. New York: Simon & Schuster.

Tallis, R. (1999). *Enemies of hope: A critique of contemporary pessimism*. London: MacMillan Press LTD.

Wilson, E. O. (1998). *Consilience: The unity of knowledge*. New York: Vintage Books.

Windschuttle, K. (1996). *The killing of history: How literary critics and social theorists are murdering our past*. San Francisco, CA: Encounter Books.

Wolin, R. (2004). *The seduction of unreason: The intellectual romance with facism from Nietzsche to postmodernism*. Princeton, NJ: Princeton University Press.

Part III

STRENGTHENING SPECIAL EDUCATION'S EMPIRICAL BASE

There is nothing magical, nor even particularly complicated, about the idea that educational practice should be based on scientific evidence. Indeed, one would think that there would be consensus that, all things being equal, it is generally better to use methods of instruction that have been tested and proven effective in rigorous experimental studies than to use untested interventions. Unfortunately, there appears to be no such consensus among important education policy- and decision-makers, and the research-to-practice gap has become a consistent topic of debate and discussion in the field of special education. Kauffman (1996) has gone so far as to suggest that the frequency with which practices are implemented in schools may, in fact, have an inverse relationship to the extent to which they are empirically supported.

What drives this gap, and prevents us from closing it? At a fundamental level, there are arguments that science is not a useful tool for determining what works (e.g., Gallagher, 1998). Kauffman has been among the most vocal and erudite critics of those who eschew scientific thinking in education, noting in *Education Deform* (2002) that "nonscientific thinking and aggressively *anti*-scientific beliefs are very strong today, and these sentiments or frames of mind pose a significant threat to any real progress in education" (p. 233). He has not been alone in this observation. Gersten (2001), commenting that even within schools of education are found diametrically opposed views toward empiricism, suggested that it is not surprising that "many students of education leave universities feeling bewildered, betrayed, or both" (p. 45).

But even if scholars grounded in the ways of Enlightenment science carry the day, several thorny issues remain. How will scientifically based research be translated into practice? More specifically, how will decisions be made about which educational practices have enough evidence to be deemed effective? This latter question is addressed directly by the chapters in this section, all of which include some reference to or consideration of the series of papers on quality indicators for educational research that were published in *Exceptional Children* in 2005. In their lead chapter, Forness and Beard discuss what constitutes evidence, and how we determine whether and when a practice can be deemed evidence-based. Drawing from psychopharmacology, and in particular studies comparing psychopharmacological and cognitive-behavioral interventions, Forness and Beard point out that complementary disciplines (e.g., child psychiatry and mental health) are well ahead of special education in ramping up to the systematic conduct of the randomized controlled trials (RCTs) that many argue are needed to establish truly evidence-based practice. Forness and Beard's overview of several psychopharmacological studies includes the call for special educators to become familiar with this research and to become more active collaborators with professionals from these complementary disciplines.

In chapter 10, Cook and Tankersley take on the challenge of interpreting and applying the quality indicators for group experimental research (Gersten et al., 2005) in the context of intervention research with students with EBD. The series of quality indicators papers published in *Exceptional Children* in 2005 represent a critical step in our efforts to formalize and legitimize a scientific research base in special education. In one of the most thorough applications to date of these quality indicators to published research studies, Cook and Tankersley note that further refinement, operationalization, and piloting are surely needed, but laud Gersten et al. for carrying the field forward in efforts to identify research-based practices.

In chapter 11, Lane, Barton-Arwood, Rogers, and Robertson provide an overview of literacy intervention research for students who are identified with or are at risk for emotional and behavioral disorders. Lane et al. also relied on the quality indicators papers to guide their coding and analysis of this literature. In addition to five group experimental or quasi-experimental design studies, for which they relied on the Gersten et al. (2005) quality indicators paper, Lane et al. also review 12 single-subject design studies, relying on the quality indicators for single-subject designs, authored by Horner, Carr, Halle, McGee, Odom, and Wolery (2005). This chapter is particularly compelling in that it not only takes a systematic look at empirical evidence, but focuses in particular on academic intervention research with students with EBD. The focus on academic instruction, Kauffman (2003) has pointed out repeatedly, has not received the attention it warrants.

In sum, the chapters in this section do much to further the reform of special education into a field where practice is based on evidence. Reflecting on his roughly four decades in the field in 2003, Kauffman stated that he "thought that the scientific base of special education would be almost universally accepted by now and that it would be stronger" (p. 325). We regret that we and our colleagues have not done more across that time span, but are heartened that scholars like Forness and Beard; Cook and Tankersley; and Lane, Barton-Arwood, Rogers, and Robertson continue to push the field of special education in the directions that Kauffman imagined and hoped it would go.

REFERENCES

Gallagher, D. (1998). The scientific knowledge base of special education: Do we know what we think we know? *Exceptional Children, 64,* 493–502.

Gersten, R. (2001). Sorting out the roles of research in the improvement of practice. *Learning Disabilities Research & Practice, 16*(1), 45–50.

Gersten, R., Fuchs, L. S., Compton, D., Coyne, M., Greenwood, C., & Innocenti, M. S. (2005). Quality indicators for group experimental and quasi-experimental research in special education. *Exceptional Children, 71,* 149–164.

Horner, R. H., Carr, E. C., Halle, J., McGee, G., Odom, S., & Wolery, M. (2005). The use of singe-subject research to identify evidence-based practice in special education. *Exceptional Children, 71*, 165–179.

Kauffman, J. M. (1996). Research to practice issues. *Behavioral Disorders, 22*, 5–60.

Kauffman, J. M. (2002). *Education deform: Bright people sometimes say stupid things about education*. Lanham, MD: Scarecrow Press.

Kauffman, J. M. (2003). Reflections on the field. *Education and Treatment of Children, 26*, 325–329.

Chapter 9

Strengthening the Research Base in Special Education: Evidence-Based Practice and Interdisciplinary Collaboration

Steven R. Forness
University of California, Los Angeles

Kelli Y. Beard
California State University, Dominguez Hills

More than a decade ago, our friend and colleague Jim Kauffman (1993) wrote a compelling article on reform in special education. In it, he decried false criticisms of special education that largely confused where students were taught with how they were taught, suggested simplistic solutions to complex problems, or denigrated the research evidence then available in special education. Jim then suggested his own strategies for substantive reform. These included more careful consideration of needs of students with different disabilities, of special education foundations, and of the evidence base necessary for advancing special education practice.

This chapter focuses on Jim's third suggested strategy, strengthening the research base. In it, we intend to review very briefly where we have come in the past decade or so in terms of our conceptualization

169

of evidence-based practice, particularly in the area of emotional or behavioral disorders (EBD). This is the category of special education in which Jim and we have spent most of our professional lives, and it is arguably among the most contentious categories in the profession. Because our field also focuses primarily on behavioral or cognitive behavioral interventions as our primary practice approach, we also briefly review some recent randomized clinical trials in which these interventions have been directly compared with psychopharmacologic treatments. We do this for two reasons. The first is that psychopharmacology is increasing exponentially as a treatment for children and adolescents with emotional or behavioral disorders in both general and special education classrooms (Zito & Safer, 2005). The second is that psychopharmacologic treatment, as we discuss, may well surpass our best behavioral or cognitive behavioral interventions in efficacy if not effectiveness; *combining* both types of treatments may, in most cases, produce better results than using either one alone; and such knowledge may be necessary to our full understanding of the evidence base in special education. We conclude with some comments on the emerging field of school mental health.

Other chapters in this section of the book provide an excellent overview of current behavioral and academic research in our field and thoughtful insights about issues in evidence-based practice. Our intent, however, is to supplement these views with insights from psychopharmacologic research and thus underline the importance not only of our interdependence in this effort but also of our need to collaborate more fully with our interdisciplinary and interagency professional colleagues in mental health.

ORIGINS OF EVIDENCE-BASED PRACTICE IN SPECIAL EDUCATION

Although professionals in the field of special education for children with emotional or behavioral disorders have referred in the past to "best practices" as a means of highlighting use of acceptable interventions, this term has recently evolved into "evidence-based practice" to denote use of only those interventions that meet a standard of empirical support from research studies. This reflects, in part, a certain confidence in the growth of our research base in this field. It also reflects professional embrace of standards for evidence-based practice by the field of medicine, including our sister profession, child psychiatry (Hamilton, 2004, 2005; McClellan & Werry, 2003). The field of mental health in general, of which we are arguably a part, has also embraced evidence-based practice and has begun to provide inventories of practices that meet criteria for these standards (Hoagwood & Johnson, 2003–2004; Kazdin & Weisz, 2003; Wasserman, Ko, & Jensen, 2001; Weisz, 2004). The gold standard for such practices in these professional fields has generally been that the intervention in question has been subjected to at least two randomized clinical trials in which it surpasses existing practice by a statistically significant, if not a clinically significant, margin.

Thus, as we see in studies to be discussed in the next section, most studies in psychiatry have even begun to focus on how many children are "normalized" by the practice, that is, how many children with a psychiatric disorder as measured on a standardized behavioral rating scale no longer meet clinical criteria for that disorder on that scale after intervention, as compared to controls. It should be noted that standards for evidence-based practice do not necessarily adopt all-or-none criteria. There is instead a hierarchy of evidence in which the criterion of two randomized clinical trials is at the top but in which evidence from other studies that suffer from less rigorous randomization or other experimental bias can still count. Such evidence may support the practice as "partially evidence-based."

Meta-analyses or syntheses of large numbers of research studies also play a role, as it has in special education (Forness, 2001). Weisz (2004), for example, synthesized 14 studies on standard psychotherapy for children and adolescents. In such therapy, the business-as-usual approach is for the therapist to interview parents and/or the child or adolescent, provide an accepting atmosphere in which the child or adolescent can discuss his or her difficulties or express them indirectly during play, and respond to these difficulties through reflection or reframing. The effect size for such psychotherapy across the 14 studies, of which 6 were randomized, was –0.03, suggesting virtually no effect. Weisz then reported several syntheses of structured therapies, either behavioral or cognitive behavioral interventions, which in most cases were either manualized or at least described in step-by-step detail. More than 350 such studies have been conducted, each using at least some form of experimental control, with a significant number being randomized in at least some fashion. Effect sizes for these ranged from 0.71 to 0.84, generally considered in the range of "large" as opposed to "medium" or "small" effects. As Weisz observed, therapists often resist using such therapies because they are predicated on time-limited goals and leave little flexibility for the therapist to exercise his or her creativity, clinical insights, or other personal skills. What Weisz was probably too polite to mention is that such therapy is also more difficult and demanding for the therapist, requiring active structuring and teaching in each session rather than simply reactive responding. One could unfortunately make the same analogy between the whole language approach to teaching reading, in which the teacher provides a language-rich environment in response to the child's interests, and the more demanding phonics-based direct-instructional approach (Shaywitz, 2003).

In special education, we do not seem yet to be at a level where we can construct inventories of evidence-based practice, although our field has begun to delineate parameters for effective research and at least some preliminary standards for determining if a practice is evidence-based (Odom et al., 2005). In a special issue of *Exceptional Children*, four articles have recently been published on different types of research and on proposed, acceptable standards for determining evidence-based practice from each type. In this special issue, Gersten, Fuchs, Compton, Coyne, Greenwood, and Innocenti (2005) suggest both essential and desirable standards for group experimental and quasi-experimental studies and propose that four acceptable quality studies or two high-quality studies, all with significant effect sizes, constitute evidence-based practice. In their scheme, "acceptable" and "high-quality" studies are essentially differentiated by number of research quality indicators that have been met. Thompson, Diamond, McWilliam, Snyder, and Snyder (2005) discuss quality issues for sophisticated correlational studies using techniques such as structural equation modeling, in which relationships between interventions and outcomes in nonrandomized conditions can be carefully modeled to determine causal factors. Two other papers in this issue on single-subject research (Horner et al., 2005) and on qualitative studies (Brantlinger, Jimenez, Klingner, Pugach, & Richardson, 2005) do an excellent job of delineating quality indicators for each type of research, but neither seems to make a compelling enough case for determining evidence-based practice from such research, as has been discussed elsewhere (Forness, 2005). For example, the standard cited for evidence-based in single-subject research involved a minimum of only five studies with a total of 20 participants.

Polsgrove and Forness (2004) have also proposed criteria for evidence-based practice. In their scheme, "evidence-based" practice should be based on at least two well-designed randomized clinical trials, with no comparable evidence to the contrary, or on a meta-analysis of at least 12 group-experimental or quasi-experimental studies with a mean effect size of 0.7 or higher. A single-subject synthesis of at least 20 well-designed single-subject studies with a minimum of 60 participants and a mean percent of nonoverlapping data (PND) between baseline and intervention phases of at least 80% could also substitute for one randomized clinical trial. A "partially evidence-based" practice would be based on only one randomized clinical trial or four quasi-experimental studies or a meta-analysis of 12 studies with an effect size of 0.4 or higher or a single-subject synthesis of 12 studies with a PND of 70% or higher. Each of the items just discussed, as noted before, should have no comparable evidence to the contrary. Thus two randomized clinical trials with negative effect sizes could potentially negate two trials with positive findings and two such trials with small effect sizes could drop the practice into the lower category of "partially supported." In their scheme, Polsgrove and Forness also suggest two other categories of "promising" practice, in which at least some positive empirical research exists in the early stages of its development, and "unsupported or unevaluated" practice, in which the practice does not seem to have significant supportive empirical evidence.

THE CURRENT EVIDENCE BASE
IN SPECIAL EDUCATION

It is interesting to note that the field of special education for children with emotional or behavioral disorders has focused a great deal of its energies in the past few years on three notable areas of practice: functional behavioral assessment, positive behavioral support, and academic remediation for children with emotional or behavioral disorders. Functional behavioral assessment is a process in which the teacher is encouraged to systematically analyze antecedent and consequent events surrounding misbehavior or noncompliance in order to develop hypotheses about behavior as a basis for planning more effective motivational or instructional programs (Fox & Gable, 2004; Scott et al., 2004; Scott, Liaupsin, Nelson, & Jolivette, 2003; Scott, McIntyre, Liaupsin, Nelson, & Conroy, 2004; Sugai et al., 2000; Sugai & Horner, 1999/2000). Functional behavioral assessment, however, has received some criticism regarding its empirical research base for children with emotional or behavioral disorders (Barton-Arwood, Wehby, Gunter, & Lane, 2003; Conroy & Stichter, 2003; Sasso, Conroy, Stichter, & Fox, 2000). It appears that functional behavioral assessment may at best only meet criteria as a partially evidence-based practice in our field, and there is even some suggestion that it may be just a promising practice, despite the attention given to it.

In its simplest terms the second approach, positive behavioral support, is a practice, currently applied classroom-wide or even school-wide as a preventative approach, in which consensus about desirable rules for positive behavior is developed and these rules are then promulgated and reinforced as a means of reducing undesirable behavior (Horner, Sugai, Lewis-Palmer, & Todd, 2001; Horner, Sugai, Todd, & Lewis-Palmer, 2004; Lewis & Newcomer, 2005; Liaupsin, Jolivette, & Scott, 2004; Nelson, Martella, & Marchand-Martella, 2002; Safran & Oswald, 2003; Scott, 2003; Sugai & Horner, 2002a, 2002b; Sugai et al., 2000). Although positive behavioral support has been widely and effectively disseminated, the evidence thus far has not included what one would consider a well-designed, randomized clinical trial, though a number of quasi-experimental designs have apparently been conducted in which reductions in office disciplinary referrals and increases in attendance or school-wide academic testing have been reported in schools adopting this practice. Thus it may currently qualify only as a partially evidence-based practice. It should be noted, however, that individual (as opposed to classroom-wide or school-wide) positive interventions, such as the recent First Step program, seem to have comparably more supportive evidence (Beard & Sugai, 2004; Walker, 2002; Walker, Ramsey, & Gresham, 2004).

Finally, the third practice, academic remediation, involves adapting evidence-based reading practices from the field of learning disabilities for instruction of children with emotional or behavioral disorders. This practice has been subject not only to well-designed controlled studies (Lane, O'Shaughnessy, Lambros, Gresham, & Beebe- Frankenberger, 2001; Lane et al., 2002; Nelson, Benner, & Gonzalez, 2005; O'Shaughnessy, Lane, Gresham, & Beebe-Frankenberger, 2003; Scott & Shearer-Lingo, 2003) but also to research syntheses (Lane, 2004; Pierce, Reid, & Epstein, 2004; Ryan, Reid, & Epstein, 2004). From initial review of this evidence, it appears that this practice, albeit originally developed in the learning disability field, may well qualify as evidence-based when applied to instruction of children with emotional or behavioral disorders.

Despite the fact that children with emotional or behavioral disorders continue to have possibly the worst outcomes of any category of children in special education (Wagner, Kutash, Duchnowski, & Epstein, 2005), currently popular practices in this category seem to be somewhat less than fully evidenced-based. Lewis, Hudson, Richter and Johnson (2004) have also evaluated a number of potentially evidence-based classroom practices in our field using admittedly rather less demanding standards, and have reached much the same conclusion. This does not so much reflect on the quality of research in special education in our field as it does on our ability to marshall our research efforts in the service of developing evidence-based practice (Brigham, Gustashaw, & Brigham, 2004; Landrum & Tankersly, 2004; Tankersly, Landrum, & Cook, 2004). We would now like to turn to a brief review of recent research in the field of child psychiatry, particularly in the area of psychopharmacology, in which research efforts have, for a variety of reasons, focused more directly on developing an evidence base to guide practice.

RANDOMIZED CLINICAL TRIALS COMPARING BEHAVIORAL AND PSYCHOPHARMACOLOGIC INTERVENTIONS

We intend here to review very briefly five relatively recent randomized clinical trials in child and adolescent psychiatry. Such research is extremely relevant to our own field of special education for children with emotional and behavioral disorders for at least two reasons. The first relates to the preceding discussion on evidence-based practice, in that such research is very much focused on randomized clinical trials; and some aspects of it may serve as models for our own research efforts. The second involves direct comparison of psychopharmacologic treatment with behavioral or cognitive behavioral interventions. The behavioral interventions are relatively similar to those used in our field of special education for children with externalizing disorders (Forness & Kavale, 2002; Walker, Ramsey, & Gresham, 2004) and the cognitive behavioral interventions are relatively similar to those used in our field for children with internalizing disorders (Gresham & Kern, 2004; Polsgrove & Smith, 2004). Such comparisons may lead to a more fully developed sense of our current interventions in the context of interdisciplinary or interagency care for children with emotional or behavioral disorders.

Of the five randomized clinical trials, three involve children with ADHD (attention deficit hyperactivity disorder) and oppositional defiant disorders, and two involve children with depression and anxiety disorders, respectively. As we see, all five represent rather compelling evidence that psychopharmacology and not behavioral or cognitive behavioral intervention is probably the critical treatment element.

The first randomized clinical trial is the MTA (multimodal treatment of ADHD) study on which a 10-month follow-up has recently been published (MTA Cooperative Group, 2004). In the original study, there were 579 children, age 7–9 years, who were all carefully diagnosed for ADHD (MTA Cooperative Group, 1999a, 1999b). They were randomly assigned to one of four groups: (a) a community control group who were paid to participate in the assessments over the 14-months of the study and who were offered no treatment but could obtain treatment in the community at their own expense if they so desired; (b) a behavioral treatment group who received teacher and parent behavioral consultation, a home-school behavioral program, a classroom aide, and a summer-camp that involved both academic and behavioral intervention; (c) a medication group who received Ritalin or related drugs according to a best-practice algorithm; and (d) a combined treatment group that received both the behavioral and the medication interventions. Note that these children were seen at six different university sites and reflected a diverse sample with 39% children of color, 31% from single-parent families, and 54% with oppositional defiant or related disorders.

At the end of the original 14-month treatment phase, children were rated as "responders" if they were no longer in the clinical range on a rating scale of ADHD or oppositional defiant disorder symptoms (Swanson et al., 2001). The results showed responders in the community and behavioral groups at 25% and 34%, respectively, and in the medication and combined groups at 56% and 68%, respectively. In addition to symptoms, children were also rated on a composite score of multiple home and school outcomes with essentially the same results (Conners et al., 2001). At a 10-month follow-up involving 540 of the original 579 children, responders in the community and behavioral groups were relatively unchanged at 28% and 32%, respectively, but medication and combined groups slipped somewhat to 37% and 48%, respectively (MTA Cooperative Group, 2004). Note, however, that all of these data represent an "intent-to-treat" analysis in which children were counted even if they did not fully comply with their original treatment, as a way to measure impact of social validity of each treatment. Further analysis of data over the 24 months showed that many children in the first two groups sought out medication at their own expense over the 10-month follow-up, whereas some children in the second two groups did not comply with medication treatment when they no longer received it free-of-charge during follow-up (MTA Cooperative Group, 2004).

In the second randomized clinical trial, the intent was to study what additional benefit, if any, occurred when 4 hours per week of after-school academic or behavioral interventions were added to existing medication treatment (Ritalin). The study, known as the MPT (multimodal psychosocial treatment) study, began with 129 children, ages 7–9 years, of whom 103 (80%) responded to Ritalin and were used in the study (Klein, Abikoff, Hechtman, & Weiss, 2004). They were randomly assigned to one of three groups: (a) a group who received only medication during the 24 months of the study; (b) a group who received Ritalin plus 4 hours per week in the first year and 4 hours per month in the second year divided among academic tutoring, behavioral parent-training, social-skills training, and individual problem-solving therapy; and (c) an attention-control group who received Ritalin plus 4 hours of "sham" treatment of comparable intensity but without the active treatments received by the second group.

There were almost 20 different measures across academic (Hechtman, Abikoff, Klein, Weiss, et al., 2004), parent-management, social-skills (Abikoff, Hechtman, Klein, Gallagher, et al., 2004) and behavioral-disorder outcomes (Abikoff, Hechtman, Klein, Weiss, et al., 2004). At the end of the 24 months of treatment, there was virtually no difference among the three groups. All improved significantly on almost all measures but at identical rates and final outcomes. For example, all three groups of children had comorbid oppositional defiant disorders at rates slightly above 50% prior to the study, but all three groups had rates at outcome of only 14 to 17%. Thus, not only did academic and behavioral interventions not add any additional impact to outcome already provided by Ritalin, but the attention-control added just as much as the active behavioral interventions, a potential lesson we have not widely explored in our own field.

The third randomized clinical trial for children with ADHD involved 36 very young children, ages 5 and 6 years (Chacko et al., 2005). Known as the STP (summer treatment program) study, its intent was to study what additional benefit, if any, occurred when medication treatment was added to ongoing academic or behavioral interventions in a summer-camp program almost identical to that used as one of the components of the MTA behavioral program, just described. The 36 children were randomly assigned to one of three groups: (a) a group who received a placebo pill plus 9-hours per day over an 8-week summer program of morning academic and related classroom intervention and afternoon games and sports, with an intensive behavioral reinforcement program in effect throughout the day; (b) a group who received the same intervention but with a low dose of Ritalin beginning in the third week; and (c) a group with the same intervention but a high dose of Ritalin also beginning in the third week. After 8 weeks, children were measured across both academic and behavioral outcomes according to a within-subject, placebo-controlled, double-blind, daily cross-over design. Some 6 of 7 measures significantly favored the two medication groups over the academic or behavioral intervention group on placebo, with the high-dose group performing better on 3 of 6 measures than the low-dose group (Chacko et al., 2005). In a final consensus outcome based on all measures, children who responded best to either of the medication conditions or who were able to respond to only the academic or behavioral intervention, without active medication, were 72% and 28%, respectively.

RANDOMIZED CLINICAL TRIALS COMPARING COGNITIVE BEHAVIORAL AND PSYCHOPHARMACOLOGIC INTERVENTIONS

There were also two randomized clinical trials involving children with depression and anxiety disorders, respectively. The TADS (treatment of adolescents with depression study) involved 439 adolescents, ages 12–17 years, who were randomly assigned to one of 4 groups across 13 university sites throughout the country (Treatment for Adolescents with Depression Study Team, 2004). The four groups were as follows: (a) a placebo group; (b) a cognitive behavioral therapy group who received 15 sessions over the 12 weeks of the study, devoted to depression and its causes, mood monitoring, and cognitive restructuring; (c) a medication group who received Prozac; and (d) a combined group who received both of the active medication and cognitive behavioral treatments. Note that participants in this study were 54% female with 26% being adolescents of color and 52% being diagnosed with other comorbid disorders including oppositional defiant disorder.

In TADS, outcome was based on both parent and adolescent interviews and ratings, with responders defined on a clinical global improvement rating within the nonclinical range at outcome. Analysis of responders showed 35% and 43% for the placebo and CBT groups, respectively, and 61% and 71% for the Prozac and combined groups, respectively. It is worth noting that suicidality among the 4 groups was carefully monitored throughout the study and decreased significantly in all four groups but that the combined group did slightly better than the other three groups on this outcome (Treatment for Adolescents with Depression Study Team, 2004).

The other randomized clinical study involved OCD (obsessive compulsive disorder) that is generally considered one of the more serious anxiety disorders with several adverse implications for school functioning (Adams, 2004). The POTS (Pediatric OCD Treatment Study) involved 112 children and adolescents, age 7 to 17 years, with 50% males and 80% with at least one other comorbid psychiatric disorder including depression and oppositional defiant disorder (Pediatric OCD Treatment Study Team, 2004). Only 8% were children or adolescents of color. Participants at three different university sites were randomly assigned to one of four groups: (a) a placebo group; (b) a cognitive behavioral therapy group who received 14 sessions of CBT over the 12 weeks of the study, devoted to OCD and its causes, target symptoms, cognitive restructuring, and response prevention; (c) a medication group who received Zoloft, a drug in the same class as Prozac; and (d) a combined group who received both of the active medication and cognitive behavioral treatments.

In POTS, outcome was based on both symptom ratings and structured interviews, and clinical responders were measured by remission of symptoms. Responders in the placebo group were 4% compared to 21% in the Zoloft group, 39% for cognitive behavioral therapy, and 54% for combined treatment. As opposed to studies discussed earlier, there were some site differences for CBT alone and Zoloft alone at two sites; but combined groups were still superior. Note that this is the only study of the five randomized clinical trials described here in which medication alone was not superior to a behavioral or cognitive behavioral intervention alone. It is worth noting, however, that Zoloft has not necessarily been considered the best of medications for OCD and that other selective serotonin reuptake inhibitors, such as Luvox or Paxil, are generally considered better first-line medications for this disorder though this may differ for adolescents versus children (Konopasek & Forness, 2004).

CONCLUSION

In regard to evidence-based practice, these five studies are illustrative. All are randomized clinical trials. All involve relatively impressive design features with four of the five studies applying practices that are essentially manualized and with four of the five studies using an intent-to-treat analysis designed to take both acceptability and social validity of the practice into account. With one or two exceptions, most have participants that reflect diverse community samples with multiple disorders. All use at least some measure of functional impairment (Winters, Collett, & Myers, 2005) rather than just measures of symptoms, in order to assess outcomes more comprehensively. All but one are collaborative efforts across universities with different geographic sites to enhance generalization. Moderator and mediator variables were generally well analyzed and, for the most part, nonsignificant except in one or two instances. No racial or ethnic differences were found, however, in response to treatment. One is left hard pressed to recall equally impressive studies in our own field.

On balance, four of the five studies also suggest that psychopharmacologic treatment may indeed be at least slightly superior to behavioral or cognitive behavioral interventions similar to those used in our own field, and, in most cases, combined treatment may be superior to either used alone, though this may still be an open question. These findings point to the need for special educators to become much more familiar with such treatment, and their role in interdisciplinary collaboration (Forness, Walker, & Kavale, 2003–2004; Konopasek & Forness, 2004). Psychopharmacologic treatment, however, is decidedly not without its problems, and issues of side effects, substandard practice, and gaps in collaboration among physicians, parents, and school or related professionals need to be systematically and continually addressed in evidence-based practice (Riba & Balon, 2005).

In the decade or so since Jim Kauffman's (1993) original call to strengthen the research base, we have made some progress; but we still seem not to have entirely learned, as Jim put it, "a lesson here for today's special education in which our advocacy for new strategies and practices is very far ahead of reliable data" (Kauffman, 1993, p. 11). Our colleagues in mental health, particularly in regard to psychopharmocology, seem not only to be further ahead of us in advancing evidence-based practice but also in developing practices that may rival or exceed our own for at least some children with emotional or behavioral disorders. The School Mental Health Alliance (2004) was recently founded and composed of several national professional associations in general education, special education, school psychology, school counseling, psychology, psychiatry, pediatrics, and related fields, including parent organizations. It is intended to bring evidence-based mental health prevention and treatment efforts into schools in a collaborative manner. Such collaboration should also help to bring special education to a new recognition of its interdisciplinary connectedness in the larger context of mental health.

Finally, we would like to add our praise for Jim Kauffman as a colleague and mentor and our personal affection for Jim Kauffman as a friend. As is evident from the breadth and insight of the other chapters in this book, the chapter authors are professionals of the highest caliber. That they are so is testimony not only to Jim's influence in both their lives and their careers but also to the astounding reach of his mentorship across this field. Jim usually described himself as "a small, shy man," but, to us, his impact on us and on our profession will forever be big and bold.

REFERENCES

Abikoff, H., Hechtman, L., Klein, R., Gallagher, R., Fleiss, K., Etcovitch, J., et al. (2004). Social functioning in children with ADHD treated with long-term methylphenidate and multimodal psychosocial treatment. *Journal of the American Academy of Child and Adolescent Psychiatry, 43,* 820–829.

Abikoff, H., Hechtman, L., Klein, R., Weiss, G., Fleiss, K., Etcovitch, J., Cousins, L., et al. (2004). Symptomatic improvement in children with ADHD treated with long-term methylphenidate and multimodal psychosocial treatment. *Journal of the American Academy of Child and Adolescent Psychiatry, 43,* 802–811.

Adams, G. B. (2004). Identifying, assessing and treating obsessive-compulsive disorder in school-aged children: The role of school personnel. *Teaching Exceptional Children, 37,* 46–53.

Barton-Arwood, S. M., Wehby, J. H., Gunter, P. L., & Lane, K. L. (2003). Functional behavior assessment rating scales: Intrarater reliability with students with emotional or behavioral disorders. *Behavioral Disorders, 28,* 386–400.

Beard, K. Y., & Sugai, G. (2004). First step to success: An early intervention for elementary children at risk for antisocial behavior. *Behavioral Disorders, 29,* 396–409.

Brantlinger, E., Jimenez, R., Klingner, J., Pugach, M., & Richardson, V. (2005). Qualitative studies in special education. *Exceptional Children, 71,* 195–207.

Brigham, F. J., Gustashaw III, W. E., & Brigham, M. S. P. (2004). Scientific practice and the tradition of advocacy in special education. *Journal of Learning Disabilities, 37,* 200–206.

Chacko, A., Pelham, W. E. Jr., Gnagy, E. M., Greiner, A., Vallano, G., Bukstein, O., et al. (2005). Stimulant medication effects in a summer treatment program among young children with attention-deficit/hyperactivity disorder. *Journal of the American Academy of Child and Adolescent Psychiatry, 44,* 249–257.

Conners, C. K., Epstein, J. N., March, J. S., Angold, A., Wells, K. C., Klaric, J., et al. (2001). Multimodal treatment of ADHD in the MTA: An alternative out-come analysis. *Journal of the American Academic of Child and Adolescent Psychiatry, 40,* 159–167.

Conroy, M. A., & Stichter, J. P. (2003). The application of antecedents in the functional assessment process: Existing research, issues, and recommendations. *The Journal of Special Education, 37,* 15–25.

Forness, S. R. (2001). Special education and related services: What have we learned from meta-analysis? *Exceptionality, 9,* 185–197.

Forness, S. R. (2005). The pursuit of evidence-based practice in special education for children with emotional or behavioral disorders. *Behavioral Disorders, 30,* 311–330.

Forness, S. R., & Kavale, K. A. (2002). Impact of ADHD on school systems. In P. S. Jensen & J. R. Cooper (Eds.), *Attention deficit hyperactivity disorder: State of the science; best practices* (pp. 24, 1–20). Kingston, NJ: Civic Research Institute.

Forness, S. R., Walker, H. M., & Kavale, K. A. (2003/2004). Psychiatric disorders and their treatment: A primer for school professionals. *Report on Emotional and Behavioral Disorders of Youth, 4,* 3–6, 20–23.

Fox, J. J., & Gable, R. A. (2004). Functional behavioral assessment. In R. B. Rutherford, M. M. Quinn, & S. R. Mathur (Eds.), *Handbook of research in emotional and behavioral disorders* (pp. 143–162). New York: Guilford.

Gersten, R., Fuchs, L. S., Compton, D., Coyne, M., Greenwood, C., & Innocenti, M. S. (2005). Quality indicators for group experimental and quasi-experimental research in special education. *Exceptional Children, 71,* 149–164.

Gresham, F. M., & Kern, L. (2004). Internalizing behavior problems in children and adolescents. In R. B. Rutherford, M. M. Quinn, & S. R. Mathur (Eds.), *Handbook of research in emotional and behavioral disorders.* (pp. 262–281). New York: Guilford.

Hamilton, J. D. (2004). Evidence-based thinking and the alliance with parents. *Journal of the American Academy of Child and Adolescent Psychiatry, 43,* 105–108.

Hamilton, J. D. (2005). Clinicians' guide to evidence-based practice. *Journal of the American Academy of Child and Adolescent Psychiatry, 44,* 494–498.

Hechtman, L., Abikoff, H., Klein, R. G., Greenfield, B., Etcovitch, J., Cousins, L., et al. (2004). Children with ADHD treated with long-term methylphenidate and multimodal psychosocial treatment: Impact on parental practices. *Journal of the American Academy of Child and Adolescent Psychiatry, 43,* 830–838.

Hechtman, L., Abikoff, H., Klein, R. G., Weiss, G., Respitz, C., Kouri, J., Blum, C., et al. (2004). Academic achievement and emotional status of children with ADHD treated with long-term methylphenidate and multimodal psychosocial treatment. *Journal of the American Academy of Child and Adolescent Psychiatry, 43,* 812–819.

Hoagwood, K. (2003/2004). Evidence-based practice in child and adolescent mental health: Its meaning, application, and limitations. *Report on Emotional and Behavioral Disorders in Youth, 4*, 7–8, 24–26.

Horner, R. H., Carr, E. G., Halle, J., McGee, G., Odom, S., & Wolery, M. (2005). The use of single-subject research to identify evidence-based practice in special education. *Exceptional Children, 71*, 165–179.

Horner, R. H., Sugai, G., Lewis-Palmer, T., & Todd, A. W. (2001). Teaching school-wide behavioral expectations. *Report on Emotional and Behavioral Disorders in Youth, 1*, 77–79, 93–96.

Horner, R. H., Sugai, G., Todd, A. W., & Lewis-Palmer, T. (2004). School-wide positive behavior support: An alternative approach to discipline in schools. In L. Bambara & L. Kern (Eds.), *Positive behavior support* (pp. 10–22). New York: Guilford.

Kadzin, A. E., & Weisz, J. R. (2003). *Evidence-based psychotherapies for children and adolescents*. New York: Guilford.

Kauffman, J. M. (1993). How we might achieve the radical reform of special education. *Exceptional Children, 60*, 6–16.

Klein, R. G., Abikoff, H., Hechtman, L., & Weiss, G. (2004). Design and rationale of controlled study of long term methylphenidate and multimodal psychosocial treatment in children with ADHD. *Journal of the American Academy of Child and Adolescent Psychiatry, 43*, 792–801.

Konopasek, D. E., & Forness, S. (2004). Psychopharmacology in the treatment of emotional and behavioral disorders. In R. B. Rutherford, M. M. Quinn, & S. R. Mathur (Eds.), *Handbook of research in emotional and behavioral disorders* (pp. 352–368). New York: Guilford.

Landrum, T. J., & Tankersley, M. (2004). Science in the school house: An uninvited guest. *Journal of Learning Disabilities, 37*, 207–212.

Lane, K. L. (2004). Academic instruction and tutoring interventions for students with emotional and behavioral disorder: 1990 to the present. In R. B. Rutherford, M. M. Quinn, & S. R. Mathur (Eds.), *Handbook of research in emotional and behavioral disorders* (pp. 462–486). New York: Guilford.

Lane, K. L., O'Shaughnessy, T. E., Lambros, K. M., Gresham, F. M., & Beebe-Frankenberger, M. E. (2001). The efficacy of phonological awareness training with first-grade students who have behavioral problems and reading difficulties. *Journal of Emotional and Behavioral Disorders, 9*, 219–231.

Lane, K. L., Wehby, J. H., Menzies, H. M., Gregg, R. M., Doukas, G. L., & Munton, S. M. (2002) Early literacy instruction for first-grade students at risk for antisocial behavior. *Education and Treatment of Children, 25*, 438–458.

Lewis, T. J., Hudson, S., Richter, M., & Johnson, N. (2004). Scientifically supported practices in emotional and behavioral disorders: A proposed approach and brief review of current practices. *Behavioral Disorders, 29*, 247–259.

Lewis, T. J., & Newcomer, L. L. (2005). Reducing problem behavior through school-wide systems of positive behavior support. In P. Clough, P. Garner, T. Pardeck, & K. O. Yuen. (Eds.), *Handbook of emotional & behavioural difficulties* (pp. 100–114). Thousand Oaks: Sage.

Liaupsin, C. J., Jolivette, K., & Scott, T. M. (2004). Schoolwide systems of behavior support: maximizing student success in schools. In R. B. Rutherford, M. M. Quinn, & S. R. Mathur (Eds.), *Handbook of research in emotional and behavioral disorders* (pp. 487–501). New York: Guilford.

McClellan, J. M., & Werry, J. S. (2003). Evidence-based treatments in child and adolescent psychiatry: An inventory. *Journal of the American Academy of Child and Adolescent Psychiatry, 42,* 1388–1400.

MTA Cooperative Group. (1999a). A 14-month randomized clinical trial of treatment strategies for attention-deficit/hyperactivity disorder. *Archives of General Psychiatry, 56,* 1073–1086.

MTA Cooperative Group. (1999b). Moderators and mediators of treatment response for children with attention-deficit/hyperactivity disorder. *Archives of General Psychiatry, 56,* 1088–1096.

MTA Cooperative Group. (2004). National Institute of Mental Health Multimodal Treatment Study for ADHD follow-up: Changes in effectiveness and growth after the end of treatment. *Pediatrics, 113,* 762–769.

Nelson, J. R., Benner, G. J., & Gonzalez, J. (2005). An investigation of the effects of a prereading intervention on the early literacy skills of children at risk of emotional disturbance and reading problems. *Journal of Emotional and Behavioral Disorders, 13,* 3–12.

Nelson, J. R., Martella, R. C., & Marchand-Martella, N. E. (2002). Maximizing student learning: The effects of a comprehensive school-based program for preventing disruptive behaviors. *Journal of Emotional and Behavioral Disorders, 10,* 136–148.

Odom, S. L., Brantlinger, E., Gersten, R., Horner, R. H., Thompson, B., & Harris, K. R. (2005). Research in special education: Scientific methods and evidence-based practices. *Exceptional Children, 71,* 137–148.

O'Shaughnessy, T., Lane, K. L., Gresham, F. M., & Beebe-Frankenberger, M. (2003). Children placed at risk for learning and behavioral difficulties: Implementing a school-wide system of early identification and prevention. *Remedial and Special Education, 24,* 27–35.

Pediatric OCD Treatment Study (POTS) Team. (2004). Cognitive-behavior therapy, Sertraline, and their combination for children and adolescents with obsessive-compulsive disorder: The pediatric OCD treatment study (POTS) randomized controlled trial. *Journal of the American Medical Association, 292,* 1969–1976.

Pierce, C. D., Reid, R., & Epstein, M. (2004). Teacher-mediated interventions for children with EBD and their academic outcomes: A review. *Remedial and Special Education, 25,* 175–188.

Polsgrove, L., & Forness, S. R. (2004, November). *Evidence-based practice in special education*. Presented at Annual Teacher Educators of Children with Behavioral Disorders Conference on Severe Behavior Disorders of Children and Youth, Tempe, AZ.

Polsgrove, L. & Smith, S. W. (2004). Informed practice in teaching self-control to children with emotional and behavioral disorders. In R. B. Rutherford, M. M. Quinn, & S. R. Mathur (Eds.), *Handbook of research in emotional and behavioral disorders* (pp. 399–425). New York: Guilford.

Riba, M. B., & Balon, R. (2005). *Competency in combining pharmacotherapy and psychotherapy: Integrated and split treatment core competencies in psychotherapy.* Washington, DC: American Psychiatric Association.

Ryan, J. B., Reid, R., & Epstein, M. H. (2004). Peer-mediated intervention studies on academic achievement for students with EBD: A review. *Remedial and Special Education, 25,* 330–341.

Safran, S. P., & Oswald, K. (2003). Positive behavior supports: Can schools reshape disciplinary practices? *Exceptional Children, 69,* 361–373.

Sasso, G. M., Conroy, M. A., Stichter, J. P., & Fox, J. J. (2000). Slowing down the bandwagon: The misapplication of functional assessment for students with emotional or behavioral disorders. *Behavioral Disorders, 26,* 282–296.

School Mental Health Alliance. (2004). *Working together to promote learning, socioemotional competence, and mental health for all children.* Available from Center for Advancement of Children's Mental Health, Columbia University New York State Psychiatric Institute, 1051 Riverside Drive, New York, NY, 10032.

Scott, T. M. (2003). Making behavior intervention planning decisions in a schoolwide system of positive behavior support. *Focus on Exceptional Children, 36*(1), 1–20.

Scott, T. M., Bucalos, A., Liaupsin, C., Nelson, C. M., Jolivette, K., & DeShea, L. (2004). Using functional behavior assessment in general education settings: Making a case for effectiveness and efficiency. *Behavioral Disorders, 29,* 189–201.

Scott, T. M., Liaupsin, C. J., Nelson, C. M., & Jolivette, K. (2003). Ensuring student success through team-based functional behavioral assessment. *Teaching Exceptional Children, 35,* 16–21.

Scott, T. M., McIntyre, J., Liaupsin, C. J., Nelson, C. M., & Conroy, M. (2004). An examination of functional behavior assessment in public school settings: Collaborative teams, experts, and methodology. *Behavioral Disorders, 29,* 384–395.

Scott, T. M., & Shearer-Lingo, A. (2003). The effects of reading fluency instruction on the academic and behavioral success of middle school students in a self-contained EBD classroom. *Preventing School Failure, 46,* 167–173.

Shaywitz, S. (2003). *Overcoming dyslexia: A new and complete science-based program for reading problems.* New York: Knopf.

Sugai, G., & Horner, R. H. (1999/2000). Special issue: Including the functional behavioral assessment technology in schools. *Exceptionality, 8,* 145–229.

Sugai, G., & Horner, R. H. (2002a). The evolution of discipline practices: School-wide positive behavior supports. *Child and Family Behavior Therapy, 24,* 23–50.

Sugai, G., & Horner, R. H. (2002b). Introduction to the special series on positive behavior support in schools. *Journal of Emotional and Behavioral Disorders, 10,* 130–135.

Sugai, G., Horner, R. H., Dunlap, G., Hieneman, M., Lewis, T. J., Nelson, C. M., et al. (2000). Applying positive behavioral support and functional behavioral analysis in schools. *Journal of Positive Behavioral Interventions, 2,* 131–143.

Swanson, J. M., Kraemer, H. C., Hinshaw, S. P., Arnold, L. E., Conners, C. K., et al. (2001). Clinical relevance of the primary findings of the MTA: Success rates based on severity of ADHD and ODD symptoms at the end of treatment. *Journal of the American Academy of Child and Adolescent Psychiatry, 40,* 168–179.

Tankersley, M., Landrum, T. J., & Cook, B. G. (2004). How research informs practice in the field of emotional and behavioral disorders. In R. B. Rutherford, M. M. Quinn, & S. R. Mathur (Eds.), *Handbook of research in emotional and behavioral disorders* (pp. 98–113). New York: Guilford.

Thompson, B., Diamond, K. E., McWilliam, R., Snyder, P., & Snyder, S. W. (2005). Evaluating the quality of evidence from correlational research for evidence-based practice. *Exceptional Children, 71,* 181–194.

Treatment for Adolescents with Depression Study Team. (2004). Fluoxetine, cognitive-behavioral therapy, and their combination for adolescents with depression: Treatment for Adolescents with Depression Study (TADS) randomized controlled trial. *Journal of the American Medical Association, 292,* 807–820.

Wagner, M., Kutash, K., Duchnowski, A. J., & Epstein, M. H. (2005). The special education elementary longitudinal study and the national longitudinal transition study: Study designs and implications for children and youth with emotional disturbance. *Journal of Emotional and Behavioral Disorders, 13,* 25–41.

Walker, H. M. (2002). The first step to success program: Preventing destructive social outcomes at the point of school entry. *Report on Emotional & Behavioral Disorders in Youth, 2,* 3–6, 22–23.

Walker, H. M., Ramsey, E., & Gresham, F. M. (2004). *Antisocial behavior in school: Evidence-based practices* (2nd ed.). Belmont, CA: Wadsworth/Thompson.

Wasserman, G. A., Ko, S. J., & Jensen, P. S. (2001). Columbia guidelines for child and adolescent mental health referral. *Report on Emotional and Behavioral Disorders in Youth, 2,* 9–14, 23.

Weisz, J. R. (2004). *Psychotherapy for children and adolescents: Evidence-based treatments and case studies.* New York: Cambridge University Press.

Winters, N. C., Collett, B. R., & Myers, K. M. (2005). Ten-year review of rating scales, VII: Scales assessing functional impairment. *Journal of the American Academy of Child and Adolescent Psychiatry, 44,* 309–338.

Zito, J. M., & Safer, D. J. (2005). Recent child pharmacoepidemiological findings. *Journal of Child and Adolescent Psychopharmacology, 15,* 5–9.

Chapter 10

A Preliminary Examination to Identify the Presence of Quality Indicators in Experimental Research in Special Education

Bryan G. Cook
University of Hawaii

Melody Tankersley
Kent State University

James M. Kauffman has profoundly influenced the education of students with emotional and behavioral disorders (EBD) and the field of special education over the past 37 years. In particular, he has played a leading role in reminding educators not to embrace fads too quickly, to examine closely the policy initiatives they undertake and encounter, and to apply science and reason to direct their interactions with students with disabilities (e.g., Kauffman, 1996a, 1997, 1999a, 2002, 2003, 2004). Of the many ways that Kauffman has provided prescient direction for our field, we will focus on one: the application of evidence-based practices to bridge the research-to-practice gap. Before the terms "evidence-based practice" and "research-to-practice gap" were staples of educational parlance, and long before they became a focus

189

of legislation like the No Child Left Behind Act, Kauffman discussed the critical need for teachers, especially of students with EBD, to implement instructional techniques that were shown by research to be effective (e.g., Kauffman, 1996b). Through the rise of constructivism in schools and post-modernism in academic circles, he remained steadfast that scientific research was the necessary barometer to gauge what practices should be used with students (e.g., Kauffman & Sasso, 2006). Kauffman clearly stated this notion in the article that serves as the focus of this book. "Reliable quantitative and qualitative research data are needed to judge the extent to which special education is having its intended results" (Kauffman, 1993, p. 12).

Ever wary of fads, but aware of the attraction that novel approaches hold for policy makers and for those concerned about children with disabilities, Kauffman (1993) warned, "Established programs and policies and those proposed as trustworthy alternatives carry equal burdens of proof of their effectiveness; the different demands no special grace when it is said to be an improvement over the extant" (p. 13). Jumping on bandwagons comprised of unproven practices, Kauffman realized, often results in students not achieving the outcomes they would have attained had evidence-based, effective teaching techniques been implemented.

Advocating that practice be based on research—in other words, that only evidence-based practices be utilized in classrooms—begs a critical question: what practices are, in fact, evidence-based? Although some might argue otherwise (e.g., Gallagher, 2006), we assume that research results are the basis by which a practice can most reliably be deemed effective or evidence-based. But how should research findings be synthesized to determine the effectiveness of a practice? One traditional method has been the literature review. Due to the subjectivity involved in selecting, interpreting, and synthesizing studies, however, literature reviews can yield unreliable and even conflicting conclusions.

Meta-analyses (Glass, 1976; Kavale, 2001) have become popular for synthesizing research findings. By yielding an overall effect size across studies examined, meta-analytic results have allowed the field of special education to make significant advances in our collective understanding of what works (see Forness, Kavale, Blum, & Lloyd, 1997). However, meta-analyses have no established procedure for determining the quality of studies that are synthesized (Cooper & Hedges, 1994). In most meta-analyses, for example, a poorly designed or executed study can influence the overall effect size as much as or more than a well-designed study implemented with rigor. Moreover, no firm guidelines have been established to determine how many studies must be included in a meta-analysis to render the findings reliable. Can a practice be considered effective or evidence-based on the basis of a meta-analysis involving, say, four studies, especially if two of the studies are methodologically flawed?

To address these issues, researchers in other fields have begun to develop and implement criterion-based frameworks for determining effective or evidence-based practices. For example, the Division 12 Task Force of the American Psychological Association (APA) recommended that for a treatment to be considered *well-established*, at least one of two empirical criteria must be met (see Chambless et al., 1998):

1. Two or more good group design experiments must demonstrate that the treatment is either (a) significantly superior to pill, placebo, or other treatment, or (b) equivalent to a previously established treatment.
2. More than nine single-subject design studies demonstrating experimental control and favorably comparing the intervention to another treatment.

Utilizing these criteria, 108 empirically supported treatments have been identified and recommended for practice with adults, and another 37 for children (Chambless & Ollendick, 2001). Other fields have developed and are beginning to implement similar frameworks, most notably the What Works Clearinghouse in general education (see an overview of their review standards at http://www.whatworks.ed.gov/reviewprocess/study_standards_final.pdf).

One prominent difference in the research traditions in special and general education lies in the use of single-subject research. Given the low incidence of many disabilities, single-subject research, a research design that exhibits experimental control, has been prominently applied in special education to examine the effectiveness of many practices (e.g., Lloyd, Tankersley, & Talbott, 1994; Odom & Strain, 2002; Tawney & Gast, 1984). Single-subject research has been utilized less frequently in general education and, accordingly, the What Works Clearinghouse does not consider single-subject research results when determining whether a practice works. For these and other reasons, many scholars in special education saw the need to develop a framework for determining what works in special education that was generated by special educators uniquely for the field of special education.

Under the auspices of the Council for Exceptional Children's Division for Research (CEC-DR), groups of prominent special education scholars with expertise in various research designs authored papers on quality indicators for experimental, single-subject, correlational, and qualitative research that must be present for a study to be considered of high quality in special education. The resulting papers were published in a special issue of *Exceptional Children* (Graham, 2005).

In their article on quality indicators for experimental research, Gersten et al. (2005) suggested that for a practice to be considered evidence-based on the basis of experimental research, the following two criteria must be met:

1. There are at least two *high-quality studies* or four *acceptable quality studies* that support the practice.
2. The weighted effect size is significantly greater than zero.

For a practice to be considered promising, two similar, but less rigorous, criteria must be met:

1. There are at least two *high-quality studies* or four *acceptable quality studies* that support the practice.
2. There is a 20% confidence interval for the weighted effect size that is greater than zero.

High-quality studies must meet all but one of what Gersten et al. deemed Essential Quality Indicators (EQIs) and demonstrate at least four of what were called Desirable Quality Indicators. To be considered acceptable, a study must meet all but one of the EQIs and demonstrate at least one of the Desirable Quality Indicators.

We believe that establishing parameters for high-quality research and criteria for determining evidence-based practice, such as those proposed in the special issue of *Exceptional Children*, are important and necessary endeavors (see Lloyd, Pullen, Tankersley, & Lloyd, 2006). Special educators are indebted to Gersten et al. (2005) for their cogent, ground-breaking work in generating proposed standards for determining evidence-based practices on the basis of experimental research. To build on this foundation, it appears to us that the next step in this process is to pilot or field test the proposed quality indicators by applying them to published studies. We believe that the criteria Gersten et al. proposed for determining whether a practice is evidence-based need to be examined and piloted as well, but it seems that the first logical action is to study the quality indicators themselves, as they determine whether individual studies are of high or acceptable quality, which, using Gersten et al.'s scheme, are prerequisite decisions for determining whether a practice is evidence-based.

Although an initial review of the preliminary quality indicators was conducted at the 2004 Office of Special Education Programs (OSEP) Research Project Director's Meeting (see Odom et al., 2004), it is possible that piloting the quality indicators will identify issues not recognized during the meeting. If meaningful difficulties are encountered during pilot testing, the quality indicators can then be revised before being applied on a larger scale in order to optimize their reliability and validity. Piloting and possibly revising the quality indicators as may be needed seem to reflect the process that Gersten et al. (2005) envisioned when they stated, "It is our intent that this standard for evidenced-based practice and the indicators be reviewed, revised as needed, and adopted by the field of special education" (p. 149). In the following sections, we therefore provide an overview of the EQIs proposed for experimental research, accompanied by a description of our initial attempt to assess the presence of the EQIs in actual research studies.[1]

QUALITY INDICATORS FOR EXPERIMENTAL RESEARCH

In this section, we examine the degree to which the EQIs, presented in Table 10.1, are present in two experimental studies, both examining

---

[1]Examination of the eight Desirable Quality Indicators was not included due to space limitations. Interested readers should contact the lead author for a description of applying the Desirable Quality Indicators.

TABLE 10.1

Essential Quality Indicators Proposed by Gersten et al. (2005)

1. *Describing Participants*

    1.1. Was sufficient information provided to determine/confirm whether the participants demonstrated the disability(ies) or difficulties presented?

    1.2. Were appropriate procedures used to increase the likelihood that relevant characteristics of participants in the sample were comparable across conditions?

    1.3. Was sufficient information given characterizing the interventionists or teachers provided? Did it indicate whether they were comparable across conditions?

2. *Implementation of Intervention and Description of Comparison Conditions*

    2.1. Was the intervention clearly described and specified?

    2.2. Was the fidelity of implementation described and assessed?

    2.3. Was the nature of services provided in comparison conditions described?

3. *Outcome Measures*

    3.1. Were multiple measures used to provide an appropriate balance between measures closely aligned with the intervention and measures of generalized performance?

    3.2. Were outcomes for capturing the intervention's effect measured at the appropriate time?

4. *Data Analysis*

    4.1. Were the data analysis techniques appropriately linked to key research questions and hypotheses? Were they appropriately linked to the unit of analysis in the study?

    4.2. Did the research report include not only inferential statistics but also effect size calculations?

the effects of preventive behavioral programs with school-age children. In the first study, Kamps, Kravits, Stolze, and Swaggart (1999) examined the effect of universal interventions (classroom management, social skills training, peer tutoring in reading) for students with and at risk for emotional and behavioral disorders in urban schools. Target students were drawn from three elementary schools, whereas the students in the control groups attended five elementary schools that had not yet received the interventions (but would the following school year). Results showed that students who had received the intervention had significantly more positive post-test scores than those who did not on rates of engagement, aggression, being out-of-seat, and positive interaction and play at recess; and teacher ratings of requests for attention, being out-of-seat, not following directions, and disruptions. In the second study, Walker, Kavanagh, Stiller, Golly, Severson, and Feil (1998) exposed two cohorts of 46 kindergarten students at-risk for antisocial behavior to a 3-month *First Step to Success* program that consisted of three modules: screening, school intervention, and home intervention. Half of the children in each cohort were randomly assigned to the experimental group and half to a wait-list control group who received the intervention program later in the school year. Results indicated that children in the experimental group made significantly greater improvements than those in the control group on teacher ratings of adaptive behavior, maladaptive behavior, and aggression, as well as proportion of classroom time spent academically engaged. No differences were found in changes in teacher ratings of withdrawn behavior.

Describing Participants

The first of three EQIs in the area of *describing participants* deals with how the disabilities or difficulties of the participants were determined and described. Gersten et al. (2005) stated that, "researchers must move beyond school-district provided labels. Researchers need to provide a definition of the relevant disability(ies) or difficulties and then include assessment results documenting that the individuals included in the study met the requirements of the definition" (p. 154). Furthermore, Gersten et al. indicated that enough information should be provided about participants so that readers can identify the population to which results can be generalized. Such information "may include, but is not limited to" (p. 155): age, race, gender, subsidized lunch status, English language learner status, special education status, comorbid disability status, and scores on academic assessments. Gersten et al. also specified that, as part of describing participants, group difference on salient variables must also be presented. . . . comparability of groups on key demographic variables must be examined ... It is also the researchers' responsibility to document sample comparability at pretest on at least one outcome measure (or key predictor of outcome). (p. 155)

Kamps et al. (1999) identified students as being at risk for EBD using the Systematic Screening for Behavior Disorders (SSBD) (Walker & Severson, 1992) with some modifications. Students in participating schools who were identified as EBD were also automatically included in the study. The gender, special education status, grade level, ethnicity, and SSBD mean adaptive and maladaptive scores were provided for the target and control groups separately. After providing means and ranges for adaptive behavior and maladaptive scores on the SSBD, Kamps et al. reported that, "a *t*-test that was conducted for these variables indicated no statistically significant differences between these groups" (p. 179), indicating that students in both conditions were equivalent. Although Kamps et al. adequately described the sample and demonstrated comparability across conditions, this study appears not to have met a strict application of this first EQI in that "students identified as having EBD were automatically included" (p. 179), apparently regardless of their scores on the SSBD.

Walker et al. (1998) identified participants (two cohorts of kindergarten students with antisocial behaviors considered at-risk for having behavior disorders) using the Early Screening Project procedure (ESP; Walker et al., 1994). This procedure involved three hierarchical stages: (a) teachers ranking their highest five students on externalizing and internalizing behaviors; (b) teachers rating those students on adaptive behavior, maladaptive behaviors, and aggression; and (c) observations of academic engaged time. Scores on standardized instruments for each cohort of participants were provided for teacher ratings of aggression, as well as percentage of academic engaged time. Gender, percentage receiving supplementary school services, percentage minority status, percentage receiving free or reduced lunch, and number of students identified as having a disability were provided for the entire sample (across cohorts). No data related to comparability of participants in the two conditions are presented in the Methods section. However, in a table in the Results section, mean baseline scores on all outcome measures were provided for both conditions. Although baseline differences were not analyzed statistically or discussed, they do not appear to be meaningfully different. We do not believe that Walker et al. meet this EQI due to demographic data not being reported separately by condition. Readers cannot, therefore, determine whether the groups were comparable on key demographic variables.

The second EQI in the category *describing participants* focuses on using procedures to increase the likelihood that participants are comparable across conditions. Specifically, Gersten et al. (2005) indicated that random assignment at some level, be it individual, classroom, or school, is optimal. However, in cases in which random assignment is not feasible, "it is then the researchers' responsibility to describe how participants were assigned to study conditions" (p. 155). Kamps et al. (1999) did not randomly assign participants, schools, or classrooms to conditions, and provided no rationale or description for how students, classrooms, or schools were assigned other than this notation: "The target group was recruited during Year 1 of the program ... with the control group recruited in new schools in the second year" (p. 181). As such, this EQI is not met by the Kamps et al. investigation. Walker et al. (1998) "randomly assigned" participants "to experimental and wait-list control groups," (p. 67) thereby satisfying the second EQI.

The final EQI in the area of *describing participants* deals with the sufficiency of information provided and comparability across conditions for teachers/interventionists. Specifically, Gersten et al. (2005) indicated that relevant characteristics of teachers/intervention providers (e.g., age, gender, race, educational background, professional experience), how intervention providers were assigned to conditions, and evidence of comparability of interventionists must be documented. Kamps et al. (1999) provided no information on the teachers or providers of interventions. This EQI is, therefore, not met. Walker et al. (1998) involved consultants, teachers, and parents in delivering interventions. The backgrounds of the eight program consultants were noted (graduate students, teachers, school counselors, and teacher aides), but no other information was provided (a) about other intervention providers or (b) that could be used to determine how intervention providers were assigned to conditions or whether they were comparable across conditions. Therefore, this EQI is not met in the Walker et al. study either.

Implementation of Intervention and Description
of Comparison Conditions

The first of three EQIs in the category of *implementation of intervention and description of comparison conditions* asks whether the intervention was clearly described and specified along a number of dimensions (including conceptual underpinnings, detailed instructional procedures, teacher actions and behaviors, use of instructional materials, and student behaviors). Kamps et al. (1999) summarized each of the three interventions associated with the prevention program—classroom behavior management, social skills training, and ClassWide Peer Tutoring in reading—noting specific key aspects of each intervention. For instance, the authors indicated that the behavior management system consisted of a point/token system, a level system, a home–school communication system, and other miscellaneous programs for students earning rewards (e.g., desk charts). However, Kamps et al. did not describe the interventions along each of the dimensions noted by Gersten et al. (2005). For example, the conceptual underpinnings of the specific intervention techniques were not discussed nor were detailed instructional procedures described. Moreover, references for ClassWide Peer Tutoring were provided rather than discussing the intervention in detail. Strictly speaking, then, Kamps et al. appear not to have met this EQI because the conceptual underpinnings, detailed instructional procedures, and other specifics regarding the interventions were not discussed in detail.

In addition to a brief overview in the Methods section, Walker et al. (1998) described the interventions or modules utilized (i.e., screening; school intervention, including consultant, teacher, and maintenance phases; and home intervention) in the *First Step to Success* program in detail in an appendix. In this appendix, the authors discussed the instructional procedures and materials, teacher actions and behavior, and student behaviors. Nonetheless it is difficult to clearly determine whether the conceptual underpinnings of the interventions were sufficiently described; they were mentioned in relation to some interventions or aspects of interventions and not others. For example, in discussing the maintenance phase of the classroom intervention, Walker et al. noted that "an attempt is made during this phase to reduce the child's dependence on the program by substituting adult praise for points, reducing the amount of daily feedback given, and making occasional rewards available contingent on exemplary performance" (p. 79). Moreover, the conceptual justification for involving parents, teachers, and peers in the intervention process was provided: "to successfully divert at-risk children and youth from a path leading to antisocial behavior, it is necessary to directly involve the three social agents who have the greatest influence on the developing child's life: parents, teachers, and peers" (Walker et al., p. 78). However, there is no mention of the conceptual underpinnings of other aspects of the intervention program (e.g., the home-based module). Although one could argue that in the strictest sense this EQI was not adequately addressed because some of the conceptual underpinnings may not have been provided, on balance we believe that Walker et al. provided a detailed description of the intervention procedures and touched on each aspect prescribed by Gersten et al. (2005), therefore satisfying this EQI.

The next EQI in the area of *implementation of intervention and description of comparison conditions* is concerned with whether and how the fidelity of implementation was described and assessed. Gersten et al. (2005) stated that, "at the least, researchers should observe the intervention using a checklist of treatment components and record whether the most central aspects of the intervention occurred" (p. 157). Kamps et al. (1999) did assess treatment fidelity. For example, it was noted that 92.5% of students in the target group received classroom behavior management programs, 78.5% received social skills training at least weekly, and 64% received ClassWide Peer Tutoring. How these data were collected, and whether data collection involved observing the frequency with which the central aspects of the interventions occurred, however, was not specified. Given the lack of clarity regarding how treatment fidelity was assessed, it is not clear that this EQI was met in the Kamps et al. study.

Walker et al. (1998) noted that training, monitoring, supervision, and other additional methods (e.g., a daily log completed by consultants on which the student's progress in the program was monitored and recorded) were used to support implementation fidelity. Yet it is not apparent how treatment fidelity was monitored throughout the project. For example, there was no mention of using a checklist of treatment components to determine whether and how often the most critical aspects of the interventions were implemented.

Although Walker et al. briefly discuss how treatment fidelity was supported, they presented no data regarding the degree to which program components were actually implemented. As such, Walker et al. do not meet this EQI.

In regard to the final EQI in this area, which deals with the nature of services provided in the comparison group, Gersten et al. (2005) indicated that, "at a minimum, researchers should examine comparison groups to determine what instructional events are occurring, what texts are being used, and what professional development and support is provided to teachers" (p. 158). Kamps et al. (1999) noted the frequency with which target interventions occurred for students in the comparison group (i.e., 75% received classroom behavior management programs, 30% received social skills training at least once a week, and 0% received ClassWide Peer Tutoring). Furthermore, Kamps et al. stated that, "Although some teachers in the control group had programs in place, no assistance in terms of behavioral consultation or quality enhancements were provided by the research staff" (p. 181). It was not evident whether teachers in comparison schools engaged in any other professional development activities. Although Kamps et al. did not indicate what texts were being used with the comparison students, the focus of the project was not academic in nature and textbook selection may not be relevant. The classroom behavior management programs in comparison classes were described as consisting of "points or reprimand-level systems for many of the students" (p. 181). No mention was made of what type of social skills training programs were utilized with the 30% of comparison students who received these programs at least weekly. We believe that Kamps et al. met the spirit of this EQI by providing data that give the reader a good idea of the relevant conditions in the comparison classrooms. However, it could be argued that this EQI was not met by Kamps et al., as specific information on the behavioral and social programs received by comparison students (e.g., what type of social skills training) was not provided. Walker et al. (1998) provided no description of the instruction received by students assigned to the wait-list control group in their study, thereby not satisfying this EQI.

Outcome Measures

The first of two EQIs in the area of *outcome measures* assesses whether multiple measures were used—specifically, whether at least one measure of generalized performance that is not tightly aligned with the intervention was utilized. Gersten et al. (2005) specified that outcome measures should be "sufficiently broad and robust" (p. 158) to avoid criticisms of teaching to the test and to show that generalizable skills were targeted. Kamps et al. (1999) utilized a number of outcome measures, including direct observations of "students' compliance with academic and behavioral requests; academic engagement; rates of aggression, negative verbal remarks, and out-of-seat behaviors; and positive and negative peer interactions at recess" (p. 179). Teacher ratings of students' behaviors and teacher estimates of frequency of inappropriate behavior were also assessed. Clearly, multiple outcome measures were used. Although exactly what constitutes a measure of generalized performance is difficult to determine conclusively, it appears to us that measures such as direct observations of on-task behavior and teachers' ratings of students' production of acceptable quality work are robust, generalizable, and not tightly aligned with the interventions; and therefore satisfy this EQI. Walker et al. (1998) also utilized multiple outcome measures, collecting five dependent variables: teacher ratings of adaptive, maladaptive, aggressive, and withdrawn behaviors; and direct observations of academic engaged time. Although it could be argued that the interventions targeted just these outcomes, it seems that, as with Kamps et al., the dependent variables employed by Walker et al. are sufficiently robust and generalizable to meet this EQI.

Measuring outcomes at the appropriate time for capturing the interventions' effects is the focus of the second EQI regarding *outcome measures*. Kamps et al. (1999) reported that schools attended by target students were recruited in Year 1 of a 4-year program and began implementing interventions during that year. Comparison schools were recruited in Year 2 (and received interventions in the subsequent year). Outcome measures used in the analyses reported by Kamps et al. occurred in the spring of Year 2 of the project. Timing of outcome measurement appears appropriate in that interventions had been in place for at least a year for target students. It is not clear whether collecting (and analyzing) both pre- and post-test data is required to meet this EQI. Gersten et al. (2005) did not clearly specify that this is necessary, but it may have been implied by this statement, used to qualify a recommendation for collecting follow-up measures: "For some studies, it may be appropriate to collect data at only pre- and post-test" (p. 159). Kamps et al. analyzed only post-test measures, which does not allow for evaluating change in outcome measures. However, it should be noted that Kamps et al. did report that no significant differences existed between target and comparison groups on pre-test measures of two of the dependent variables—adaptive and maladaptive behaviors. Although analyzing pre- and post-test measurements would have been preferable, especially given the nonrandom assignment of participants to conditions, it is unclear whether it is required to satisfy this EQI. We therefore conclude that Kamps et al. did meet it.

Walker et al. (1998) collected baseline data before the intervention program was implemented and again approximately 3 months later after children in the experimental group finished the intervention program (this process was completed with two different cohorts of students in each of 2 years). The pre-test measures served as covariates in the ANCOVA analyses used to assess the impact of the intervention program. Follow-up measures were conducted one (for the first and second cohort) and two (for the first cohort only) years following the intervention. However, it is important to note that the control group received the intervention program after the initial post-test data were collected, so it is difficult to interpret the follow-up measures. It could be argued that follow-up measures involving a control group are a critical evaluation component for a program that aimed to, among other things, "divert antisocial kindergartners from an antisocial behavior pattern during their subsequent school careers" (Walker et al., p. 67). Gersten et al. (2005) recommended that researchers "should consider collecting data at multiple points across the course of the study, including follow-up measures" (p. 159), but do not seem to absolutely require it (in fact, conducting follow-up measures is the focus of a Desirable Quality Indicator). Therefore, it seems to us that Walker et al. meet this EQI.

Data Analysis

The first of two EQIs in the area of *data analysis* asks if a proper rationale was provided for data analysis techniques, linking them to key research questions and hypotheses. Gersten et al. (2005) also emphasized that "appropriate statistical techniques" be used to "adjust for any pretest differences on salient predictor variables" (p. 160). Kamps et al. (1999) did not provide a rationale for the statistical techniques (i.e., ANOVAs) used to compare the observed behaviors and teacher ratings of behavior for students in the target and comparison groups (although ANOVAs appear to be an appropriate procedure to analyze the data). Similarly, although Walker et al. (1998) seem to have used appropriate statistical procedures (ANCOVAs utilizing pre-test scores as covariates), there was no rationale presented for doing so. A loose interpretation of this EQI might suggest that both studies met the criteria, in that an appropriate analysis was used, even if a rationale was not provided. However, Gersten et al. stated that, "a brief rationale for major analyses and for selected secondary analyses is critical" (p. 161), indicating that, strictly speaking, this EQI is not met in either study.

The final EQI requires that effect sizes be calculated in addition to inferential statistics. Kamps et al. (1999) did not present effect sizes. However, the required data for calculating effect sizes (i.e., means and standard deviations on all measures for target and comparison students) are provided. Nonetheless, this EQI is not met in the Kamps et al. study. Effect sizes were calculated by Walker et al. (1998), thereby meeting this EQI.

DISCUSSION OF APPLYING QUALITY INDICATORS

We selected these two studies (i.e., Kamps et al., 1999; Walker et al., 1998) to review based only on the criteria that they examined an outcome in which Kauffman is interested (i.e., prevention of EBD; Kauffman, 1999b), their design is experimental or quasi-experimental, and that they appeared to be of high quality after an initial reading. It should be noted that our cursory search of the literature did not reveal a large selection of experimental and quasi-experimental studies in the EBD literature. It would be very difficult, we believe, to locate more than a few group experimental studies pertaining to the vast majority of behaviorally focused instructional practices. As such, regardless of how quality of relevant experimental studies is assessed, determining whether educational treatments that target the behavioral characteristics of students with EBD are evidence-based on the basis of group experimental studies will likely be problematic. As is true in other areas of special education, more group studies with a control or comparison group are needed to establish what works with students with EBD.

Neither of the studies reviewed was determined to be of high or acceptable quality according the quality indicators and criteria set forth by Gersten et al. (2005). In fact, neither study came close to qualifying as high or acceptable quality. For an experimental study to be considered of high or acceptable quality, it must meet all but one of the EQIs (see Table 10.2 for a summary of the quality indicators that the studies did or did not meet in our judgment). It appears to us that Kamps et al. satisfied three of the 10 EQIs, whereas Walker et al. met five. A number of possible explanations exist as to why so few quality indicators were present in the studies we examined. For example, it may be that the studies we selected happened not to be of very high methodological quality. In other words, perhaps applying the quality indicators correctly identified the designs and procedures of these studies as being unacceptable. We do not think this is the case.

A second possible reason that the studies we reviewed were found to be of unacceptable methodological quality is that the quality indicators are excessively rigorous. There are obvious dangers for setting the bar for methodological rigor too high—meaningful studies are excluded from consideration when determining whether a practice is evidence-based. Of course there are contrasting threats posed by the bar being too low; namely, flawed research would have the same influence for determining effective practice as high-quality studies. It is, then, important that the quality indicators reflect all and only the most essential methodological considerations. It might be prudent to review the current quality indicators to determine whether some considerations can be eliminated or met differently. Although we agree with the spirit of all the proposed quality

TABLE 10.2

Summary of Essential Quality Indicators Met by
Kamps et al. (1999) and Walker et al. (1998).

Quality Indicator	Kamps et al. (1999)	Walker et al. (1998)
Description of participants	No	No
Assignment of participants to condition	No	Yes
Description and comparability of teachers/interventionists	No	No
Intervention clearly described	No	Yes
Treatment fidelity	No	No
Description of instruction in control group	Yes	No
Use of multiple outcome measures	Yes	Yes
Outcomes measured at appropriate times	Yes	Yes
Rationale for data analyses	No	No
Effect sizes reported	No	Yes

indicators, we believe that research reports that do not address all but one EQI (as we interpreted the EQIs) can still be meaningful.

For example, we certainly concur with Gersten et al. (2005) that interventions should be clearly described. Specifically, Gersten et al. required that the intervention be clearly described and specified along a number of dimensions, including conceptual underpinnings, detailed instructional procedures, teacher actions and behaviors, use of instructional materials, and student behaviors. Walker et al. (1998) devoted a separate appendix to describing their multilevel intervention program. In fact, the description of the intervention stood out to us as inordinately extensive. Moreover, Walker et al. touched on each of the aspects of intervention description specified by Gersten et al. However, although the conceptual underpinnings of the project as a whole and of some specific components of the project were briefly noted, the conceptual or theoretical foundations of some aspects of the study, such as the home-based facet, were not discussed at all. Does this mean that the quality indicator for describing the interventions used was not met? It certainly could be argued that Walker et al. did not meet this quality indicator (although we believe that they did). Is it critical, especially in the case of multicomponent intervention programs, that the conceptual underpinnings of each component, as well as detailed instructional procedures, teacher actions and behaviors, use of instructional materials, and student behaviors, be thoroughly described?

A third possibility for why the studies we reviewed did not meet many quality indicators is that we misinterpreted and/or misapplied some of the quality indicators. That is, there were instances in which it was difficult to determine whether particular quality indicators were met and we may have erred in concluding that they were not present in the studies. We see confusion in applying the quality indicators arising from two primary sources: (a) lack of clarity/completeness in reporting the investigations, and (b) lack of clarity/objectivity in describing the quality indicators. Often, when the information reported in the articles was insufficient for us to clearly conclude whether a quality indicator had been addressed, the shortcoming appears to have been a function of reporting, rather than reflecting a significant methodological inadequacy in the studies. For example, neither Kamps et al. (1999) nor Walker et al. (1998) reported a rationale for their data analyses. These skilled and experienced researchers certainly could have justified their analyses, which seem to us to be appropriate; they simply did not report a rationale. Similarly, Walker et al. did not compare the demographic characteristics of the control group with that of the experimental group. Because demographic data were provided for the entire sample, we assume that Walker et al. could have made such a comparison, but simply did not report the data in that form.

It is important to consider that the page limitations of most academic journals and concerns regarding the "readability" of articles often compromise authors' abilities to report every aspect of a research study in detail. It may be problematic to penalize, in a sense, previously published studies for not reporting information that the authors did not know they might be required to present. Perhaps the most obvious example of the difficulty in "retro-fitting" quality indicators to previously conducted studies is the requirement to report effect sizes. Until 2001, the American Psychological Association (APA), the primary writing style of special education scholarship, did not require researchers to report effect sizes. As such, in past decades, very few experimental studies included effect sizes as outcome results, but now it is expected that they be reported. Once special education scholars have disseminated a set of agreed-on quality indicators, future studies should be held accountable for them. However, it seems to us that the treatment of previously conducted and published research is a thorny issue with which the field will have to grapple in determining the evidence-base of practices. It seems ill-advised to discount studies because of incomplete reporting, when the missing information does not represent an important methodological flaw. Yet it is also hazardous to provide reviewers carte blanche in evaluating previously conducted studies and risk lending credence to research that does not meet the high standards set by the field.

The other primary source of difficulty for us in determining whether the quality indicators were met in the studies reviewed were the instances in which we were not clear regarding what was required to meet the quality indicators. For example, one experimental research quality indicator which we had difficulty interpreting deals with measuring outcomes at the appropriate time. Gersten et al. (2005) did not unequivocally state that pre- and post-test measures be analyzed, but they implied that this was to be the case when advocating for the use of follow-up measures ("For some studies, it may be appropriate to collect data at only pre- and post-test," p. 159). It was difficult, then, to determine whether Kamps et al. (1999), who did not analyze pre-test data, met this quality indicator. We also had trouble determining whether EQI 2.3, regarding description of comparison conditions, was met. Gersten et al. stated that a study must "at a minimum, ... examine comparison groups to determine what instructional events are occurring, what texts are being used, and what professional development and support is provided to teachers" (p. 158). Kamps et al. did not describe what textbooks were being used in comparison classrooms, but did provide information on the other elements required. Should the Kamps et al. study have met this EQI? We thought so, but a strong argument could also be made for why it should not. We believe that reviewers of studies will encounter similar problems regarding whether all of the elements of an EQI have to be met for the EQI to be addressed in EQI 1.1 (regarding description and comparability of groups), 1.3 (description and comparability of interventionists/teachers), 2.1 (description of intervention), and 2.3 (the conditions in the comparison group).

Other questions that we anticipate reviewers who apply the EQIs as presented by Gersten et al. (2005) will ask include:

- Under what conditions are nonrandom assignment of participants to groups justifiable? When random assignment is not feasible, what procedures for assigning participants to groups are acceptable? (EQI 1.2)
- Is there a minimum level of implementation fidelity that is acceptable? (EQI 2.2)
- What is meant by a broad and robust outcome measure that is not tightly aligned with the dependent variable? (EQI 3.1)
- Is a rationale for the type of data analysis necessary if it is a standard and appropriate analysis? (EQI 4.1)
- Is presenting data necessary for computing an effect size sufficient for meeting EQI 4.2?

Generating operational definitions of the quality indicators could potentially answer these and other questions that we imagine will be encountered when applying the quality indicators. Indeed, the articles describing the quality indicators were not intended to provide an operational definition of the quality indicators, rather they were intended to create and briefly describe the most critical methodological features of special education research (S. L. Odom, personal communication, April 7, 2006). Accordingly, we recommend that a knowledgeable and broadly representative group of special education scholars construct, pilot, and refine operational definitions for the quality indicators. However, operationally defining the quality indicators will inevitably involve some level of interpretation that will have a decided impact on the meaning and utility of the quality indicators. For example, decisions such as whether studies (a) must rigorously describe the conceptual underpinnings, detailed instructional procedures, teacher actions and behaviors, use of instructional materials, and student behaviors or (b) just describe some of these aspects in moderate depth will likely influence which and how many studies are considered to be of high or acceptable quality.

Operationally defining the quality indicators and having researchers base their reporting of studies on the basis of the established quality indicators and their definitions will undoubtedly remove much of the difficulty we came upon in applying them to existing studies. Indeed, one of the benefits of having a clearly delineated set of broadly endorsed quality indicators will be that researchers' reports (as well as reviewers' evaluations) of studies is guided by the quality indicators, thereby enhancing the methodological quality of the research base in special education. However, we doubt whether all ambiguity can be eliminated from the process. Too much prescriptive detail in the operational definitions stipulating what exactly is required may not allow for the flexibility necessary to apply the quality indicators to the diverse range of experimental research that has been and will be conducted in the field of special education. Still, criteria that are too general or subjective leave too much discretion to the reviewer and will not be applied reliably. Continued piloting and revision of the quality indicators and their operational definitions will be essential in determining the appropriate balance between prescriptive, specific criteria and conceptual, general standards. Moreover, to have confidence in the reliability of the quality indicators, adequate inter-rater reliability must be established across a range of studies. Operationally defining the quality indicators, piloting them, and establishing reliability among raters is needed in order to then identify meaningfully which studies in special education are of sufficiently high quality to be considered in determining which educational practices "work" for students with disabilities.

CONCLUSION

It is important that we reiterate our admiration and gratitude for the pioneering work of Gersten and his colleagues (2005) in developing quality indicators for experimental research, as well as Kamps et al. (1999) and Walker et al. (1999) for conducting such important research that has benefitted children with EBD. As Gersten et al. suggested, now that the quality indicators have been proposed, the next step lies in examining, refining, and ultimately applying them. On the basis of reviewing two studies, we believe that operationally defining the proposed EQIs is needed. Furthermore, we recommend that the quality indicators be examined to determine whether they are too rigorous—especially in relation to how they are "retro-fitted" to existing research. We conjecture that, as currently formulated and as applied to studies conducted in the past, the quality indicators will deem some meaningful studies to be of insufficient quality (probably too often based on reporting deficiencies rather than methodological flaws) and therefore discount them in determining whether a practice is evidence-based.

Regardless of how the quality indicators may or may not be refined in the future, it is imperative that special education researchers reach consensus on quality indicators for group experimental research, and develop a process for determining evidence-based practices in special education on the basis of research that has met the quality indicators (see Cook & Schirmer, 2006; Lloyd et al., 2006). As Kauffman (e.g., Kauffman, 1996a, 1997, 1999a, 2002, 2003, 2004) has consistently recognized and advocated, identifying evidence-based practices and using them as the basis for teacher preparation, professional development, and classroom instruction will allow for meaningful improvements in the outcomes of students with EBD and other disabilities. As with most worthwhile endeavors, accomplishing this goal will be difficult and time-consuming, but—thanks to Kauffman and other pioneers like him who have highlighted the need for a scientifically-based method for determining evidence-based practices—it is one that will ultimately result in improved outcomes and life opportunities for students with disabilities.

REFERENCES

Chambless, D. L., Baker, M. J., Baucom, D. H., Beutler, L., Calhoun, K. S., Crits-Christoph, P., et al. (1998). Update on empirically validated therapies II. *Clinical Psychologist, 51*, 3–16.

Chambless, D. L., & Ollendick, T. H. (2001). Empirically supported psychological interventions: Controversies and evidence. *Annual Review of Psychology, 52*, 685–716.

Cook, B. G., & Schirmer, B. R. (2006). An overview and analysis of the role of evidence-based practices in special education. In B. G. Cook & B. R. Schirmer (Eds.), *What is special about special education: The role of evidence-based practices* (pp. 175–185). Austin, TX: PRO-ED.

Cooper, H., & Hedges, L. V. (Eds.). (1994). *The handbook of research synthesis.* New York: The Russell Sage Foundation.

Forness, S. R., Kavale, K. A., Blum, I. M., & Lloyd, J. W. (1997). Mega-analysis of meta-analyses: What works in special education and related services. *Teaching Exceptional Children, 29,* 4–10.

Gallagher, D. J. (2006). If not absolute objectivity, then what? A reply to Kauffman and Sasso. *Exceptionality, 14,* 91–107.

Gersten, R., Fuchs, L. S., Compton, D., Coyne, M., Greenwood, C., & Innocenti, M. S. (2005). Quality indicators for group experimental and quasi-experimental research in special education. *Exceptional Children, 71,* 149–164.

Glass, G. V. (1976). Primary, secondary, and meta-analysis of research. *Educational Researcher, 5,* 3–8.

Graham, S. (2005). Criteria for evidence-based practice in special education [special issue]. *Exceptional Children, 71.*

Kamps, D., Kravits, T., Stolze, J., & Swaggart, B. (1999). Prevention strategies for at-risk students and students with EBD in urban elementary schools. *Journal of Emotional and Behavioral Disorders, 7,* 178–188.

Kauffman, J. M. (1993). How we might achieve the radical reform of special education. *Exceptional Children, 60,* 6–16.

Kauffman, J. M. (1996a). Think about these things: Gentleness, truth, justice, excellence. *Education and Treatment of Children, 19,* 218–232.

Kauffman, J. M. (1996b). Research to practice issues. *Behavioral Disorders, 22,* 55–60.

Kauffman, J. M. (1997). Caricature, science, and exceptionality. *Remedial and Special Education, 18,* 130–132.

Kauffman, J. M. (1999a). Today's special education and its messages for tomorrow. *Journal of Special Education, 32,* 244–254.

Kauffman, J. M. (1999b). How we prevent prevention of emotional and behavioral disorders. *Exceptional Children, 65,* 448–468.

Kauffman, J. M. (2002). *Education reform: Bright people sometimes say stupid things about education.* Lanham, MD: Scarecrow Education.

Kauffman, J. M. (2003). Reflections on the field. *Education and Treatment of Children, 26,* 4, 325–329.

Kauffman, J. M. (2004). The president's commission and the devaluation of special education. *Education and Treatment of Children, 27,* 307–324.

Kauffman, J. M. & Sasso, G. M. (2006). Toward ending cultural and cognitive relativism in special education. *Exceptionality, 14,* 65–90.

Kavale, K. A. (2001). Meta-analysis: A primer. *Exceptionality, 9,* 177–183.

Lloyd, J. W., Pullen, P., C., Tankersley, M., & Lloyd, P. A. (2006). Critical dimensions of experimental studies and research syntheses that help define effective practices. In B. G. Cook & B. R. Schirmer (Eds.), *What is special about special education* (pp. 136–154). Austin, TX: PRO-ED.

Lloyd, J. W., Tankersley, M., & Talbott, E. (1994). Using single-subject methodology to study learning disabilities. In S. Vaughn & C. Bos (Eds.), *Research issues in learning disabilities: Theory, methodology, assessment, and ethics* (pp. 163–177). New York: Springer-Verlag.

Odom, S. L., Brantlinger, E., Gersten, R., Horner, R. D., Thompson, B., & Harris, K. (2004, Fall). *Quality indicators for research in special education and guidelines for evidence-based practices: Executive summary.* Retrieved February 24, 2006, from http://education.uoregon.edu/grantmatters/pdf/DR/Exec_Summary.pdf.

Odom, S., & Strain, P. S. (2002). Evidence-based practice in early intervention/early childhood special education: Single-subject design research. *Journal of Early Intervention, 25,* 169–179.

Tawney, J. W., & Gast, D. L., (1984). *Single-subject research in special education.* Columbus, OH: Merrill.

Walker, H. M., Kavanagh, K., Stiller, B., Golly, A., Severson, H. H., & Feil, E. G. (1998). First step to success: An early intervention approach for preventing school antisocial behavior. *Journal of Emotional and Behavioral Disorders, 6,* 66–80.

Walker, H. M., & Severson, H. H. (1992). *Systematic screening for behavior disorders: User's guide and technical manual.* Longmont, CO: Sopris West.

Chapter 11

Literacy Interventions for Students with and At-Risk for Emotional or Behavioral Disorders: 1997 to Present

Kathleen Lynne Lane
Sally M. Barton-Arwood
Leslie A. Rogers
E. Jemma Robertson
Peabody College of Vanderbilt University

Students with emotional or behavioral disorders (EBD) have been recognized historically for their social and behavioral deficits. Specifically, these children and youth are noted for impaired relationships with peers and adults; tendencies to misinterpret neutral social interactions (e.g., being bumped into in a hallway) as hostile; and high levels of noncompliance, physical aggression, and verbal aggression. Collectively, these behavior patterns pose tremendous challenges for teachers, peers, parents, and the community as a whole (Kauffman, 2004; Lane, 2004; Walker, Ramsey, & Gresham, 2004).

Over the past 25 years teacher training programs and research agendas addressed the social and behavioral concerns of students with and at-risk for EBD (Lane, Gresham, & O'Shaughnessy, 2002). Teacher training programs have largely emphasized topics such as anger management, conflict resolution, social skills instruction, and classroom management techniques. Although important content areas, the lack of attention to teaching core academic skills to this population is alarming. With the exception of Wallace and Kauffman's (1986) textbook, *Teaching Students With Learning and Behavior Problems* (3rd ed.), university-level text books dedicated towards preparing teachers to work with students with emotional and behavioral disorders published before 2002 addressed academic instruction of these students in a cursory manner. As Kauffman (2003) more recently noted, "Either academic instruction was never sufficiently important to us or we have lost a focus on it. I suspect that it never was sufficiently important in our field and that the lack of focus on instruction in special education has exacerbated the problem" (p. 206).

Similarly, in the research community, advances have been made in how to identify students with these concerns (e.g., the Systematic Screening for Behavior Disorders, SSBD; Walker & Severson, 1992; the Early Screening Project, ESP; Walker, Severson, & Feil, 1995) and how to address their social and behavioral needs (Gresham, Cook, Crews, & Kern, 2004; Landrum, Tankersley, & Kauffman, 2003; Mathur, Kavale, & Quinn, 1998). Yet, it has only been in the last 10 years that increased attention has been devoted to serving these students' academic needs. This is concerning given that students with EBD also exhibit academic deficits.

ACADEMIC CONCERNS

Although most recognized for their social and behavioral concerns, students with or at-risk for EBD across the kindergarten through twelfth-grade span also have broad academic deficits. These academic deficits tend to remain stable over time, with students making minimal to no progress (Lane, 2004). Specifically, compared to their general education peers, students with EBD demonstrate significant academic deficits across the core content areas (e.g., reading, writing, mathematics, and science; Coutinho, 1986; Greenbaum et al.,

1996; Landrum, Tankersley, & Kauffman, 2003; Mattison, Spitznagel, & Felix, 1998; Mattison, Hooper, & Glassberg, 2002; Nelson, Benner, Lane, & Smith, 2004; Reid, Gonzalez, Nordness, Trout, & Epstein, 2004; Scruggs & Mastorpieri, 1986; Wagner, 1995; Wagner & Davis, 2006). Further, research also suggests that students with emotional disturbance (ED), which qualifies a student for special education services per the Individuals with Disabilities Education Act (IDEA, 1997), may exhibit greater academic deficits than students with other high incidence disability categories such as learning disabilities (LD) and mild mental retardation (MMR; Gajor, 1979). However, other investigations have found that academic performance levels of students with ED and LD are parallel (Lane, Carter, Pierson, & Glaeser, 2006). Still others have found that students with ED actually outperform students with LD (Epstein & Cullinan, 1983) and MMR (Wagner, 1995).

Although the nature of differences in academic deficits among students with ED and other high incidence disabilities is unclear, what is clear is that students with ED and EBD in general, do not tend to improve their academic performance levels over time. At best the academic deficits characteristic of this population remain stable over time (Mattison et al., 2002); at worst, they deteriorate (Greenbaum et al., 1996; Nelson et al., 2004). Whereas students with LD improve their reading skills over time, students with ED do not show similar improvement (Anderson, Kutash, & Duchnowski, 2001). In sum, "students with EBD probably experience less school success than any other subgroup of students with or without disabilities" (Landrum et al., 2003, p. 148).

A Negative Path

Collectively, the behavioral, social, and academic deficits characteristic of these students coupled with the lack of progress over time, set the stage for a range of negative outcomes within and beyond the school setting (Lane, 2004; Kauffman, 2005; Walker et al., 2004). Namely, students with EBD have poor school attendance, earn lower grades, have higher failure rates, are more likely to be retained in grade, and have higher school dropout rates than any other disability category (Wagner, 1995; Wagner & Davis, 2006). In addition,

students with EBD also have highly negative postsecondary outcomes, including high rates of unemployment, negative employment experiences, poor community adjustment, substance abuse,
and need for mental health services (Bullis & Yovanoffm, 2006;
Kauffman, 2005; Walker et al., 2005; Zigmond, 2006).

As stated by Kauffman (2004), these concerns are alarming on two
fronts. First, "a substantial portion of children and youth with EBD
receive neither special education nor mental health services; second,
the problems that these children and youth cause themselves and
others are many and expensive" (p. 13). The human and financial
costs associated with failing to adequately serve students with EBD
are substantial, posing individual risks to this group of youngsters as
well as society as a whole (Kauffman, 2004; Quinn & Poirier, 2004).
Thus, we cannot afford to overlook these youngsters' educational
needs. Fortunately, the field of EBD has made substantial progress
in how to address both social and behavioral needs. Now, it is time to
focus our attention on identifying evidenced-based best practices in
the area of academic instruction—particularly academic instruction
in the area of reading given that reading is a seminal skill that allows
a student to access all other learning (Foorman, Francis, Shaywitz,
Shaywitz, & Fletcher, 1997; Lyon, 1996; O'Shaughnessy, Lane,
Gresham, & Beebe-Frankenberger, 2002).

A Focus on Academic Instruction

During the past 25 years the field of EBD has examined the relationship between academic underachievement and problem behaviors
(Ayllon & Roberts, 1974; Hinshaw, 1992; Lane, Gresham, &
O'Shaughnessy, 2002; Lane & Wehby, 2002). Although the exact nature of the relationship between achievement and behavior is yet to
be determined, what is clear is that (a) a relationship does exist and
(b) these variables should not be viewed or treated as mutually exclusive concerns. Kauffman contends that "the first question we need to
ask when confronted by any behavior management problem is
whether the student is being given good academic instruction"
(Kauffman, Mostert, Trent, & Hallahan, 2002). Yet, even though
many people now recognize that learning and behavior are not separate entities, there has been insufficient attention devoted to academic interventions with students with EBD. It is imperative that we

make academic instruction a top priority in the field of EBD, given the academic characteristics of these students and the short- and long-term negative consequences associated with school failure (Wagner & Davis, 2006).

Rather than devoting substantial attention to where students with EBD are educated, it would be wise to focus our efforts on validating effective, efficient methods of instructing students as they progress across the kindergarten through twelfth-grade span (Lane, 2004). As a field, we must identify the most parsimonious methods of teaching our students core skills that will allow them to acquire the skills necessary to meet the academic task demands of the school setting. This is particularly critical in light of the inclusive schools movement (MacMillan, Gresham, & Forness, 1996), which calls for all students with exceptionalities, including those with EBD, to be educated in the general education environment to the maximum extent possible. As Kauffman (2004) noted,

> location, better known as the full inclusion movement, has become more important than instruction to most special educators. The focus on place rather than on instruction is perverse because it short-changes the students we serve. Elevating place over instruction is a serious problem in our field. All is not lost, however, because I have younger colleagues who understand both the primary role of instruction in special education for students with emotional or behavioral disorders and the importance of empirically validated instructional methods. (p. 206)

Fortunately, the field has been making progress in the area of reading as evidenced by the influx of treatment-outcome studies conducted during the past 8 years. Kauffman contends that the emphasis on instruction is apt to continue for two primary reasons. First, researchers are now aware that sound instruction is the "first line of defense in behavior management" (Kauffman, 2005, p. 55). Second, empirical evidence is mounting to support "an instructional approach to behavioral problems" (Kauffman, 2005, p. 55). Thus, the field is attending to the academic and behavioral needs of students with EBD, recognizing the importance of identifying sound instruction procedures to meet these students' total educational needs. At the same time, the field of special education has also issued a call for scientific rigor in educational research.

A Call for Scientific Rigor

Although many teachers are well-trained and have a vast array of teaching experiences with the EBD population, most teachers do not develop effective, feasible instruction procedures (Kauffman, 2004). Therefore, if the goal is to improve the academic skill set of students with EBD, it is necessary for researchers to identify sound instructional practices. In order to identify these practices, empirically sound methodologies must be employed to determine the efficacy of proposed instructional strategies. Fortunately, quality indicators are now available for identifying evidence-based practices using group experimental and quasiexperimental (Gersten et al., 2005) and single-subject (Horner et al., 2005) research methodologies. These indicators include quality indicators such as description of participants and settings; dependent variables; independent variables; comparison or baseline conditions; experimental control; data analysis techniques; as well as internal, external, and social validity. Thus, although it appears that establishing and implementing evidenced-based practices is a "Herculean" task (Kauffman, 2004; Tankersley, Landrum, & Cook, 2004)—particularly in light of the popularity of anti-scientific views (Kauffman, 2003)—the bar is set. It is our responsibility as researchers to meet the call of improving the quality and quantity (Sasso, 2003), of treatment-outcome studies by designing, implementing, and evaluating intervention studies that adhere to these indicators. In the words of Kauffman (2004), it "is time to recognize the importance of scientific rigor in our field" (p. 12).

Purpose

The purpose of this chapter is to respond to James Kauffman's call for scientific rigor in how we support and improve the literacy skills of students with or at risk for EBD. This chapter evaluates systematically the current knowledge base using the quality indicators provided by Gersten et al. (2005) and Horner et al. (2005) as guideposts. Specifically, this chapter provides (a) a systematic review of the reading instruction studies conducted since the passage of IDEA 1997 and (b) recommendations for further developing interventions to improve the literacy skills of students with and at-risk for EBD.

METHOD

Article Selection

We conducted a systematic literature review to identify refereed intervention articles published between 1997 and 2005 that focused on reading and writing interventions for students with or at-risk for emotional or behavioral disorders. Electronic searches were conduced in psychology and education (Psyc INFO, ProQuest, and Education full-text) data bases using all derivatives and combinations of these three sets of terms (a) reading, literacy, academic, or writing; (b) intervention, treatment, study, training, or instruction; and (c) emotional or behavioral disorders, emotionally disturbed, antisocial, problem behavior, or aggression. Next, independent hand searches were conducted by the first and second authors in *Behavioral Disorders* and *Journal of Emotional and Behavioral Disorders*. A total of 23 articles were identified and read in entirety for possible inclusion in this review.

Inclusion Criteria

Articles in this review met the following criteria: (a) described school-based literacy interventions focusing on either reading or writing skills that were implemented by an interventionist, teacher, or peer; (b) reported academic or academic-related outcome measures; (c) involved school-aged students with or at-risk for emotional or behavioral disorders, and (d) were published in a peer-reviewed journal between 1997 and 2005. These are the same review criteria used by Lane (2004) in a more comprehensive review of all academic interventions (reading, writing, and mathematics) implemented with this population.

School-Based Literacy Interventions.   School-based literacy interventions referred to reading or writing interventions conducted in a school setting. Interventions included in this review involved instruction led by an interventionist, teacher, or peer in either reading or writing skills. Interventions involving environmental modifications (e.g., Ervin et al., 2000), choice (Kern, Bambara, & Fogt, 2002), task modifications (Miller, Gunter, Venn, Hummel, & Wiley, 2003;

Umbreit, Lane, & Dejud, 2004), assignment demands (e.g., Teeple & Skinner, 2004), and self-regulatory procedures (e.g., Levendoski & Cartledge, 2000) were omitted, as were packaged interventions involving academic and behavioral components (e.g., self-monitoring, task modifications) if the design did not allow the impact of the academic component to be evaluated separate from that of the behavioral component (e.g., Kamps, Kravits, Rauch, Kamps, & Chung, 2000; Kamps, Kravits, Stolze, & Swaggart, 1999; Penno, Frank, & Wacker, 2000). Interventions including reinforcement procedures to motivate participation were included. Finally, the interventions could have been conducted in general education, self-contained classrooms, self-contained schools, or alternative schools. Interventions implemented in juvenile detention centers or clinics (e.g., Malmgren & Leone, 2000) were excluded.

Outcome Measures. All studies must also have reported academic (e.g., correct words read per minute) or academic-related (e.g., task engagement) outcome measures as part of the outcome data. Although many of the studies included academic and behavioral outcome measures; studies were excluded if they only reported behavioral outcomes and did not include academic measures. Studies that described outcomes in narrative context without including actual data (e.g., Edwards & Chard, 2000) were also excluded.

School-Age Students with Behavioral Issues. Student participants included kindergarten through twelfth-grade students who met one of the following behavioral categories that have been used in previous reviews of the EBD literature (Lane, 2004; Lane, Umbreit, & Beebe-Frankenberger, 1999): (a) at-risk for behavioral problems; (b) emotionally disturbed (Individuals with Disabilities Education ACT [IDEA], 1997), which qualifies students to receive special education services; (c) emotional or behavioral disorders (EBD), a more inclusive term to describe students with behavioral concerns; (d) psychiatric diagnoses specified in the *Diagnostic and Statistical Manual of Mental Health* (*DSM–TR*, American Psychiatric Association, 2001) such as oppositional defiant disorder (ODD) and conduct disorder (CD); (e) EBD and another disability specified in IDEA (e.g., learning disability, other heath impairment, or speech and language disorder) except for students with a dual diagnosis of mental retardation as these students typically participate in life skills curricula rather than traditional core curricula; (f) a general behavioral concern (e.g., noncompliance) and attention-deficit/hyperactivity disorder (ADHD), a group of students with attentional and behavioral concerns that place them at heightened risk for behavior disorders; and (g) a psychiatric (e.g., ODD, CD) or educational (ED) condition that co-occurs with ADHD. If a study included student participants that did and did not meet the inclusion criteria, the study was included provided that outcome data were reported in a manner that the effects on the target student could be identified. If data were presented in a format that did not allow the effects on students with or at-risk for EBD to be identified, the study was excluded (e.g., O'Connor & Padeliadu, 2000).

Time Frame. Articles were included if they were published in referred journals between 1997 and 2005. The intent was two-fold. First we sought to examine the quality of intervention studies with this population due to the emphasis on (a) access to and success for all students in the general curriculum, and (b) implementation of research-based practices in schools as stipulated in IDEA 1997 and the Individuals with Disabilities Education Improvement Act (IDEIA, 2004). Second, we wanted to avoid excessive overlap with other review articles (e.g., Coleman & Vaughn, 2000; Lane, 2004; Ruhl & Berlinghoff, 1992). Sources that were not subject to the peer review process (e.g., dissertation, book chapters, and unpublished manuscripts) were also excluded to maintain high inclusion standards and allow valid inferences to be drawn about the quantity and quality of intervention studies devoted to literacy skills of students with or at-risk for EBD.

Coding Procedures

Articles that met the inclusion criteria were read by all three authors and coded for the following variables: (a) purpose; (b) participant characteristics (number, gender, ethnicity, age, grade, intervention window [within: through age 8; beyond: beyond age 8, Kazdin (1987)], classification as just described, instructional setting, and participant selection criteria); (c) intervention and baseline/ comparison conditions (descriptions, setting, interventionist, dosage, treatment integrity, and baseline or comparison group); (d) measures (outcomes and social validity); (e) experimental design and analysis (group or single case methodology; analysis procedures; and generalization and maintenance); (f) outcomes. These coding categories were developed based on criteria established to identify evidence-based practice in single-subject research (Horner et al., 2005) and quality indicators for group experimental and quasi-experimental (Gersten et al., 2005) in special education.

RESULTS

Of the 25 articles read, 68% ($n = 17$) met inclusion criteria and were coded subsequently by all four authors. Any coding discrepancies were discussed and consensus obtained. The 17 articles contained data on 246 participants. All interventions focused on reading skills and none on writing instruction. This chapter reviews the participant characteristics, intervention, outcome measures, experimental design and analysis, and outcomes of literacy interventions for students with or at-risk for EBD.

Participant Characteristics and Instructional Setting

Only two articles were published between 1997 and 1999 (Lane, 1999; Skinner, Cooper, & Cole, 1997) followed by six articles in the next 3-year period (2000–2002; Babyak, Koorland, & Mathes, 2000; Dawson, Venn, & Gunter, 2000; Falk & Wehby, 2001; Lane, O'Shaughnessy, Lambros, Gresham, & Beebe-Frankenberger, 2001; Lane, Wehby, Menzies, Gregg, Doukas, & Munton, 2002; Scott & Shearer-Lingo, 2002) and nine in the final 3-year period (2003–2005; Barton-Arwood, Wehby, & Falk, 2005; Hale, Skinner, Winn, Oliver, & Allin, 2005; Nelson, Benner, & Gonzalez, 2005; Nelson, Stage, Epstein, & Pierce, 2005; Spencer, Scruggs, & Mastropieri, 2003; Strong, Wehby, Falk, & Lane, 2004; Trout, Epstein, Mickelson, Nelson, & Lewis, 2003; Wehby, Falk, Barton-Arwood, Lane, & Cooley, 2003; Wehby, Lane, & Falk, 2005). These 17 studies included 246 student participants, with the majority of participants (78. 05%; $n = 192$) being male. The majority of the participants were Caucasian; however, ethnicity was reported in only 10 studies. Students ranged in age from

5 to 14 years of age, with the majority of studies ($n = 10$) intervening during the window of opportunity to prevent the development of anti-social behavior tendencies (Kazdin, 1987; Walker et al., 2004). Five of these studies involved kindergarten students (Falk & Wehby, 2001; Nelson et al., 2004; Nelson et al., 2005; Trout et al., 2003; Wehby et al., 2005). In six studies intervention occurred beyond the window of prevention; four of the six focused on middle school students (Hale et al., 2005; Scott & Shearer-Lingo, 2002; Spencer et al., 2003; Strong et al., 2004). One study included some participants within and some participants beyond the window, intervening with students in second through fourth grade (Wehby et al., 2003).

One hundred and one (41.06%) students were at risk for emotional or behavioral disorders; 77 (31.30%) had ED as either a primary or secondary handicapping condition; 11 (4.47%) were labeled EBD or this label was inferred based on the school that they attended (e.g., self-contained schools for students with EDB; Scott & Shearer-Lingo, 2002; Wehby et al., 2003); 21 (8.54%) were labeled EBD and also had disabilities specified in IDEA (e.g., Specific Learning Disability, Speech and Language Impairment, or Other Health Impaired); 6 (2.44%) were typical students who were controls; and 30 (12.20%) had a classification of ED or EBD with either a psychiatric or educational condition, although in this study the number of students in each category was not stated (Spencer et al., 2003).

Students were educated in a range of instructional settings including general education classrooms ($n = 170$, 69.11%; Lane, 1999; Lane et al., 2001; Lane et al., 2002; Nelson et al., 2004; Nelson et al., 2005; Trout et al., 2003); resource rooms ($n = 4$, 1.63%; Dawson et al., 2000); self-contained classrooms on general education campuses ($n = 10$, 4.07%; Falk & Wehby, 2001; Wehby et al., 2005); and day schools serving students with EBD ($n = 55$, 22.36%; Babyak et al., 2000; Barton-Arwood et al., 2005; Skinner et al., 1997; Spencer et al., 2003; Strong et al., 2004; Wehby et al., 2003). In two studies, it was not possible to determine whether the students were in self-contained classroom on general education campuses or in day schools dedicated to students with EBD ($n = 7$, 2.85%; Hale et al., 2005; Scott & Shearer-Lingo, 2002).

Intervention

Eleven studies examined the efficacy of specific curricular programs such as Torgesen and Bryant's (1994) *Phonological Awareness Training for Reading* (Lane, 1999; Lane et al., 2001; Wehby et al., 2005), *Stepping Stones to Reading* (Nelson et al., 2004; Nelson et al., 2005), *Great Leaps* with direct instruction (Trout et al., 2003), *Teach Your Child to Read in 100 Easy Lessons* (Scott & Shearer-Lingo, 2002), John Shefelbine's *Phonics Chapter Books* (Lane et al., 2002), and Becker and Carnine's (1980) *Corrective Reading and Repeated Readings* (Strong et al., 2004). The remaining two curricula, *Open Court* (Wehby et al., 2003) and *Horizons* (Barton-Arwood et al., 2005), were used in conjunction with *Peer Assisted Learning Strategies* (PALS; Fuchs et al., 2001). Two studies used peer tutoring interventions in isolation (Falk & Wehby, 2001; Spencer et al., 2003). The other four studies focused on listening interventions (Hale et al., 2005; Scott & Shearer-Lingo, 2002), reading previews (Dawson et al., 2000), and story mapping (Babyak et al., 2000).

In eight studies, at least part of the intervention was delivered in the instructional setting. In seven studies, the entire intervention was implemented in a separate location such as a separate classroom, library, conference room, or cafeteria (Babyak et al., 2000; Hale et al., 2005; Lane, 1999; Lane et al., 2001; Skinner et al., 1997; Scott & Shearer-Lingo, 2002; Trout et al., 2003). The intervention location was not described in two studies (Nelson et al., 2004; Nelson, 2005).

University personnel (research assistants, experimenters, and primary investigators) conducted the interventions in the majority of studies. In five studies, school personnel (e.g., classroom teacher or paraprofessionals) conducted part (Barton-Arwood et al., 2005; Strong et al., 2004; Wehby et al., 2003) or all (Dawson et al., 2000; Lane et al., 2002; Spencer et al., 2003) of the intervention.

Intervention dosage was either stated or sufficient information provided to compute dosage in eight (47.06%) studies (Babyak et al., 2000; Barton-Arwood et al., 2005; Lane, 1999; Lane et al., 2001; Lane et al., 2002; Spencer et al., 2003; Trout et al., 2003; Wehby et al., 2005). In nine other studies partial information was provided; however, it was not possible to determine the actual intervention length due to insufficient information (e.g., session lengths that were presented as a range rather than a fixed time interval; Falk & Wehby,

2001; Hale et al., 2005; Nelson et al., 2005; Strong et al., 2004). In one case, intervention dosage was not mentioned (Skinner et al., 1997). For the studies that did report dosage, the length of intervention time ranged from 5.83 (Spencer et al., 2003) to 47.5 hours (Trout et al., 2003), with a median intervention time of 15 hours.

Treatment integrity was mentioned and reported in the majority ($n = 13$, 76.47%) of studies with checklists and tapes (Hale et al., 2005; Skinner et al., 1997) being the most common type of method used to collect treatment integrity data. Several studies also evaluated treatment integrity from multiple perspectives (e.g., self-evaluations and outside observers; Lane et al., 2002; Nelson et al., 2004; Nelson et al., 2005; Wehby et al., 2005). Three studies mentioned treatment integrity, but did not report the level of fidelity (Scott & Shearer-Lingo, 2002; Spencer et al., 2003; Trout et al., 2003). Only one study neither mentioned nor reported treatment integrity (Dawson et al., 2000).

Description of baseline or comparison group practices was reported in all but two studies (Lane et al., 2001; Lane et al., 2002). However, the level of precision varied greatly from general descriptions (e.g., Nelson et al., 2004; Spencer et al., 2003; Trout et al., 2003) to reporting the dosage of current practices in the baseline phase (e.g., Wehby et al., 2005).

Measures

As stated in the inclusion criteria, all 17 studies reported academic (e.g., letter naming fluency, correct words read per minute) or academic-related (e.g., task engagement) outcome measures. Other studies also reported collateral effects on behaviors such as inappropriate behavior (e.g., Barton-Arwood et al., 2005; Wehby et al., 2003). Four studies included behavioral (direct observations of disruption and teacher-completed behavior rating scales) and social measures (e.g., negative social interactions; Lane, 1999; Lane et al., 2001; Lane et al., 2002; Nelson et al., 2005).

Social validity data were assessed and reported in six (35.29%) studies. Common measures included the *Intervention Rating Profile-15* (IRP-15; Martens, Witt, Elliott, & Darveaux, 1985), the *Children's Intervention Rating Profile* (CIRP; Witt & Elliott, 1985; e.g., Lane, 1999; Lane et al., 2001; Lane et al., 2002; Wehby et al., 2005),

general surveys (Babyak et al., 2000; Spencer et al., 2003), and interviews (Lane, 1999; Lane et al., 2001; Wehby et al., 2005).

Eleven studies (64.71%) explicitly stated the role of the person(s)
conducting the assessments. In all but one study (Dawson et al.,
2000), university personnel administered the assessments.

Experimental Design and Analysis

The majority ($n = 12$) of studies used single case methodology to examine intervention outcomes. Multiple baseline designs were the
most commonly used methodology followed by alternating treatments (Dawson et al., 2000; Hale et al., 2005) and multi-element
(Skinner et al., 1997) designs. As expected, the most common
method of data analysis was visual inspection techniques followed by
mean and slope comparisons (Babyak et al., 2000; Barton-Arwood et
al, 2005; Hale et al., 2005; Lane et al., 2001; Lane et al., 2002; Strong
et al., 2004; Wehby et al., 2003; Wehby et al., 2005) and effect size
calculations (Hale et al., 2005; Lane et al., 2001; Lane et al., 2002;
Strong et al., 2004). Other methods of analysis included percentage
of non-overlapping data points (Babyak et al., 2000) and
goals-to-achievement calculations (Lane et al., 2001). Only three of
the single case studies (Lane et al., 2001; Lane et al., 2002; Wehby et
al., 2005) examined maintenance of effects, and none examined
generalization of responses, behaviors, or settings.

Of the five studies using group designs, two employed a pre-post
design (Nelson et al., 2004; Nelson et al., 2005), one used a
pre-post-follow-up design with teacher as the unit of random assignment (Lane, 1999), one used a crossover design (Spencer et al.,
2003), and one used a group hybrid quasi-experimental design
(Trout et al., 2003). Data analysis techniques included analysis of
variance (Lane, 1999; Nelson et al., 2004; Nelson et al., 2005;
Spencer et al., 2003) and effect size calculations (Lane, 1999;
Spencer et al., 2003; Trout et al., 2003)—some of which included
95% confidence bands (Nelson et al., 2004; Nelson et al., 2005). Only
one group design study examined maintenance of effects over time
(Lane, 1999), and none examined generalization of responses,
behaviors, or settings.

Outcomes

Although the studies reviewed were few in number ($n = 17$), academic instruction in literacy skills was associated with improved literacy skills. However, a consistent pattern was not observed with respect to collateral effects on behavior. We highlight briefly key outcomes associated with various intervention foci.

Studies examining the impact of specific curricular programs produced improved early literacy skills (e.g., Lane et al., 2001; Lane et al., 2002; Nelson et al., 2004; Nelson et al., 2005; Trout et al., 2003; Scott & Shearer-Lingo, 2002), increased on-task behavior (Scott & Shearer-Lingo, 2002), decreased disruptive classroom behavior (Lane et al., 2001; Lane et al., 2002), and improved social interactions in recreational settings (Lane et al., 2001; Lane et al., 2002). However, some studies did not produce consistent increases on all measures of literacy skills (Wehby et al., 2005), particularly in studies involving junior high students (Strong et al., 2004). Further, of the group design studies, one did not produce consistent effects on social outcomes (Lane, 1999) and another showed only small behavioral improvements for students in the treatment group with greater gains exhibited by students in the control condition (Nelson et al., 2005).

Two studies examined the utility of *Open Court* (Wehby et al., 2003) and *Horizons* (Barton-Arwood et al., 2005) when implemented in conjunction with *Peer Assisted Learning Strategies* (PALS; Fuchs et al., 2001). The former study produced moderate improvements in literacy measures, slight improvements in attending, and no improvements in inappropriate behavior. The latter study yielded improvements in literacy measures, with some decreases in total inappropriate classroom behavior (Barton-Arwood et al., 2005).

Peer tutoring interventions implemented in isolation from packaged curricula were associated with modest improvements for the majority of students in letter-sound and blending skills (Falk & Wehby, 2001), increases in quizzes and multiple choice test scores (Spencer et al., 2003), and higher levels of engagement (Spencer et al., 2003).

Only three studies examined reading comprehension as an outcome measure (Babyak et al., 2000; Hale et al., 2005; Strong et al.,

2004). A story mapping intervention improved the comprehension skills of all participants with outcome measures including story retells and passage comprehension probes (Babyak et al., 2000). Strong and colleagues (2004) used a combination of *Corrective Reading* and repeated readings to produce slight increases in four out of six participants. An intervention focusing on listening interventions found that listening only and listening while reading produced higher comprehension levels than silent reading (Hale et al., 2005) as measured by level and rate of passage comprehension.

Two studies focused on reading accuracy (Dawson et al., 2000; Skinner et al., 1997). Reading previews, whether conducted by a teacher or a computer, produced the highest number of words and the percentage of words read compared to no modeling. However, the teacher modeling technique produced greater levels of improvement than the computer modeling method (Dawson et al.). Listening previews yielded greater increases in rate of reading accuracy as compared to silent reading previews (Skinner et al., 1997).

Although the magnitude of change varied across studies, the interventions were largely effective in producing the desired changes on academic outcome measures. Further, of the six studies examining collateral effects of behavior (Barton-Arwood et al., 2005; Lane, 1999; Lane et al., 2001; Lane et al., 2002; Nelson et al., 2005; Wehby et al., 2003), three studies (all of which used single case methodology) reported that improvements in reading were associated with some changes in social and/or behavioral performance levels (e.g., Barton-Arwood et al., 2005; Lane et al., 2001; Lane et al., 2002). However, both group designed studies that used rating scales to assess behavioral performance (Lane, 1999; Nelson et al., 2005) as well as one single case study did not report consistent, collateral effects on behavior.

DISCUSSION AND IMPLICATIONS

Students with and at-risk for EBD pose significant challenges to the educational system, due to their limited academic skills, behavioral excesses and deficits, and limited social competencies. Although the field of EBD has made progress in meeting their behavioral and social needs, less attention has been devoted to meeting their academic needs—particularly in terms of literacy skills (Lane, 2004; Kauffman, 2005). This lack of attention to literacy skills is concerning given that reading is a seminal skill that enables students to access all other learning (Lyon, 1996) and writing is an essential skill for communicating information to others (Tindal & Crawford, 2002). Given that students with EBD have poorer academic skills than their typically developing peers and other students with high-incidence disabilities, and further that their skill sets do not appear to improve over time (Nelson & Benner, 2005), the field of EBD needs to develop the instructional knowledge base. In doing so, it is important for rigorous investigations to be conducted using the proposed quality indicators (Gersten et al., 2003; Horner et al., 2005) to ensure that accurate conclusions are drawn about intervention outcomes with the goal of providing evidenced-based practices for practitioners.

In this review, a number of concerns are illustrated. First, it is apparent that although still in fledgling stage, the knowledge base about reading interventions is developing. In contrast, the knowledge base about how to teach writing skills to students with EBD is quite lacking. Second, additional rigor is needed when describing the population of students we are attempting to serve. Third, greater precision is necessary when describing both the intervention practices as well as the baseline or comparison conditions. Fourth, the measures used to evaluate intervention outcomes demands improvement. Finally, if the goal is to draw causal inferences about treatment-outcomes studies, the methodologies and data analysis techniques utilized need to be rigorous enough to move beyond associations. We discuss each of these concerns and provide recommendations for future intervention efforts.

Intervention Focus

All 17 studies reviewed focused on reading interventions that emphasized base-level skills (e.g., decoding, fluency building), whereas few focused on comprehension skills (Babyak et al., 2000; Hale et al., 2005; Strong et al., 2004). In addition, the majority of studies ($n = 10$) were conducted during the early elementary years when behaviors are most amenable to change (Kazdin, 1987). Of all the intervention studies, only four studies took place with middle school students (Hale et al., 2005; Scott & Shearer-Lingo, 2002; Spencer et al., 2003; Strong et al., 2004) and none were conducted at the high school level. Although intervening at the high school poses unique challenges (e.g., high rates of absenteeism; Lane et al., 2006), it is imperative that empirically validated techniques be identified to develop literacy skills of secondary students with EBD (Lane & Carter, in preparation). Given the negative postsecondary experiences awaiting most students with EBD, the field of EBD must make literacy instruction a priority across the kindergarten through twelfth-grade age span and include a focus on the full range of reading skills.

In addition, intervention efforts should target writing as well as reading domains. The value of reading is clear and a number of studies have been conducted to determine how to teach students with EBD to become more skilled readers, with some studies examining the corresponding effects on behavior (Barton-Arwood et al., 2005; Lane, 1999; Lane et al., 2001; Lane et al., 2002; Nelson et al., 2005; Wehby et al., 2003). Yet, there were no published instructional interventions focused on teaching students with and at-risk for EBD how to write. This is a serious omission given that writing is a common method for communicating what one learns and can also be a powerful tool for analyzing one's feelings and behavior patterns (Tindal & Crawford, 2002).

Moving forward, we recommend that the field attend to Kauffman's call for understanding "the primary role of instruction in special education for students with emotional or behavioral disorders and the importance of empirically validated instructional methods ..." (Kauffman, 2003, p. 206). Instruction—particularly in literacy skills—should be one of the top priorities for educators. Accordingly, researchers must conduct rigorous, systematic investigations across the developmental continuum (Bullis & Walker, 1994) to identify the most effective, efficient methods of developing both basic and sophisticated academic skill sets for students with and at-risk for EBD. In doing so, we must first have clarity on the population we are attempting to serve.

Population of Students

There are a variety of terms used to describe students with and at-risk for EBD including those from the educational (e.g., ED), research (e.g., internalizing and externalizing), and psychiatric (e.g., CD, ODD) communities. This lack of consistent terminology used across the communities intended to serve these youngsters creates challenges for professionals and researchers alike (Lane, 2004). Given the breadth of terms used to describe students with behavior concerns and the lack of precision with which these labels are assigned (Gresham, MacMillan, & Bocian, 1998), a recommendation has been made to focus on a broader range of students (e.g., EBD rather than only ED) when conducting treatment-outcome studies (Lane, 2004). Although the goal of avoiding false negatives is a sound decision in prevention research (Walker & Severson, 2002), it also demands a high degree of precision when reporting intervention outcomes.

Specifically, it is critical that sufficient detail be provided regarding both participant selection criteria and the characteristics of participants (Gersten et al., 2005; Horner et al., 2005). These two indicators are essential to allow for precise replication, which is necessary to establish external validity. Further, these indicators are also necessary to draw accurate conclusions about the populations, settings, and other circumstances with which intervention efforts are apt to be successful. If either of these indicators are lacking in detail, it becomes difficult to establish the external validity of the findings.

Intervention Practices and Baseline or Comparison Conditions

Another concern identified in this review was the lack of detail offered in describing both intervention practices and baseline or comparison conditions. Study authors rarely provided a thorough description of the interventions that included descriptions of the setting, interventionist, dosage, and treatment fidelity data. The absence of this information hampers future replication efforts, and limits readers' ability to draw accurate conclusions about intervention outcomes and generalize findings to other circumstances. In short, the absence of this information limits the internal and external validity of the studies (Lane, Bocian, & MacMillan, 2004).

The same is true when describing baseline or comparison conditions. In single case design, the assumption is that only one change is made between baseline and intervention phases—namely, the intervention (Lane, Wolery, Riechow, & Rogers, in press). If the baseline condition is not described in sufficient detail, it may not be possible to determine whether the intervention was the only change between phases, which in turn limits any inference about a functional relationship. Similarly, if comparison conditions in group design studies lack sufficient detail it is not possible to determine whether treatment contamination exists or even to understand to what the intervention is being compared. Gersten, Baker, and Lloyd (2000) contend that, although far from glamorous, the comparison condition must be described in sufficient detail (e.g., Wehby et al., 2005) to clearly understand and interpret the effects of the intervention.

Moving forward, we recommend that the field of EBD afford greater precision when describing the intervention condition—particularly when describing intervention dosage and treatment fidelity. We also recommend that the field attend to the issues of baseline descriptions in single case research (Horner et al., 2005) and descriptions of control or comparison conditions when conducting quasi-experimental and experimental group studies (Gersten et al., 2005) for the reasons just discussed.

Outcome Measures

Another area that requires additional attention is outcome measures. In group design studies, it is important to include multiple measures to assess both the immediate, closely aligned effects of the intervention as well as generalized intervention outcomes (Gersten et al., 2005). In addition, it is important that outcome measures (a) have psychometrically sound properties with good evidence of reliability (e.g., coefficient alpha reliabilities of .6 or greater) and validity (e.g., concurrent validity); (b) be administered at the correct time to detect differences by research assistants blind to intervention conditions; and (c) include documentation of interscorer agreement. Yet, too often, researchers spend insufficient time in selecting and developing outcome measures (Gersten et al., 2005; Klienbaum et al., 1998). The group design studies in this review often selected psychometrically sound instruments (e.g., *Behavior and Emotional Rating Scale* [BERS; Epstein & Sharma, 1998]; *Social Skills Rating System* [SSRS; Gresham & Elliott, 1990]). However, information regarding the reliability, validity, and interscorer agreement was seldom reported. It may be that some of indicators are not included in the group design studies due to concerns about the amount of text space required to report psychometric information.

These same omissions were not as evident in the single case studies. Core quality indicators for single case designs recommend dependent variables must be (a) operationally defined with great precision, (b) assessed with a procedure that yields a quantifiable index, (c) measured frequently over time, (d) include a report of interobserver agreement of 80% or Kappa of 60% or greater, and (e) socially valid behaviors (Horner et al., 2005; Wolf, 1978). The studies in this review largely adhered to each of these indicators.

Methodology and Data Analysis

A final concern pertains to methodology and data analysis. If the goal is to draw definitive, causal conclusions about treatment outcome studies, it is essential that single case investigations include sufficient demonstrations and replications to establish generalizability of treatment outcomes. There is also a call for replications across three or more research teams (Horner et al., 2005). When using single case methodologies, we recommended that caution be taken to establish experimental control and conduct sufficient replications to establish internal and external validity (Johnston & Pennypacker, 1993).

When employing group designs, randomized trials with students as the unit of random assignment appear to be the gold standard. As is evident from this review, there are few group design studies (e.g., Lane, 1999; Nelson et al., 2004; Nelson et al., 2005; Spencer et al., 2003; Trout et al., 2003), with only three randomly assigning at the student level (Nelson et al., 2004; Nelson et al., 2005; Trout et al., 2003). Moving forward, we recommend that researchers consider not only the rigor of the group design, but also the rigor of the data analysis techniques they employ (e.g., confidence bands for effect sizes; Nelson et al., 2004; Nelson et al., 2005). It is particularly important that the analysis techniques be appropriately linked to research questions, taking into consideration the appropriate unit of analysis (Gersten et al., 2005; Klienbaum, Kupper, Muller, & Nizam, 1998). As with single case methodology, it is imperative that internal and external validity be established to draw accurate conclusions about intervention outcomes.

SUMMARY

> Is special education for students with EBD special? It certainly is. And it can become even more special if we take full advantage of the currently available technology of behavioral and instructional intervention. Indeed, we think it has the potential to become extraordinary. (Landrum et al., 2003, p. 154)

To reiterate, it is important that we continue to develop the instructional techniques we use to teach literacy skills to students with and at-risk for EBD. Although the knowledge base is building, it is important that it be grounded in greater methodological rigor in accordance with the recommendations set forth by Gersten et al. (2005) when conducting experimental and quasi-experimental studies and Horner et al. (2005) when using single case methodologies. In doing so, we challenge the field to move beyond base skill development and learn how to meet the academic needs of secondary students with and at-risk for EBD. Given the negative outcomes for students with and at-risk for EBD within and beyond the school setting, it would be irresponsible to ignore this challenge. We must focus on the primacy of academic instruction (Kauffman, 2003), a clear, ambitious, yet possible standard set by James Kauffman, a true leader in the field of EBD.

Sasso (2003) captured our sentiment when he said "this is an appropriate time for us to recognize his [Jim Kauffman's] contributions and to thank him for his intelligences, persistence, courage, collegiality, and friendship" (p. 210). To this we would add our thanks for the standards Kauffman has set for those of us who are still in the novice stage of our careers and for the gifts of passion, commitment, and kindness.

REFERENCES

American Psychiatric Association. (2001). *Diagnostic and statistical manual of mental disorders* (DSM-IV-TR) (5th ed.). Washington, DC: Author.

Anderson, J. A., Kutash, K., & Duchnowski, A. J. (2001). A comparison of the academic progress of students with EBD and students with LD. *Journal of Emotional and Behavioral Disorders, 9*, 106–115.

Ayllon, T., & Roberts, M. (1974). Eliminating discipline problems by strengthening academic performance. *Journal of Applied Behavior Analysis, 7*, 71–76.

*Babyak, A. E., Koorland, M., & Mathes, P. G. (2000). The effects of story mapping instruction on the reading comprehension of students with behavioral disorders. *Behavioral Disorders, 25*, 239–258.

*Barton-Arwood, S. M., Wehby, J. H., & Falk, K. B. (2005). Reading instruction for elementary-age students with emotional and behavioral disorders: Academic and behavioral outcomes. *Exceptional Children, 72*, 7–27.

Becker, W. C., & Carnine, D. W. (1980). Direct instruction. In B. B. Lahey & A. E. Kazdin (Eds.), *Advances in clinical child psychology* (pp. 429–473). New York: Plenum.

Bullis M., & Walker, H. M. (1994). *Comprehensive school-based systems for troubled youth*. Eugene: University of Oregon, Center on Human Development.

Bullis, M. & Yovanoff, P. (2006). Idle hands: Community employment experiences of formerly incarcerated youth. *Journal of Emotional and Behavioral Disorders, 14*, 99–107.

Coleman, M. C., & Vaughn, S. (2000). Reading interventions for students with EBD. *Behavioral Disorders, 25*, 93–104.

Coutinho, M. J. (1986). Reading achievement of students identified as behaviorally disordered at the secondary level. *Behavioral Disorders, 11*, 200–207.

*Dawson, L., Venn, M. L., & Gunter, P. L. (2000). The effects of teacher versus computer reading models. *Behavioral Disorders, 25*, 105–113.

Edwards, L., & Chard, D. J. (2000). Curriculum reform in a residential treatment program: Establishing high academic expectation for students with emotional and behavioral disorders. *Behavioral Disorders, 25*, 259–263.

Epstein, M. H., & Cullinan, D. (1983). Academic performance of behaviorally disordered and learning-disabled pupils. *Journal of Special Education, 17*, 303–307.

Epstein, M. H., & Sharma, J. M. (1998). *Behavioral and emotional rating scale: A strength-based approach to assessment*. Austin, TX: PRO-ED.

Ervin, R. A., Kern, L., Clarke, S., DuPaul, G. J., Dunlap, G. J., & Friman, P. C. (2000). Evaluating assessment-based intervention strategies for students with ADHD and comorbid disorders within the natural classroom context. *Behavioral Disorders, 25*, 344–358.

*Falk, K. B., & Wehby, J. H. (2001). The effects of peer-assisted learning strategies on the beginning reading skills of young children with emotional or behavioral disorders. *Behavioral Disorders, 26*, 344–359.

Foorman, B. R., Francis, D. J., Shaywitz, S. E., Shaywitz, B. A., & Fletcher, J. M. (1997). The case for early reading intervention. In B. A. Blachman (Ed.), *Foundations of reading acquisition and dyslexia: Implications for early intervention* (pp. 243–264). Mahwah, NJ: Lawrence Erlbaum Associates.

Fuchs, D., Fuchs., L. S., Thompson, A., Svenson, E., Yen, L., Otaiba, S. A., et al. (2001). Peer-assisted learning strategies in reading: Extensions for kindergarten, first grade, and high school. *Remedial and Special Education, 22*, 15–21.

Gajar, A. (1979). Educable mentally retarded, learning disabled, emotionally disturbed: Similarities and differences. *Exceptional Children, 45*, 470–472.

Gersten, R., Baker, S., & Lloyd, J. W. (2000). Designing high-quality research in special education: Group experimental design. *The Journal of Special Education, 34*, 2–18.

Gersten, R., Fuchs, L. S., Compton, D., Coyne, M., Greenwood, C., & Innocenti, M. S. (2005). Quality indicators for group experimental and quasi-experimental research in special education. *Exceptional Children, 71*, 149–164.

Greenbaum, P. E., Dedrick, R. F., Friedman, R. M., Kutash, K., Borwn, E. C., Lardierh, S. P., et al. (1996). National Adolescent and Child Treatment Study (NACTS): Outcomes for children with serious emotional and behavioral disturbance. *Journal of Emotional and Behavioral Disorders, 4*, 130–146.

Gresham, F. M., Cook, C. R., Crews, S. D., & Kern, L. (2004). Social skills training for children and youth with emotional and behavioral disorders: Validity considerations and future directions. *Behavioral Disorders, 30*, 32–46.

Gresham, F. M., & Elliott, S. N. (1990). *Social skills rating system*. Circle Pines, MN: American Guidance Service.

Gresham, F. M., MacMillan, D. L., & Bocian, K. M. (1998). Agreement between school study team decisions and authoritative definitions in classification of students at-risk for mild disabilities. *School Psychology Quarterly, 13*, 181–191.

*Hale, A. D., Skinner, C. H., Winn, B. D., Oliver, R., & Allin, J. D. (2005). An investigation of listening and listening-while-reading accommodations on reading comprehension levels and rates in students with emotional disorders. *Psychology in the Schools, 42*, 39–51.

Hinshaw, S. P. (1992). Externalizing behavior problems and academic underachievement in childhood and adolescence: Causal relationships and underlying mechanisms. *Psychological Bulletin, 11*, 127–155.

Horner, R. H., Carr, E. C., Halle, J., McGee, G., Odom, S., & Wolery, M. (2005). The use of single-subject research to identify evidence-based practice in special education. *Exceptional Children, 71*, 165–179.

Individuals with Disabilities Education Act Amendments of 1997. Pub. L. No. 105–17, Section 20, 111 Stat. 37 (1997). Washington, DC: U.S. Government Printing Office.

Johnston, J. M., & Pennypacker, H. S. (1993). *Strategies and tactics of behavioral research* (2nd ed.). Hillsdale, NJ: Lawrence Erlbaum Associates.

Kamps, D., Kravits, T., Rauch, J., Kamps, J. L., & Chung, N. (2000). A prevention program for students with or at risk for ED: Moderating effects of variation in treatment and classroom structure. *Journal of Emotional and Behavioral Disorders, 8,* 141–154.

Kamps, D., Kravits, T., Stolze, J., & Swaggart, B. (1999). Prevention strategies for at-risk students and students with EBD in urban elementary schools. *Journal of Emotional and Behavioral Disorders, 7,* 178–188.

Kauffman, J. M. (1999). How we prevent the prevention of emotional and behavioral disorders. *Exceptional Children, 65,* 448–468.

Kauffman, J. M. (2003). Reflections on the field. *Behavioral Disorders, 28,* 205–208.

Kauffman, J. M. (2004). Introduction. In R. B. Rutherford, Jr., M. M. Quinn, & S. R. Mathur (Eds.). *Handbook of research in emotional and behavioral disorders* (pp. 11–14). New York: Guilford.

Kauffman, J. M. (2005). *Characteristics of emotional and behavioral disorders of children and youth* (8th ed.). Columbus, OH: Merrill.

Kauffman, J. M., Mostert, M. P., Trent, S. C., & Hallahan, D. P. (2002). *Managing classroom behavior: A reflective case-based approach.* (3rd ed.). Boston: Allyn & Bacon.

Kazdin, A. (1987). Treatment of antisocial behavior in children: Current status and future directions. *Psychological Bulletin, 102,* 187–203.

Kern, L., Bambara, L., & Fogt, J. (2002). Class-wide curricular modification to improve the behavior of students with emotional or behavioral disorders. *Behavioral Disorders, 27,* 317–326.

Klienbaum, D. G., Kupper, L. L., Muller, K. E., & Nizam, A. (1998). *Applied regression analysis and other multivariable methods* (3rd ed.). Pacific Grove, CA: Duxbury Press.

Landrum, T., J., Tankersley, M., & Kauffman, J. M. (2003). What is special about special education for students with emotional or behavioral disorders? *The Journal of Special Education, 37,* 148–156.

*Lane, K. L. (1999). Young students at risk for antisocial behavior: The utility of academic and social skills interventions. *Journal of Emotional and Behavioral Disorders, 7,* 211–223.

Lane, K. L. (2004). Academic instruction and tutoring interventions for students with emotional/behavioral disorders: 1990 to present. In R. B. Rutherford, M. M. Quinn, & S. R. Mathur (Eds.), *Handbook of research in emotional and behavioral disorders* (pp. 462–486). New York: Guilford.

Lane, K. L., Bocian, K. M., & Macmillan, D. L. (2004). Treatment integrity: An essential-but often forgotten-component of school-based interventions. *Preventing School Failure, 48,* 36–43.

Lane, K. L., & Carter, E. (2006). Supporting transition-age youth with and at-risk for emotional and behavioral disorders at the secondary level: A need for further inquiry. *Journal of Emotional and Behavioral Disorders, 14,* 66–70.

Lane, K. L., Carter, E., Pierson, M., & Glaeser, B. (2006). Academic, social, and behavioral profiles of high school students with emotional disturbances and learning disabilities: Are they more alike than different? *Journal of Emotional and Behavioral Disorders, 14,* 108–117.

Lane, K. L., Gresham, F. M., & O'Shaughnessy, T. E. (Eds.). (2002). *Interventions for children with or at risk for emotional and behavioral disorders.* Needham, MA: Allyn & Bacon.

*Lane, K. L., O'Shaughnessy, T. E., Lambros, K. M., Gresham, F. M., & Beebe-Frankenberger, M. E. (2001). The efficacy of phonological awareness training with first-grade students who have behavior problems and reading difficulties. *Journal of Emotional and Behavioral Disorders, 9,* 219–231.

Lane, K. L., Umbreit, J., & Beebe-Frankenberger, M. (1999). A review of functional assessment research with students with or at risk for emotional and behavioral disorders. *Journal of Positive Behavioral Interventions, 1,* 1–24.

Lane, K. L., & Wehby, J. (2002). Addressing antisocial behavior in the schools: A call for action. *Academic Exchange Quarterly, 6,* 4–9.

*Lane, K. L., Wehby, J. H., Menzies, H. M., Gregg, R. M., Doukas, G. L., & Munton, S. M. (2002). Early literacy instruction for first-grade students at-risk for antisocial behavior. *Education and Treatment of Children, 25,* 438–458.

Lane, K. L., Wolery, M., Reichow, B., & Rogers, L. (in press). Describing baseline conditions: Suggestions for study reports. *Journal of Behavioral Education.*

Levendoski, L. S., & Cartledge, G. (2000). Self-monitoring for elementary school children with serious emotional disturbances: Classroom applications for increased academic responding. *Behavioral Disorders, 25,* 211–224.

Lyon, G. R. (1996). Learning disabilities. In E. Marsh & R. Barkley (Eds.), *Child Psychopathology* (pp. 390–434). New York: Guilford.

MacMillan, D. L., Gresham, F. M., & Forness, S. R. (1996). Full inclusion: An empirical perspective. *Behavioral Disorders, 21,* 145–159.

Malmgren, K. W., & Leone, P. E. (2000). Effects of a short-term auxiliary reading program on the reading skills of incarcerated youth. *Education and Treatment of Children, 23,* 239–247.

Martens, B. K., Witt, J. C., Elliott, S. N., & Darveaux, D. (1985). Teacher judgments concerning the acceptability of school-based interventions. *Professional Psychology: Research and Practice, 16,* 191–198.

Mathur, S. R., Kavale, K. A., & Quinn, M. M. (1998). Social skills interventions with students with emotional and behavioral problems: A quantitative synthesis of single-subject research. *Behavioral Disorders, 23,* 193–201.

Mattison, R. E., Hooper, S. R., & Glassberg, L. A. (2002). Three-year course of learning disorders in special education students classified as behavioral disordered. *Journal of the American Academy of Child and Adolescent Psychiatry, 41,* 1454–1461.

Mattison, R. E., Spitznagel, E. L., & Felix, B. C. (1998). Enrollment predictors of the special education outcome for students with SED. *Behavioral Disorders, 23*, 243–256.

Miller, K., Gunter, P. L., Venn, M., Hummel, J., & Wiley, L. (2003). Effects of curricular and materials modifications on academic performance and task engagement of three students with emotional or behavioral disorders. *Behavioral Disorders, 28*, 130–149.

Nelson, J. R., & Benner, G. J. (2005). Improving the early literacy skills of children with behavioral disorders and phonological processing deficits at school entry. *Reading & Writing Quarterly, 21*, 105–108.

*Nelson, J. R., Benner, G. J., & Gonzalez, J. (2005). An investigation of the effects of a prereading intervention on the early literacy skills of children at risk of emotional disturbance and reading problems. *Journal of Emotional and Behavioral Disorders, 13*, 3–12.

Nelson, J. R., Benner, G. J., Lane, K. L., & Smith, B. W. (2004). An investigation of the academic achievement of K–12 students with emotional and behavioral disorders in public school settings. *Exceptional Children, 71*, 59–73.

*Nelson, J. R., Stage, S. A., Epstein, M. H., & Pierce, C. D. (2005). Effects of a pre-reading intervention on the literacy and social skills of children. *Exceptional Children, 72*, 29–45.

O'Connor, R. E., & Padeliadu, S. (2000). Blending versus whole word approaches in first grade remedial reading: Short-term and delayed effects on reading and spelling words. *Reading and Writing: An Interdisciplinary Journal, 13*, 159–182.

O'Shaughnessy, T., Lane, K. L., Gresham, F. M., & Beebe-Frankenberger, M. (2002). Students with or at risk for learning and emotional-behavioral difficulties: An integrated system of prevention and intervention. In K. L. Lane, F. M. Gresham, & T. E. O'Shaughnessy (Eds.), *Intervention for children with or at risk for emotional and behavioral disorder*, (pp. 3–17). Boston: Allyn & Bacon.

Penno, D. A., Frank, A. R., & Wacker, D. P. (2000). Instructional accommodations for adolescent students with severe emotional or behavioral disorders. *Behavioral Disorders, 25*, 325–343.

Quinn, S. R., & Poirier, J. M. (2004). Linking prevention research with policy: Examing the costs of the failure to prevent emotional and behavioral disorders. In R. B. Rutherford, Jr., M. M. Quinn, & S. R. Mathur (Eds.), *Handbook of research in emotional and behavioral disorders* (pp. 78–97). New York: Guilford.

Reid, R., Gonzalez, J. E., Nordness, A. T., Trout, A., & Epstein, M. H. (2004). A meta-analysis of the academic status of students with emotional/behavioral disturbance. *The Journal of Special Education, 38*, 130–143.

Ruhl, K. L., & Berlinghoff, D. H. (1992). Research on improving behaviorally disordered students' academic performance: A review of the literature. *Behavioral Disorders, 17*, 178–190.

Sasso, G. M. (2003). An examined life: A response to James Kauffman's reflections on the field. *Behavioral Disorders, 28*, 209–211.

*Scott, T. M., & Shearer-Lingo, A. (2002). The effects of reading fluency instruction on the academic and behavioral success of middle school students in a self-contained EBD classroom. *Preventing School Failure, 46,* 167–173.

Scruggs, T. E., & Mastropieri, M. A. (1986). Academic characteristics of behaviorally disordered and learning disabled students. *Behavioral Disorders, 11,* 184–190.

*Skinner, C. H., Cooper, L., & Cole, C. L. (1997). The effects of oral presentation previewing rates on reading performance. *Journal of Applied Behavior Analysis, 30,* 331–333.

*Spencer, V. G., Scruggs, T. E., & Mastropieri, M. A. (2003). Content area learning in middle school social studies classrooms and students with emotional or behavioral disorders: A comparison of strategies. *Behavioral Disorders, 28,* 77–93.

*Strong, A. C., Wehby, J. H., Falk, K. B., & Lane, K. L. (2004). The impact of a structured reading curriculum and repeated reading on the performance of junior high students with emotional and behavioral disorders. *School Psychology Review, 33,* 561–581.

Tankersley, M., Landrum, T., J., & Cook, B. G. (2004). How research informs practice in the field of emotional and behavioral disorders. In. R. B. Rutherford, M. M. Quinn, & S. R. Mathur (Eds.), *Handbook of research in emotional and behavioral disorders* (pp. 98–113). New York: Guilford.

Teeple, D. F., & Skinner, C. H. (2004). Enhancing grammar assignment perceptions by increasing assignment demands: Extending additive interspersal research to students with emotional and behavioral disorders. *Journal of Emotional and Behavioral Disorders, 12,* 120–127.

Tindal, G., & Crawford, L. (2002). Teaching writing to students with behavior disorders: Metaphor and medium. In K. L. Lane, F. M. Gresham, & T. E. O'Shaughnessy (Eds.), *Interventions for children with or at risk for emotional and behavioral disorders* (pp. 3–17). Boston, MA: Allyn & Bacon.

Torgesen, J. K., & Bryant, B. R. (1994). *Phonological awareness training for reading.* Austin, TX: ProEd.

*Trout, A. L., Epstein, M. H., Mickelson, W. T., Nelson, J. R., & Lewis, L. M. (2003). Effects of a reading intervention for kindergarten students at risk for emotional disturbance and reading deficits. *Behavioral Disorders, 28,* 313–326.

Umbreit, J., Lane, K. L., & Dejud, C. (2004). Improving classroom behavior by modifying task difficulty: The effects of increasing the difficulty of too-easy tasks. *Journal of Positive Behavior Interventions, 6,* 13–20.

Wagner, M. M. (1995). Outcomes for youths with serious emotional disturbance in secondary school and early adulthood. *The Future of Children, 5,* 90–111.

Wagner, M. M., & Davis, M. (2006). How are we preparing students with emotional disturbances for the transition to young adulthood? Findings from the National Longitudinal Transition Study-2. *Journal of Emotional and Behavioral Disorders, 14,* 86–98.

Walker, H. M., Ramsey, E., & Gresham, F. M. (2004). *Antisocial behavior in schools: Evidence-based practices* (2nd ed.). Florence, KY: Wadsworth/ Thompson Learning.

Walker, H. M., & Severson, H. (1992). *Systematic Screening for Behavior Disorders: Technical Manual*. Longmont, CO: Sopris West.

Walker, H. M., Severson, H. H., & Feil, E.g. (2005). *Early screening project: A proven child find process: Technical Manual*. Longmont, CO: Sopris West.

Wallace, G., & Kauffman, J. M. (1986). *Teaching students with learning and behavior problems* (3rd ed.). Columbus, OH: Merrill.

*Wehby, J. H., Falk, K. B., Barton-Arwood, S., Lane, K. L., & Cooley, C. (2003). The impact of comprehensive reading instruction on the academic and social behavior of students with emotional and behavioral disorders. *Journal of Emotional and Behavioral Disorders, 11*, 225–238.

*Wehby, J. H., Lane, K. L., & Falk, K. B. (2005). An inclusive approach to improving early literacy skills of students with emotional and behavioral disorders. *Behavioral Disorders, 30*, 155–169.

Witt, J. C., & Elliott, S. N. (1985). Acceptability of classroom intervention strategies. In T. R. Kratochwill (Ed.), *Advances in school psychology* (Vol. 4, pp. 251–288). Hillsdale, NJ: Lawrence Erlbaum Associates.

Wolf, M. M. (1978). Social validity: The case for subjective measurement or how applied behavior analysis is finding its heart. *Journal of Applied Behavior Analysis, 11*, 203–214.

Zigmond, N. (2006). Twenty-four months after high school: Paths taken by youth diagnosed with severe emotional/behavioral disorders. *Journal of Emotional and Behavioral Disorders, 14*, 99–107.

Note: * Denotes articles included in this review.

Part IV

KAUFFMAN'S CONTRIBUTIONS
TO SPECIAL EDUCATION

Authors of chapters in previous sections of this volume have raised and explored several of the issues for which James M. Kauffman has contributed insight and leadership as scholar, special educator, and advocate for children and youth. The chapters also stand as testimony to the continuing influence of Kauffman's ideas to special education research, policy, and practice, creating a strong countervailing force against a toxic mix of poor thinking and ideologically motivated pronouncements, that rather than improve the lives of children with disabilities produce instead what Kauffman called *educational deform* (see Kauffman, 2002). As a special educator, he continues to articulate the logic and necessity, as well as the humanistic intent, of special education and the policies that support it. He continues to strenuously argue why providing effective specially designed instruction is a valuable and integral component of comprehensive educational systems (see Kauffman & Hallahan, 2005). As an advocate for children and youth, especially for children with emotional and behavior disorders, he continues to challenge the field to rise to the themes he articulated in 1993, those themes around which these authors have assembled their tribute.

Most importantly, Kauffman continues to call on the field to recognize the truth of differences, that some differences among children with disabilities, and indeed some of the differences between children with and without disabilities, have ultimate importance for an education system that aspires to educate all children. He laments that the field is buffeted by fashion and political ill will and seems at times adrift, inviting harsh critiques and damning attacks both from within and outside of special education. Kauffman offers unapologetic assertions of the valid historical and conceptual foundations on which modern special education was built, and calls urgently for its intellectual and practical reclamation. The previous chapters demonstrate that this call continues to be heard and answered with a high level of commitment

The final chapter of our *Festschrift* is authored by Kauffman's long-time colleagues and friends at the University of Virginia, John W. Lloyd and Daniel P. Hallahan. In reflecting on long-standing problems that still confront the field of special education Lloyd and Hallahan structure their chapter around concepts of *advocacy*, which captures the nature and tone of most of Kauffman's writings, and *reform*, the goal toward which Kauffman has consistently pushed the field. Their analysis of advocacy and overview of several proposed reforms highlights, we think, a theme that pervades all of Kauffman's work: Basing reforms on science instead of on emotion provides the only basis for truly achieving the radical reform of special education (Kauffman, 1993).

REFERENCES

Kauffman, J. M. (1993). How we might achieve the radical reform of special education. *Exceptional Children, 60,* 6–16.

Kauffman, J. M. (2002) *Education deform: Bright people sometimes say stupid things about education.* Lanham, MD: Scarecrow Press.

Kauffman, J. M., & Hallahan, D. P. (2005). *Special education: What it is and why we need it.* Boston: Pearson.

Chapter 12

Advocacy and Reform of Special Education

John Wills Lloyd
Daniel P. Hallahan
University of Virginia

Advocacy in special education is important, but it is also fraught with problems. As special educators, we are responsible for promoting awareness of the difficulties faced by individuals with disabilities, their families, and other educators and to advance policies that help address these difficulties. Some special educators may devote relatively greater emphasis to advocacy, but virtually all special educators advocate for children with disabilities and their families in one way or another, whether by encouraging parents to stand up for their rights, publishing scholarly work, or testifying to government agencies. An important aspect of this advocacy is promoting awareness and understanding of disabilities among general educators; too often children with disabilities have been overlooked in general education, the services available in general education have been too inflexible to accommodate individuals with disabilities, and the special education services available have been inadequate. These are matters that special education advocates should address.[1]

Most of the advocacy in special education has promoted ways to reform special education. *Reform* is a popular word in rhetoric about education and special education has a ranch-hand share of reform rhetoric. Even though it included modest changes in a law written 30 years earlier, IDEA 2004 was heralded as a special education reform bill in press releases from the Committee on Education and the Workforce of the U.S. House of Representatives (EdWorkForce, 2004). Many of the initiatives supported by the U.S. Department of Education Office of Special Education Programs refer to reform in their materials—for illustration: Access Center (54 references to "reform" at its Web site); Federal Resource Center (13 references); National Center for Culturally Responsive Educational Systems (39 references); National Center on Educational Outcomes (215 references); National Dropout Prevention Center (63 references); National Institute of Urban School Reform (86 references); National Research Center on Learning Disabilities (67 references).[2] The professional literature likely has an even greater number of references to reform.

It is important to note that the references on any given Web site do not necessarily reflect the opinions of those responsible for the site. For example, a site might have a reference list of articles that include the term *reform*, even though the tenor of the Web page referring to those articles may treat some of them differently than it treats others; both articles favoring and doubting reform would be captured in such a search. That these searches capture both types of treatments does not alter our assertion that "reform" is a popular topic.

---

[1]The term *advocacy* often refers to efforts to help an individual student, as when parents hire an advocate to represent their daughter or son. This is an appropriate use of the term, but in our discussion, we use *advocacy* to refer to the idea of advocating for many children and youth with disabilities in our schools.

[2]The counts for the occurrence of "reform" in these parenthetical notes is not meant to be a thorough analysis, only to illustrate that reform is a term used commonly in special education rhetoric. On December 10, 2005, we used Google to search each site for the term *reform*. More specifically, we used the search phrase, "reform site:http://[sitename]/:" which is a query of the Google data base for any objects that include the term "reform" at the given site. Similar searches using the Yahoo database of sites yielded similar results.

Throughout its history, special education has benefitted from having advocates who promote awareness, policies, and practices that serve individuals with disabilities. Although parents (e.g., E. Tash) have been very important advocates, many professional figures—among others, Seguin, Dix, Kirk, and Cruickshank—have championed greater understanding of individuals with disabilities; helped instill laws, regulations, and rules that protect individuals with disabilities; and studied and taught about the nature and assessment of disabilities, and instructional procedures that help people to approximate their capacities more completely (Hallahan & Mercer, 2002; Kauffman & Landrum, 2006).

Advocacy for students with disabilities has changed remarkably from the time of these pioneers. Although earlier advocates promoted understanding disability and helping those who were disabled, legal constraints have had much greater influence on advocates since the 1960s and 1970s. Court cases such as the *Pennsylvania Association for Retarded Citizens v. Commonwealth of Pennsylvania* (1972) or *Mills v. Board of Education of the District of Columbia* (1972) and legislation such as PL 94–142 mark a transition from the historically important figures to those who affected special education in the last quarter of the 20th century. Advocates such as Ballard, Martin, and Weintraub promoted the legal basis for special education services. By establishing legal rights to education for students with disabilities, laws they helped write laid the foundation for contemporary special education.

As important as the foci of advocacy are, we believe that all advocacy and reform activities must be predicated on a few important principles. Those principles include legality, empiricism, rationality, and continuing concern for providing beneficial services at a given time while seeking to improve the quality of services available in the future. In this chapter, we develop this idea by examining the foundations for advocacy and examples of some proposed reforms.

ADVOCATES AND ISSUES

Advocating reform requires someone to act as advocate and something to advocate—a person and a position or issue. This raises the question of who can legitimately advocate for special education and what they can advocate. In this section, we briefly discuss advocates and issues.

Advocates

Advocacy requires a substantial understanding of the difficulties that people encounter. Sometimes some advocates scoff at the advocacy provided by individuals who do not have the personal experience of having a disability themselves. Can only those who actually have disabilities advocate effectively for individuals with disabilities? We think not.

To be sure, those who have disabilities have different experiences than those who do not. There are wonderful examples of people with disabilities and their families successfully advocating for beneficial changes. Reflect on the value that has been brought to mental retardation by U.S. and U.K. People First organizations. Consider the importance for Learning Disabilities of the advocacy provided by Eli Tash and other parents when they founded what was then known as the Association for Children with Learning Disabilities in the 1960s. Marvel on the awareness that Temple Grandin's public persona has brought to autism spectrum disorders.

It is important for special education advocates to inquire about and respect the opinions of people with disabilities and their families. Those opinions, however, represent only an incomplete understanding; for the very reason that those opinions are important to include, they cannot be the only foundation for advocacy. The opinions represent a biased view, one that both benefits from and is constrained by the condition under study. Those who doubt the authenticity of advocacy by individuals who do not have disabilities clearly do not understand an essential feature of disability: Many who have disabilities are not able to advocate for themselves.

Thus, we agree with those who warn about paternalistic advocacy, but we do not consider concerns about paternalism or lack of first-hand personal experience with disability to disqualify special educators from advocacy. In fact, special educators have what we consider a duty to champion understanding of individuals with disabilities and provision of beneficial services for them.

Positions or Issues

Ad hoc approaches have a lot of appeal, but they are not anchored in evidence. Too often, contemporary advocacy is predicated on variable principles. We need to move beyond this, get to firm guiding principles for our advocacy. People may differ about what those principles are, and that is okay. We should discuss those differences in a reasoned and evidence-based way. When we talk, we shouldn't talk dismissively, but in a constructive way. Firm bases for advocacy require us to talk about core values.

Sometimes, however, advocacy comes from an excessive reliance on the importance of just one principle. It is advocacy of this sort that forms the basis for the relatively temporary, but highly enthusiastic efforts to promote policies in special education. If we could only achieve this one fundamental reform, everything else would take care of itself. Examples of efforts that can lead to unrealistic expectations include: If educators would simply differentiate instruction, fully include all students, provide services without labels, and so forth. These views usually accord enough with reality to be attractive, and with magnifying rhetoric, their truths sound compelling.

Policies based on the primacy of one specific idea usually enjoy brief, intense support before they begin to fade under the light of careful analysis. Once their popularity has waned, however, some vestige of the idea remains in the great reservoir of special education ideas and is likely to be revived by a later advocate. A case in point is facilitated communication (FC). FC, which purportedly enables people with severe communication problems (especially autism) to express themselves by typing messages, was featured in the U.S. national magazine *Time* with a circulation in excess of 4 million at least 10 years after it had been thoroughly debunked by virtually every reputable scientist who encountered it (Wallis, 2006). The advocacy that supported FC is instructive in that it cautions us not to get too far ahead of our empirical basis. Other examples, perhaps less egregious, are still quite instructive. We take up some of these examples in the next section.

POPULAR REFORM IDEAS

Too often, special educators spout opinions that are unfounded or poorly reasoned, and these opinions pass as advocacy. It is only when special educators present carefully reasoned and evidence-based arguments that our efforts to serve children and youths with disabilities and their families and teachers actually do benefit the intended beneficiaries. In this section, we illustrate the fallacies into which reform advocacy falls using contemporary examples of recommended reforms.

Tuning Up Schools

One currently popular reform is creating schools that are said to be attuned to children's unique educational needs (Levine, 2002; Levine & Reed, 1999), an idea that at once reflects both the general perspective of special education and discredited special education interventions. For Schools Attuned, one of the core ideas is an understanding of neurological development.

> As teachers gain neurodevelopmental expertise, they are in a far better position to understand students who are struggling to keep up. Once familiar with the kinds of memory and spatial ordering needed in fifth-grade math, a teacher can inspect a student's quiz paper and determine whether his mistakes reflect problems with pattern recognition, factual recall, procedural recall, nonverbal thinking, active working memory, or automatization. A teacher then has the option to bypass the student's area of difficulty or intervene and seek to repair the student's breakdown—or, even better, do both. (All Kinds of Minds, 2006, article ID = 68)

Does Schools Attuned pass the test of having a viable psychological base? According to Willingham (2005a, 2005b), it does not. Willingham argued that the fundamental view of neuro-psychology is faulty.

> Levine's broad-strokes account of the mind agrees with that of most researchers (and for that matter, with the observant layman): There is a memory system, an attention system, and so on. But it's the detailed structure Levine claims to see within each of those systems that really drives his proposed treatments for disabled children, and on those details Levine is often wrong. ... Given the inaccurate description of the mind on which it is based, however, it seems unlikely that it will prove particularly effective. (p. Wallingham, 2005b, [introduction], para. 4)

The direct research on Schools Attuned is scarce and the effects are less than overwhelming. Reports available from the Web site (e.g., Gates, 2002; O'Sullivan & Associates, 2001a, 2001b; O'Sullivan & Page, 2002) describe non-experimental evaluations employing measures (e.g., self-report; accuracy of special education referrals; change scores) of less concern than students' performance in critical areas, not the stuff that inspires one to yell "Eureka!" To be fair, there are other evaluations in the works at the time of this writing. However, there is reason to question the benefits of basing interventions on patching up underlying processes or matching instruction to strengths and weaknesses. At its heart, the Levine approach champions an effort to reform schools so that they address students' problems, a goal shared by most special educators. At the same time, the approach recommends patch-up and match-up (or both!) teaching for underlying psychological processes similar to those that have been found wanting (see, Forness & Kavale, 1993; Hallahan & Cruickshank, 1973; Kavale, 1981; Kavale & Forness, 1987; Kavale & Mattson, 1983).

From Levine's Schools Attuned movement we can take at least two lessons about advocating reform. First, an intuitively appealing theory is a powerful magnet, but it is not enough. The theory needs to accord with psychological science. Second, advocates should do their homework; ideas touting discredited methods are likely to meet resistance. Third, calls for massive reform should have clear evidence of benefits on measures that matter (e.g., student outcomes in reading).

One can draw similar lessons from other well-intentioned reform efforts that are based on high-profile ideas. For examples, consider the ideas of multiple intelligences (Gardner, 1983, 1993, 1999) or block scheduling (Canady & Rettig, 1996). In the former case, the theory is scientifically untenable (Willingham, 2004) and practices based on it (e.g., Armstrong, 1994; New Horizons, 2006) are of no documented benefit. In the latter case, a perceived need, theory, and personal preferences drive the reform, despite data indicating that traditional scheduling yields better student academic outcomes (Lawrence & McPherson, 2000; Terrazas, Slate, & Achilles, 2003).

All Positive All the Time

One intervention that became popular around the end of the last millennium is an approach to teaching—especially, behavior management—that emphasizes use of only positive techniques. One version of this view in special education led to debate about the use of any aversive procedure (Repp & Singh, 1990). The idea of providing positive consequences to increase appropriate behavior accords with most humans' inclination to accentuate the affirmative and eliminate the negative. By judicious application of positive reinforcement, including techniques such as differential reinforcement of incompatible behavior and functional behavioral assessment, advocates hope to build environments where deviant behavior can be reduced and pro-social behaviors increased.

In its most popular incarnation, it is called "Positive Behavior Support" or PBS. PBS was popular enough that the U.S. Department of Education funded a center to disseminate information and technical assistance to schools to help them identify and employ PBS practices as a part of school-wide disciplinary programs (National Technical Assistance Center on Positive Behavioral Interventions and Supports, 2006; PBIS). We hasten to note that not all PBS is PBIS and that PBIS is more than PBS only. The approach recommended in PBIS includes other components (e.g., school-wide agreement about a shared behavior management program).

PBS itself has been advocated by colleagues whom we know and admire, but it is founded on some questionable assumptions. First, and foremost, there is ample evidence going back to the 1960s showing that positive-only approaches to behavior management have fewer and less-immediate benefits than approaches that employ a strong positive component with a judicious measure of negative consequences (Becker, Madsen, Arnold, & Thomas, 1967; Pfiffner, Rosen, & O'Leary, 1984; Rosen, O'Leary, Joyce, Conway, & Pfiffner, 1984). Second, like Schools Attuned and Multiple Intelligences, a positive-only approach appears to base part of its advocacy on the superficial appeal to uncritical, emotional factors. Is it actually possible to construct environments where there are no negatives? Even the absence of access to positive reinforcement—time out—is a negative in that it has a decellerative effect on behavior. Thus, there appears to be some smoke and mirrors to PBS, as others have noted:

Our general thesis has two parts. The first part is that whatever else it may be, PBS is not science, but rather a form of illusion that leads to dangerously biased decision making ... The second part of our analysis shows that PBS is not new, if by new, it refers to either the synthesis of values with a technology or the content adherents claim it encompasses. In establishing these points we are led...to an inescapable conclusion about PBS; namely, that it represents little more than propaganda designed to promote the professional interests of a group of social and educational reformers. (Mulick & Butter, 2005, p. 385)

From the PBS example we note again the importance of not founding one's advocacy on methods that contradict established evidence. And we learn that adopting a superficially appealing language to sell an idea, even one that has at least some merit, risks inviting skeptics' concern.

Including Reform

Clearly the foremost illustration of this approach to reform has been the inclusion movement. Representatives of the full inclusion movement (e.g., Burrello, Lashley, & Beatty, 2001; Gartner & Lipsky, 1987; Horn & Tynan, 2001; Lipsky, 2005) have called for creation of a unified system of education requiring a merger of general and special education systems. They have criticized special education as costly, ineffective, stigmatizing, the source of double standards in discipline and assessment, and other ills. The most fundamental criticism by the full-inclusion advocates is summed up in the book title, "Inclusion: A Service not a Place: A Whole School Approach" (Gartner & Lipskey, 2003).

As young special educators in the 1960s, we and our colleagues had ideals that are echoed in the inclusion movement. There is nothing particularly surprising about this. The times were idealistic and we were of an age to cleave to ideals. In our idealistic days as special educators we talked about the hope of teaching even the most seriously involved children and youth so well and explaining our techniques and procedures to our general education peers with such clarity that we would "put ourselves out of a job" by returning our students to school with their general education classmates. We endorsed the idea of returning students with disabilities to the mainstream. With the aide of early identification, prevention, and technical advances we foresaw in our behavior management and instructional methods, there would be little need for special education (Deno, 1970).

Our ideals were naïve. With the benefit of hindsight, it is clear to us now that it is neither possible nor beneficial to serve all children in general education. Even with the best-laid and best-implemented educational efforts, there will be some students who will still require special education. Some will be born with intractable problems (microcephaly, perhaps), some will not benefit from even the most powerful instructional technology we have available at the time, and others simply do not thrive in environments that cannot be controlled to a greater degree than the general education setting. Even if educators were able to produce a negative skew to the distribution of outcomes (and we hope that education is accomplishing this goal), there would still be a few cases that would fall under the elongated, flattened part of the curve on the left of the distribution. No matter how much we might hope to do so, we cannot detach the left tail of the distribution from the left wall.

It is clear to us also that the logical underpinnings of full inclusion are tenuous. Mock and Kauffman (2005) describe full inclusion advocates' attacks on the continuum of alternative placements as composed of nonsequiturs, oversimplifications, willful ignorance, and misinterpretations. Others have raised similar objections (e.g., Fuchs & Fuchs, 1994; Simpson & Sasso, 1992). How about the research basis for full inclusion? The evidence comes from studies using diverse research methods, and only a few studies measure up to the high standards on which we should base education decisions (Lloyd, Pullen, Tankersley, & Lloyd, 2006). Zigmond's summary is valuable here. As might be expected given the diversity of methods, the results are equivocal. She explains that efficacy research about the *where* to provide services mostly reveals that *where* is not the right question.

> The search for the best place in which to receive special education services has tended to be fueled by passion and principle, rather than by reason and rationality. Until educators are ready to say that receiving special education services in a particular setting is good for some students with disabilities but not for others, that different educational environments are more conducive to different forms of teaching and learning, that different students need to learn different things in different ways, and that traditional group research designs may not

capture these individual differences in useful ways, we may never get beyond the equivocal findings reported here. (2003, p. 198)

LEARNING FROM THESE EXAMPLES

What can we learn by examining these and other popular reform efforts? Beneficial reforms are those that meet criteria for establishing their value. These reform efforts we have just described have failed to meet one or more important standards, in our view.

What are those standards? We propose that they should include at least these: Advocates for special education should recommend reforms that (a) protect access to special education services; (b) recognize the unique and shared characteristics of students with disabilities; and (c) promote more accurate and useful assessment and effective services. To ensure that their recommendations for reform meet these standards, advocates must predicate their recommendations on strong empirical research.

Protect Access to Services

We believe that the basis of advocacy for students with disabilities is founded on protecting access to special education for those who need it. To do less is to allow special education to wither, to promote the demise of special education, or—worst—to fail to provide the help children and youths with disabilities need. This is to fail to accept the social obligation of watching out for one's fellow people, especially those less fortunate.

Protecting access to services requires that services are available. If there are no teachers prepared to address the problems of students with emotional and behavior disorders, providing those students with educational services is impossible. If the continuum of placements has been truncated, then there is no alternative for those—however few they may be—who can thrive only in what some might label "restrictive environments." No quantity of good intentions and rhetoric will meet those needs. At the least, we need to be able to construct these services on very short notice, if they are not available. But why should they be unavailable, given that millions of students have been identified as needing them?

Of course, we do not want to protect deleterious services. How does one decide which services are needed? This is an easily answered question: Look to the research. Although some research will provide greater guidance than other research, it is clearly possible to use research to outline the basic types of services that are beneficial to students (Lloyd et al., 2006). One cannot use the research selectively, though; for example, it is less than genuine to point to the negative *overall* effect size for special class placement and ignore the finding in the same analysis showing positive effect sizes for students with learning disabilities and for students with emotional and behavioral disorders (Carlberg & Kavale, 1980; Lloyd, Forness, & Kavale, 1998).

Recognize Students' Unique Needs

Since at least the 1960s some people have promoted the idea that sustaining categories of disability is unneeded and downright mistaken (Reynolds, 1991). In its most extreme form, advocates of this view even contend that special education is unwarranted and superfluous, that education is education; because children are mostly alike, those who are different should not be treated differently from their peers; and supple and nuanced provision of education can accommodate the full range of learners, from those in elementary school for whom formal algebra is within reach to those adolescents for whom grocery shopping is the most pressing instructional objective.

Not all those who champion this idea take it to extremes, of course. As with most ideas, there is a distribution of perspectives. Although complex, the array of arguments is founded on a relatively few shared ideas. First, there is a profound concern about separation, often stated with references to language from the landmark civil rights holding by the U.S. Supreme Court in *Brown v Board of Education*: "Separate is not equal." Second, there is the genuine hope that having individuals with and without disabilities in the same environments for the maximum amount of time possible will have beneficial effects on both students with and without disabilities by providing models of appropriate behavior for those who have problems and increasing acceptance of differences for those who do not have problems. To be sure, there are other aspects of the argument that do not usually rise to the level of advocacy; some advocates may discuss these issues—especially, finances—but treat them as secondary or tertiary concerns, subordinate to the primary matters of equity and academic and social benefits.

Our time in special education has seen the rise and rebirth of attacks on categorical special education. One of the foundational concepts, one with which we agree to at least a degree, is that students with disabilities are more alike than they are different and that there should not, for example, be a program designed for students with learning disabilities, another for students with emotional and behavioral disorders, and a third program for students with mental retardation. Indeed, according to U.S. law, students should receive an individualized education program, one designed to fit their unique needs, not their categorical labels.

At the same time, we must recognize that there are commonalities among those students whom educators identify as having emotional and behavioral disorders versus mental retardation versus learning disabilities. Indeed, empirical data about these similarities and differences show clearly that the diagnostic teams are sorting cases according to common characteristics (Sabornie, Cullinan, Osborne, & Brock, 2005; Sabornie, Evans, & Cullinan, 2006).

As a matter of advocacy at the level of the individual student, the law provides good guidance: If a student is in need of special education because of a disability, educators should identify the student's unique educational needs, plan how to address those needs, and prepare means for assessing whether the student is making adequate progress (Bateman & Linden, 2006). At the level of advocacy for students in general, however, there is substantial benefit to be gained from considering categories of special education. These include teacher preparation, protection of access to services, and so forth.

Base Reform on Strong Evidence

Many reform efforts are based on rhetoric more than on evidence. Special educators need to promote reforms that actually have a chance of improving outcomes for students. It is not enough simply to sound the horn for reform because of differences between the life outcomes of individuals with disabilities and their nondisabled peers, even if those differences are clearly discouraging (Wagner,

1995; Wagner et al., 1991). There are data showing how clearly some reforms actually affect outcomes (e.g., Comprehensive School Reform Quality Center, 2005), and it is those that deserve advocacy.

Just as special educators have insisted on incorporating measurable goals and objectives in students' IEPs, so should we require that our policies identify specific, measurable outcomes. Then, we should test whether they meet those standards. "If you're not sure where you're going, you're liable to end up someplace else—and not even know it" (Mager, 1962, p. vii).

At the core of special education, along with understanding that individuals with disabilities, despite the many characteristics that they share with other people, have unique educational needs, lives a need for effective practices. It is no mistake that other chapters in this volume and elsewhere examine practices and recommend those that are effective (see Forness & Beard, chap. 9 in this volume; Lane, Barton-Arwood, Rogers, & Robertson, chap. 11 in this volume; Sasso, chap. 8 in this volume; see also Cook & Schirmer, 2006). This core value is also reflected in the emphasis on empiricism that is routinely evident in special education and has made special education a well-spring for valuable innovations adopted throughout education (Gerber, 1999; Lloyd & Hallahan 2005). We may recognize that students with disabilities have unique educational needs, but unless special educators do something about those needs, unless special educators provide services that address those needs, special educators have failed.

REFORMING SPECIAL EDUCATION

Reform of special education is predicated on promoting better means of meeting the needs of students with disabilities. Better than what? Who cares if your reform sounds better than a straw representation of special education at some previous time? Promoting reform should be more than simply championing an alternative that is based on a theory, intuition, or bias. If there is a bias, it should be for reforms that meet standards based on the philosophical predilection for helping and the need for practices and policies that benefit outcomes.

Thus, those reforms that should be championed should advocate clearly and they should be based on empirical evidence. There are vital roles for students with disabilities, and especially their families, to play in reform of special education. Not the least of these is creating and sustaining the public pressure for effective services.

Supporting students with disabilities requires advocates to maintain equilibrium between the higher-order principles that structure our efforts and the realities of day-to-day services. Too often, advocates lean too far in one or the other direction. One must both attend to the details and deduce decisions based on higher order principles.

Although the rhetoric for reform is often overblown (Kauffman, 2002), much of the mistaken advocacy of this sort emanates from absolute positions, often using the kind of rhetoric reminiscent of introductory logic problems (e.g., "all *x* are *y*" or "no *M* should be *N*"). In special education, one can find what surely must be heartfelt but ill-reasoned attacks based on absolute adherence to one or another general principle. In the most extreme examples, some advocates are not at all supporters of special education. They argue that special education really is unnecessary and should be scuttled.

We certainly do not advocate abolishing special education. Special education provides an array of services for students with disabilities, and that array of services both meets the needs of individual students and makes it possible for education to pursue the larger goal of promoting equity and excellence for students who do and do not have disabilities. Special educators should advocate for a range of administrative arrangements to ensure that there are options available for those students with disabilities who require them; a system of identification that ensures that students with disabilities have access to special education services; a process for establishing the unique educational needs of individual students and creating a plan for how to address those unique needs; an array of continuously improving special education practices that can be employed to meet different students' unique needs; and mechanisms for recurring assessments that permit parents, teachers, and students themselves to evaluate the extent to which they are making progress toward meeting goals and objectives.

REFERENCES

All Kinds of Minds. (2006). *All kinds of minds*. Retrieved October 12, 2006, from http://www. allkindsofminds.org/.

Armstrong, T. (1994). Multiple Intelligences: Seven ways to approach curriculum. *Educational Leadership, 52,* 26–28.

Bateman, B. D., & Linden, M. A. (2006). *Better IEPs: How to develop legally correct and educationally useful programs* (4th ed.). Verona, WI: Attainment.

Becker, W. C., Madsen, C. H., Jr., Arnold, C. R., & Thomas, D. R. (1967). The contingent use of teacher attention and praise in reducing classroom behavior problems. *Journal of Special Education, 1,* 287–307.

Burrello, L. C., Lashley, C., & Beatty, E. E. (2001). *Educating all students together: How school leaders create unified systems.* Thousand Oaks, CA: Corwin.

Canady, R. L., & Rettig, M. D. (1996). *Teaching in the block: Strategies for engaging active learners.* Princeton, NJ: Eye on Education.

Carlberg, C., & Kavale, K. A. (1980). The efficacy of special versus regular class placement for exceptional children: A meta-analysis. *Journal of Special Education, 14,* 296–309.

Comprehensive School Reform Quality Center. (2005). *CSRQ report on elementary school comprehensive school reform models.* Washington, DC: Author. Retrieved November 16, 2006, from http://www.csrq.org/documents/CSRQCenterCombinedReport_Web11-03-06.pdf.

Cook, B. G., & Schirmer, B. R. (Eds.). (2006) *What is special about special education: Examining the role of evidence-based practices.* Austin, TX: PRO-ED.

Deno, E. (1970). Special education as developmental capital. *Exceptional Children, 37,* 229–237.

EdWorkForce. (2004). *President Bush signs special education reform bill: House republicans hail bipartisan achievement.* Retrieved November 11, 2005, from http://edworkforce.house.gov/press/press108/second/12dec/idea120304.htm.

Forness, S. R., & Kavale, K. A. (1993). Strategies to improve basic learning and memory deficits in mental retardation: A meta-analysis of experimental studies. *Education and Training in Mental Retardation, 28,* 99–110.

Fuchs, D., & Fuchs, L. S. (1994). Inclusive school movement and the radicalization of special education reform. *Exceptional Children, 60,* 294–305.

Gardner, H. (1983). *Frames of mind: The theory of multiple intelligences.* New York: Basic Books.

Gardner, H. (1993). *Multiple intelligences: The theory into practice.* New York: Basic Books.

Gardner, H. (1999) *Intelligence reframed: Multiple intelligences for the 21st century.* New York: Basic Books.

Gartner, A., & Lipsky, D. K. (2003). *Inclusion: A service not a place: A whole school approach.* Baltimore, MD: Brookes.

Gates, G. S. (2002). *Project style.* Sulphur Springs (TX) Independent School District. Retrieved June 6, 2006, from http://allkindsofminds.org/documents/Schools%20Attuned%20-%20Project%20Style%20Evaluation%202001.pdf.

Gerber, M. M. (1999–2000). An appreciation of learning disabilities: The value of blue-green algae. *Exceptionality, 8,* 29–42.

Hallahan, D. P., & Cruickshank, W. (1973). *Psychoeducational foundations of learning disabilities.* Englewood Cliffs, NJ: Prentice-Hall.

Hallahan, D. P., & Mercer, C. D. (2002). Learning disabilities: Historical perspectives. In R. Bradley, L. Danielson, & D. P. Hallahan (Eds.), *Identification in learning disabilities: Research to practice* (pp. 1–67). Mahwah, NJ: Lawrence Erlbaum Associates.

Horn, W. F., & Tynan, D. (2001). Time to make special education "special" again. In C. E. Finn, A. J. Rotherham, & C. R. Hokanson, (Eds.), *Rethinking special education for a new century* (pp. 23–51). Washington, DC: Fordham Foundation.

Kauffman, J. M. (1993). How we might achieve the radical reform of special education. *Exceptional Children, 60,* 6–16.

Kauffman, J. M. (2002). *Education deform: Bright people sometimes say stupid things about education.* Lanham, MD: Scarecrow.

Kauffman, J. M., & Landrum, T. J. (2006). *Children and youth with emotional and behavioral disorders: A history of their education.* Austin, TX: PRO-ED.

Kavale, K. A. (1981). Functions of the Illinois test of Psycholinguistic Abilities (ITPA): Are they trainable? *Exceptional Children, 47,* 496–510.

Kavale, K. A., & Forness, S. R. (1987). Substance over style: A quantitative synthesis assessing the efficacy of modality testing and teaching. *Exceptional Children, 54,* 228–234.

Kavale, K. A., & Mattson, P. D. (1983). "One jumped off the balance beam": Meta-analysis of perceptual-motor training. *Journal of Learning Disabilities, 16,* 165–173.

Lawrence, W. W., & McPherson, D. D. (2000). A comparative study of block scheduling and traditional scheduling on academic achievement. *Journal of Instructional Psychology, 27,* 178–192.

Levine, M. (2002). *A Mind at a time.* New York: Simon & Schuster.

Levine, M. D., & Reed, M. (1999). *Developmental variation and learning disorders* (2nd ed.). Cambridge, MA: Educators Publishing Service.

Lipskey, D. K. (2005). Are we there yet? *Learning Disability Quarterly, 28,* 156–158.

Lloyd, J. W., Forness, S. R., & Kavale, K. A. (1998). Some methods are more effective. *Intervention in School and Clinic, 33*(1), 195–200.

Lloyd, J. W. Pullen, P. L., Tankersley, M., & Lloyd, P. A. (2006). Critical dimensions of experimental studies and research syntheses the help define effective practices. In B. G. Cook & B. R. Schirmer (Eds.), *What is special about special education: Examining the role of evidence-based practices* (pp. 136–153). Austin, TX: PRO-ED.

Lloyd, J. W., & Hallahan, D. P. (2005). Going forward: How the field of learning disabilities has and will contribute to education. *Learning Disability Quarterly, 28,* 133–136.

Mager, R. (1962). *Preparing instructional objectives.* Belmont, CA: Fearon.

Mills v. Board of Education of the District of Columbia, 348 F. Supp. 866 (D. D. C. 1972).

Mock, D. R., & Kauffman, J. M. (2005). The delusion of full inclusion. In J. W. Jacobson, R. M. Foxx, & J. A. Mulick (Eds.), *Controversial therapies for developmental disabilities: Fad, fashion, and science in professional practice* (pp. 113–128). Mahwah, NJ: Lawrence Erlbaum Associates.

Mulick, J. A., & Butter, E. M. (2005). Positive behavior support: A paternalistic utopian delusion. In J. W. Jacobson, R. M. Foxx, & J. A. Mulick (Eds.), *Controversial therapies for developmental disabilities: Fad, fashion, and science in professional practice* (pp. 385–404). Mahwah, NJ: Lawrence Erlbaum Associates.

New Horizons for Learning. (2006). Teaching and learning strategies: Multiple intelligences. *New Horizons for Learning.* Retrieved February 2, 2006, from http://www.newhorizons.org/strategies/mi/front_mi.htm.

O'Sullivan and Associates. (2001a). *National Schools Attuned: Student success study: Grand Rapids, Michigan.* [No location given]: Author. Retrieved June 6, 2006, from http://allkindsofminds. org/documents/Schools%20Attuned%20-%20Student%20Success%20Study%202001.pdf.

O'Sullivan and Associates. (2001b). *North Carolina Schools Attuned: 2001 Outcome information.* [No location given]: Author. Retrieved June 6, 2006, from http://allkindsofminds.org/documents/North%20Carolina%20Schools%20Attuned%20-%202001%20Outcome%20Information.pdf.

Pennsylvania Association for Retarded Citizens v. Commonwealth of Pennsylvania, 334 F. Supp. 1257 (E. D. Pa. 1971), Consent Agreement.

Pfiffner, L. J., Rosen, L. A., & O'Leary, S. G. (1984) The efficacy of an all-positive approach to classroom management. *Journal of Applied Behavior Analysis, 18,* 257–261.

Repp, A. C., & Singh, N. N. (Eds.). (1990). *Perspectives on the use of non-aversive and aversive interventions.* Sycamore, IL: Sycamore.

Reynolds, M. C. (1991). Classification and labeling. In J. W. Lloyd, N. N. Singh, & A. C. Repp (Eds.), *The regular education initiative: Alternative perspectives on concepts, issues, and models* (pp. 29–41). Sycamore, IL: Sycamore.

Rosen, L. A., O'Leary, S. G., Joyce, S. A., Conway, G., & Pfiffner, L. J. (1984). The importance of prudent negative consequences for maintaining the appropriate behavior of hyperactive students. *Journal of Abnormal Child Psychology, 12,* 581–604.

Sabornie, E. J., Cullinan, D., Osborne, S. S., & Brock, L. B. (2005). Intellectual, academic, and behavioral functioning of students with high incidence disabilities: Cross-categorical meta-analysis. *Exceptional Children, 72,* 47–63.

Sabornie, E. J., Evans, C. E., & Cullinan, D. (2006). Comparing characteristics of high-incidence disability groups: A descriptive review. *Remedial and Special Education, 27*(2), 95–104.

Simpson, R. L., & Sasso, G. M. (1992). Full inclusion of students with autism in general education settings: Values versus science. *Focus on Autistic Behavior, 7*(3), 1–13.

Terrazas, P., Slate, J. R., & Achilles, C. M. (2003). Traditional versus the block instructional schedule: A statewide study. *Research in the Schools, 10,* 1–9.

Wagner, M. (1995). Outcomes for youths with serious emotional disturbance in secondary school and early adulthood. *The Future of Children, 5*(2), 90–112.

Wagner, M., Newman, L., D'Amico, R., Jay, E. D., Butler-Nalin, P., Marder, C., et al. (1991). *Youth with disabilities: How are they doing?* Menlo Park, CA: SRI International.

Wallis, C. (2006). Inside the autistic mind. *Time, 167*(20), 43–48.

Willingham, D. T. (2004, Summer). Reframing the mind. *Education Next.* Retrieved September 20, 2006, from http://www.educationnext.org/unabridged/20043/18.pdf.

Willingham, D. T. (2005a). A Mind at a Time. *Reading & Writing Quarterly, 21,* 197–202.

Willingham, D. T. (2005b, Spring). Mind over matter: A Popular pediatrician stretches a synapse or two. *Education Next.* Retrieved October 12, 2006, from http://www.educationnext.org/unabridged/20052/65.pdf.

Zigmond, N. (2003). Where should students with disabilities receive special education services? Is one place better than another? *The Journal of Special Education, 37,* 193–199.

Author Index

265

Subject Index